A Date Which Will Live

AMERICAN ENCOUNTERS/GLOBAL INTERACTIONS

A series edited by Gilbert M. Joseph and Emily S. Rosenberg

This series aims to stimulate critical perspectives and fresh interpretive frameworks for scholarship on the history of the imposing global presence of the United States. Its primary concerns include the deployment and contestation of power, the construction and deconstruction of cultural and political borders, the fluid meanings of intercultural encounters, and the complex interplay between the global and the local. American Encounters seeks to strengthen dialogue and collaboration between historians of U.S. international relations and area studies specialists.

The series encourages scholarship based on multiarchival historical research. At the same time, it supports a recognition of the representational character of all stories about the past and promotes critical inquiry into issues of subjectivity and narrative. In the process, American Encounters strives to understand the context in which meanings related to nations, cultures, and political economy are continually produced, challenged, and reshaped.

Emily S. Rosenberg

A Date Which Will Live

Pearl Harbor in American Memory

Duke University Press Durham & London

2003

© 2003 Duke University Press

All rights reserved

Printed in the United States of

America on acid-free paper ∞

Designed by C. H. Westmoreland

Typeset in Scala with

Franklin Gothic display

by Keystone Typesetting, Inc.

Library of Congress Cataloging-in-

Publication Data appear on the last

printed page of this book.

TO NORMAN

Contents

Acknowledgments

Many people have assisted the shaping and production of this book. As the book itself stresses the contexts of historical production, I would like to indicate some of its own background by thanking those to whom, as readers, I am directly indebted. First and foremost, I wish to thank Norman Rosenberg. It is within our continual dialogue about the meanings of history that all of my work has taken shape. Akira Iriye, long an influence on my scholarship, provided an initial invitation to join with several others in investigating a topic of historical memory related to the United States, Japan, and the Pacific War. Collaborators in this larger historical memory project commented on this work at two conferences, held in 2001 and 2002. The book benefited enormously from generous readers who made suggestions, caught errors, and provided encouragement. I especially wish to thank Paul Solon and Jerry Fisher, my colleagues at Macalester College, along with John Dower, Marc Gallicchio, Waldo Heinrichs, Akira Iriye, and Edward T. Linenthal. Ruth Rosenberg, Matt Diediker, David Itzkowitz, and Frank Costigliola alerted me to relevant materials. Two students provided valuable assistance. Katherine Forsyth, as part of our larger conversation about historical memory, co-authored chapter 8. Anthony Todd, with diligence, meticulous attention to detail, and great humor, provided help with research, computer tasks, and manuscript preparation. Finally, I am deeply indebted to Valerie Millholland at Duke University Press, who skillfully guided and facilitated this project at every stage.

Introduction

The daughter of a navy veteran, I grew up amid some of the memory-effects of World War II. During the 1960s, as I protested the Vietnam War, my father equated military action with patriotism and contributed to the navy's lobbying organization, the Navy League. In our arguments over foreign policy, foreign foes, and military spending, we had little common ground. I now understand that World War II structured his understanding of politics and values in ways that I could hardly then appreciate.

The last decade's exploding popularity of World War II "memory products" has increased my curiosity about the various cultural meanings of that war and how memories take shape and circulate. Just as an outpouring of interest and commemoration about the Civil War came during the second generation after its end, so turn-of-the-twentieth-century America has embraced a "memory boom" related to World War II. In what forms and to what effects do the language and symbolism of World War II "live" in American culture?

This book examines the construction of Pearl Harbor as an icon in historical memory, commemoration, and spectacle. As an icon—a site suggesting a cluster of meanings—Pearl Harbor has offered "rhetorical resources" to support many different narratives, drawing a multitude of lessons.[1] What were the various contexts within which the powerful symbolism around Pearl Harbor initially developed? Why did Pearl Harbor seem to assume greater and greater visibility in American culture after its fiftieth anniversary in 1991? My goal is to explore the cultural meanings—and political contests—that have been attached to the words "Pearl Harbor."

As this book was under way, the release of Jerry Bruckheimer's blockbuster film, *Pearl Harbor*, on Memorial Day 2001, turned Pearl Harbor into a veritable cultural industry. Despite almost universal disdain from critics, the film popularized imagery associated with the attack. The Mall of America near Minneapolis, Minnesota, celebrated the film's opening with a gala, complete with parade and speeches, to honor Pearl Harbor veterans. The night of the film's opening, my own town's television stations all led their local newscasts with interviews of Pearl Harbor veterans rather than with news of George W. Bush's important tax-cut legislation, which had cleared Congress the same day. Bookstores stacked up dozens of new and reissued books on Pearl Harbor, and amazon.com featured a separate "Pearl Harbor store" on its website. During the spring of 2001, any documentary and feature film with a Pearl Harbor theme bedecked video store display windows, and television—especially the History Channel— offered viewers a steady stream of new and old productions. The makers of GI Joe tried to revive sagging sales by issuing Pearl Harbor figures; fashion designers revamped their "look" to recall that of the early 1940s. Much of this activity proved ephemeral, of course, especially as Hollywood quickly directed attention to the next, and then the next, new thing.

Fascination with Pearl Harbor during the summer of 2001, however, increased its currency as an available metaphor for discussing foreign policy. The new Republican administration's secretary of defense pressed the case for a controversial high-tech missile defense system by alluding to the perils of a "space Pearl Harbor." Then, on September 11, 2001, newspapers across the country ran huge headlines reading "DAY OF INFAMY" or simply "INFAMY." Pearl Harbor became the most commonly invoked metaphor to frame the early understandings of the attacks on the World Trade Center and Pentagon, the most deadly strikes on American soil. With the sixtieth anniversary of the attack in

December 2001, likely the last major anniversary that many members of the Pearl Harbor Survivors' Association (PHSA) would be able to attend, Pearl Harbor assumed even greater visibility as an emotion-laden icon.

This study will not provide an account of the military and diplomatic encounter that has been the subject of shelves of books about Pearl Harbor. Unlike so many other writings, it neither aims nor claims to "reveal" some new "shocking truth." Rather, this book will be attentive to the processes by which a variety of stories about the past, centered on the icon of Pearl Harbor, have taken shape in American culture. A work of cultural history, it will analyze the circulation of diverse meanings through professional and popular histories, monuments, public proclamations, the Internet, films, journalism, and other media. It understands history and other forms of public memory not as avenues to "recover" some "authentic" version of the past but as ever-changing and inevitably mediated fields of contestation over how to structure the past's representation.

Historical memory and the phenomenon of the recent memory boom have been the subjects of a rich scholarly and popular literature, and dozens of writers have discussed and theorized the relationship between history and memory. Building upon the insights of Maurice Halbwachs, the first sociologist to theorize the role of social institutions and groups in the formation and perpetuation of collective memories, much work on history/memory emphasizes its ongoing social construction, the multiplicity and mutability of memory traditions, and the roles of governments, private institutions, pressure groups, and media in perpetuating and altering narratives (often conflicting and contested ones) about the past.[2] This book draws throughout, with appreciation, on the diverse insights of this scholarship, which provides context for its argument at many key points.[3] But this analysis uses the term "memory" to evoke a special interpretive stance that should here be set forth.

In recent American culture, I would contend, historical memory (to which I will refer as "memory" or "history/memory") is inseparable from the modern media, in all their forms. Even so-called "lived memory," which revolves around individual "experience" and "testimony," takes shape in interaction with diverse media effects and also must attract and be recorded in some kind of mediated form if it is to last and become part of known "history." Because media provide the matrix that collects and circulates diverse memories in America, shaping them in various ways and keeping some alive while burying others, memories are enhanced (and, perhaps, even implanted) through more rapid and widespread circulation in media. Forgetting is the condition of media death (no matter how "alive" certain memories may be within individuals). In America, there is increasingly no effective memory or history outside of media, broadly defined.

Remembering and forgetting are, of course, parts of the same process. "Memory and Oblivion," wrote the nineteenth-century historian Thomas Carlyle, "are necessary for each other's existence: Oblivion is the dark page, whereon Memory writes her light-beam characters, and makes them legible; were it all light, nothing could be read there, any more than if it were all darkness."[4] Writer Milan Kundera claims that we can analyze what we call reality only as it appears in memory. "We know reality only in the past tense. We do not know it as it is in the present, in the moment when it's happening, when it 'is.' The present moment is unlike the memory of it. Remembering is not the negative of forgetting. Remembering is a form of forgetting."[5] What becomes preserved as memory of the past cannot replicate the past but can only *select* and *structure* its remains by the simultaneity of remembering and forgetting. Silences are as important as inclusions in historical production. As anthropologist Barbara Kirshenblatt-Gimblett writes in *Destination Culture*, "Memory is not reclaimed. It is produced."[6] In America, the media matrix shapes and reshapes this social remembering and forgetting. It literally "re-members" (re-assembles) the past and provides the "texture" of memories.[7]

In the process of saving and discarding remnants of the past, media's circulatory matrix blurs the distinctions between "memory" and "history" and between "popular" and "professional." Academic historians often try to advance such distinctions. Charles Maier, expressing a view common among academics, has written that memory abets a popular and mythological nostalgia that stands in opposition to the professional and more rational exercise of history. David Lowenthal similarly contrasts memory, which is unreliable and in the "domain of psychology," with history, which is empirically testable and in the domain of historians.[8] Such separations, however, prove difficult to uphold in face of postmodern and boundary-blurring media.

I have become convinced that the distinction between "memory" and "history" is highly contingent upon time, place, and project and that for *this* project, related to American culture in the late twentieth century, it has little significance. In my writing and thinking, the two words, memory and history, seem nearly always interchangeable. Into which category, if they were to be held as distinct, would a History Channel documentary belong? Or the books and documentaries based on Tom Brokaw's *Greatest Generation?* Or a book such as Robert Stinnett's widely read *Day of Deceit?* Or an Internet discussion of Pearl Harbor in which academics and participants all debate a particular interpretation of events? Who can legitimately claim the cultural authority to decide which of these are "memory" and "popular" but not "history" and "professional"? Historians who work in the academy may resist and decry the collapse of distinctions between "high" and "low," between so-called "rational" history and "nostalgic" myth, for much of their cultural capital rests on such distinctions. But this book argues that—especially in the media nation of post–World War II America—memory, history, and media all reproduce and re-present in *intertextual* relationships among diverse kinds of cultural material. It insists that memory and history are blurred forms of representation whose structure and politics need to be analyzed not as oppositional but as interactive forms.

Media often encourage multivocality in memory/history. Pearl Harbor is certainly "a date which will live," but the particular stories that "will live" and the meanings assigned to them become highly volatile in a media-saturated culture. Pearl Harbor "lives" for most Americans in media broadly encompassing popular and professional books, films, journalism, television, memorial sites, and Internet chat rooms. It "lives" in a thousand guises and symbolizes dozens of often conflicting historical "lessons." Stories of the past that are summoned as memory and history vie for media attention, and disagreement enhances their visibility. An earlier generation of cultural critics worried that media would homogenize culture and produce conformity in habits of thought. Media, however, often generate and then flourish on controversy and multiplicity. Sites that become monumental, iconic, or spectacularized (through media) may become *more* evocative, *more* charged with the burden of heavy meaning, *more* contested.

In this sense, Pearl Harbor may be seen as a figurative site of contested meanings where power is exerted and challenged. Over time—now more than sixty years after Japan's attack—disagreements over interpretations have not mellowed. As media circulation expands and accelerates and as a variety of "memory activists" press their interpretations, the diversity of (and disagreements over) meanings and narrative structures have become more, not less, pronounced.[9] As time passes, the cultural stakes over how to recount and valorize the various possible historical "lessons" that may be embedded in the near-sacred symbol of Pearl Harbor have intensified. Since the attack, the term "Pearl Harbor" has circulated as a sometimes contradictory representation of "infamy," the obligations of national loyalty, the importance of military and foreign policy vigilance, the Roosevelt administration's ineptitude or deceit, the unfair scapegoating of the military, and the need to commemorate the courage of ordinary soldiers and sailors. Stories of Pearl Harbor have been marshaled to illustrate both the necessity of military preparedness and the importance of an antimilitarist ethic; they may carry messages about Japanese character that emphasize both a negative tendency toward "treachery" and a positive commitment to honor and precise execution of duty. They have anchored disputes among Japanese Americans over how to shape remembrance of internment. This book attempts not to stabilize some truth about this iconic event but to investigate its instability and to see what can be learned from the terms of contestation.

In researching and writing this study of the meanings of Pearl Harbor, I have struggled with the question of how the past shapes the stories called "history" and, conversely, how culturally familiar stories prestructure understandings and memories of the past. Examining the significations of Pearl Harbor in American culture suggests the usefulness of seeing a back-and-forth dynamic. The cultural and political contests reflected in the Pearl Harbor controversies preceded the attack and shaped its symbolism. Yet Pearl Harbor also focused, altered, and intensified those contests, updating contending narratives and re-presenting them to live in a new generation.

In short, this study addresses how memories of Pearl Harbor circulate in (post)modern American life. What are the cultural politics of history/memory? How do "professional" and "popular" histories (both written and visual) interact and blur with other forms of remembrance (and forgetting), such as those introduced by omnipresent cable television, film, and the Internet? *History/memory, in this investigation, is about production, contestation, and circulation in diverse print, celluloid, electronic, and commemorative media.* Memory is presented as an ever-changing process through which "realities" are remembered and forgotten, meanings are produced and contested, values are professed and debated, and political positions are expressed and challenged. Pearl Harbor "lives" less as a specific occurrence in the past than as a highly emotive and spectacularized icon in an ongoing present—always in interaction with the mediated representations that constitute memory/history.

This book is organized into two parts. The first analyzes the many meanings that became attached to Pearl Harbor in American culture during the first fifty years after the event. It sets them within four broad themes: infamy/preparedness, "backdoor" governmental deceit, commemoration, and American-Japanese relationships. The many stories of Pearl Harbor examined in this section have provided multifaceted—and highly mediated—rhetorical resources that figure in the cultural and political dynamics of postwar American history and policy.

The second part explores many of the more recent cultural contexts and contests that may have contributed to Pearl Harbor's resurgence in American memory since the fiftieth anniversary in 1991: the broad-based memory boom in American culture; the politics of the Republican revival and the determined effort to exonerate commanders Admiral Husband Kimmel and Lieutenant General Walter Short; the mobilization of military lobbying groups over issues of historical interpretation; the *"Titanic* effect" that propelled "high-concept" historical spectacles such as the film *Pearl Harbor* to the movie screen; the current stress on identity and remembrance in domestic and international politics; the post–cold war security environment; and the grasping for a historical frame through which to understand events related to September 11, 2001.

Throughout, there will be an emphasis on the interplay of three components that seem to affect remembering/forgetting and to determine visibility in mediated history/memory: (1) How does the remembering fit prior stories that already claim cultural familiarity? (2) What are the activities of various (sometimes contesting) memory activists who have a stake in maintaining or promoting particular historical formulations? (3) How are stories repeated and circulated through various print, celluloid, electronic, and commemorative media? Familiarity, promotion, and intertextual circulation will be the guiding, if not always explicit, concerns of this study.

I

Signifying Pearl Harbor

The First Fifty Years

As dawn broke over Honolulu on December 7 (December 8 Japanese time), Lieutenant Commander Mitsuo Fuchida, the lead pilot in a fleet of Japanese aircraft, looked into the distance as the U.S. Pacific Fleet came into view. Seeing planes neatly grouped on the runway and naval vessels tranquilly lined up along "Battleship Row," he radioed the code word signifying that a complete surprise had been achieved: "Tora, Tora, Tora." At 7:55 A.M. the first Japanese raid swooped down, interrupting the USS *Nevada's* brass band playing "The Star-Spangled Banner" for flag raising. "Air raid, Pearl Harbor. This is no drill," blared a radio message three minutes later. After an hour, a second Japanese raid circled in. Within less than two hours, 18 U.S. battleships, cruisers, and destroyers lay in ruins; 188 planes were hit; and some 2,400 Americans died. U.S. aircraft carriers, luckily, were out of port. In Washington, Secretary of State Cordell Hull, who had been negotiating with Japanese diplomats, grimly heard the news. When Japanese envoys arrived to present Japan's final terms in the ongoing negotiation, an hour after the attack had started, Hull ordered them out of his office. Throughout the government, anger flared at Japan's "treachery"—apparently covering a carefully planned "sneak attack" with the appearance of continued negotiation. At that moment, few Americans knew much about Hawaii, America's distant island possession. Fewer yet had ever heard of Pearl Harbor.

The words "Pearl Harbor" quickly became one of the most emotive icons in American culture, and the dramatic story of the attack has subsequently been told and retold in thousands of print and visual representations. It should be emphasized that formulations in memory and history are seldom clear-cut. Neither people nor societies remember or recount things in only one way but can sometimes hold in their memories many meanings at once and invoke them in variable, even inconsistent, contexts. During the first fifty years, Pearl Harbor narratives came to offer rhetorical resources related to national security preparedness, to assignment of blame to the Roosevelt administration in Washington or to the commanders at Pearl Harbor, to characterization of Japan and its relations with the United States, and to commemoration of war dead.

1 Infamy

Reinvigorating American Unity and Power

President Franklin Delano Roosevelt, a master of persuasion, seized the opportunity of the surprise Japanese attack to appeal to Americans to join together in a war against the empire of Japan. In penning his six-and-one-half-minute speech to Congress asking for a state of war against Japan, he chose his words carefully. The address opened: "Yesterday, Dec. 7, 1941—a date which will live in world history—the United States of America was suddenly and deliberately attacked by naval and air forces of the Empire of Japan." FDR crossed out "world history" and substituted "infamy."[1]

"A date which will live in infamy"

Infamy became the theme of the address. FDR did not ask Americans to go to war to protect the national interest, to stop Japan's imperial ambitions, to protect vital resources, to avenge Japan's atrocities in China, or to stand firm against aggression from a Tripartite alliance of dictators. He did not ask Americans to save democracy or civilization. Although any of these themes might have been invoked to rally Americans around familiar foreign policy traditions and to provide a persuasive framework, he did not choose them. Perhaps Roosevelt feared recalling President Woodrow Wilson's rhetoric during World War I. Wilson's war message of April 1917 had detailed the strategic threat posed by the enemy, agonized over the violence of war, and advanced idealistic and lofty goals to justify participation. During the 1930s, however, the country's strong antiwar, isolationist, and anti-Wilsonian sentiment had made such themes a political liability. In this initial speech to Congress, Roosevelt avoided echoes of Wilson's war message and, instead, adopted the sole framework of "infamy"—a rhetorical tradition closely related to America's frontier-fighting heritage.

In a very short appeal that contained no details about America's security interests or the lives and equipment lost, the president called on Americans to avenge "infamy," "treachery," and "an unprovoked and dastardly attack." Roosevelt summoned the nation to fight not just an enemy nation, but a treacherous people who would deceitfully negotiate for peace while preparing a surprise war. "Always will we remember the *character* of the onslaught against us" (italics mine). In emphasizing the "character" of the attack by Japan and promising that such "infamy" needed to be followed through to "inevitable triumph," Roosevelt structured his narrative to recall America's most celebrated frontier legends: Custer's Last Stand and the Alamo. These, too, were terrible defeats that provided rallying cries for overwhelming military counterforce leading to total victory. Memory research confirms that people remember events in ways that fit already familiar patterns and narrative structures. The infamy framework for Pearl Harbor was perhaps so powerful because it already circulated widely in frontier lore.

By referring to an "infamy framework," I am not suggesting that Japan's attack was in any way unreal or that "infamy" was not an appropriate descriptor. Rather, I use the term "infamy framework" as a shorthand for the various rhetorical and narrative components that came to structure the most influential remembering of the attack. Later chapters will examine other frameworks, some more and some less compatible with this one.

Historian Richard Slotkin (among others) has shown how the

defeat of General George Armstrong Custer's Seventh Cavalry regiment by a large force of Indians led by Sitting Bull at the Battle of the Little Big Horn in 1876 had become the iconic object called "Custer's Last Stand." Shaped by mass-marketed and highly partisan newspapers during the late nineteenth century, the last-stand legend buttressed a familiar frontier perspective on late nineteenth-century debates over Indian policy: progress in America could be achieved not through accommodation and philanthropy toward so-called "noble savages." Instead, it could come only through regenerative, violent warfare against these barbaric racial others. In the traditional version of that legend, writes Slotkin, the battle occurs "in the margins of civilization, which poses the most extreme test of the culture's value and its power to shape history." This frontier challenge summoned men to marshal their assertively masculine traits and to reject soft, feminized values and policies. The Custer created in the legend, with his blond hair and youthful vigor, gallantly sacrificed his men in a defeat that would subsequently be gloriously avenged by vigorous military counterforce. The last-stand legend taught that strong, frontier-hardened men needed to secure civilization against barbarous attacks and to oppose the compromises proposed by (feminized) weaklings in the East.[2]

During the late nineteenth and early twentieth centuries, this last-stand legend became widely memorialized in journalism, histories, textbooks, Wild West shows, and visual images of all kinds.[3] Slotkin shows how it became an available metaphor not only to support the federal government's determined warfare to end Indian resistance, but also to justify the use of force against whomever—labor militants, for example—seemed to threaten the established order.[4]

The metaphor provided by the last-stand legend also contributed to reshaping the historical memory of an earlier event—the siege at the Alamo. In March 1836, during the struggle over the independence of Texas, Mexico's general Antonio López de Santa Anna had led an attack on some two hundred Texans at an old mission in San Antonio called the Alamo. All of the Alamo's defenders, including the legendary frontier figures James Bowie and Davy Crockett, were killed. The Alamo became a rallying cry for a counterattack by Sam Houston's army, which defeated Santa Anna and secured the independence of Texas later that spring. An event of mostly regional significance for most of the rest of the nineteenth century, the battle of the Alamo was shaped by a concerted effort of Texan elites during the 1890s into a legend of national visibility and significance. Like the Last Stand, the Alamo became a metaphor for a massacre by racialized primitives that rallied righteous revenge by men of heroic, masculine qualities.[5] "Remember the Alamo!" became a slogan known to most Americans, and on the eve of the War of 1898 a similarly structured call to action, "Remember the *Maine!*" whipped up nationalistic anger against a (mis)alleged Spanish "attack" on a U.S. ship in Cuba.

Nearly half a century later, the Pearl Harbor narrative became a refreshed version of these familiar cautionary tales. Physical defeat justified righteous revenge, even expressed as divine retribution. It became a marker of the nation's moral superiority and its unjust victimization. In the late 1930s the Fiesta San Jacinto pilgrimage to the Alamo had become a popular annual event celebrated each April 22. Hollywood's rendition of Custer's Last Stand, *They Died with Their Boots On* (1941), starring Errol Flynn, played to packed theaters just before the Pearl Harbor attack.[6] Understood through the prism of the Last Stand and the Alamo, the Pearl Harbor attack gained emotive power as an icon. It, too, promised fierce revenge against another humiliating defeat visited upon Americans. In the final revision of his speech, Roosevelt handwrote: "No matter how long it may take us to overcome this premeditated invasion, the American people in their righteous might will win through to absolute victory." The Custer/Alamo/Pearl Harbor narrative was simple and nationalistic: Don't mess with Americans or they will rightly rise up to destroy you.

Roosevelt's speech also emphasized that the attack hit U.S. territory itself. Roosevelt's fear that the damage might not be perceived as hitting close enough to home to crush isolationist sentiment guided his revisions. Three times in his first draft, Roosevelt wrote that attacks came against Hawaii and the Philippines. On revision, the Philippines (a U.S. colony but not a territory) was deleted, and it was only mentioned later in a list of other Japanese attacks throughout the Pacific. The infamy trope worked better if the attack was positioned clearly on American soil. Again, this emphasis recalled another episode in U.S.-Texas-Mexican relations when President James Polk used the rallying cry that a Mexican attack had "shed American blood on American soil" (actually it was disputed ground). Demanding revenge for a highly personal attack by people of bad character stirs emotions.

A persuasive speech, such as Roosevelt's, is meant to mobilize. It necessarily aims to simplify, to flatten complexity and reduce ambivalence. If the story it tells is already familiar as a background legend in the culture, the work of persuasion becomes less difficult. The infamy trope, this insult to the nation—and implicitly to divine will—became a battle cry that, drawing upon popular rhetorical structures and historical legends, built recognition among Americans that few presidential proclamations can boast.

The president's message was especially memorable because words, not photographs, sketched the initial public image of the attack. The Navy Department did not release photos that provided a view of the damage at Pearl Harbor for several weeks, and not until the first anniversary of the attack did an extensive photo spread appear in *Life* magazine.[7] It was the words "infamy" and "treachery," rather than visual images, that reverberated from Roosevelt's speech into most representations of Pearl Harbor during the war and after, providing a long-lasting framework shaping the imagery of history and remembrance.

One implication of the infamy framework has been that, for most Americans, the historical narrative of World War II often *begins* with the Pearl Harbor attack, establishing American military action as reactive and defensive. Yet few other national histories in the world view Pearl Harbor as a beginning in the story of World War II. Yukiko Koshiro writes that "there is no single war to remember. . . . This diverse thrust has given rise to diverse names [for the war], all of them heavily charged with meaning and often incommensurable."[8] For most Chinese people, the war began in the early 1930s as Japan's offensive against China; many in Japan saw (and continue to see) the attack as a defensive measure against a longer series of U.S. provocations that, in effect, began hostilities. For most Europeans, Pearl Harbor is simply one of several turning points of a conflict that began in 1939. Literary theorists emphasize that where a story begins and ends is vital to its structuring elements, to what is both remembered and suppressed. The infamy and retaliation structure draws power from its simplicity and its highly national-centric beginning (later wrapped up with its definitive atomic bomb ending).

Examining the structure of Roosevelt's war message, however, highlights a curious omission. Although in countless anthologies, websites, and collected papers, the speech is called "Roosevelt's Pearl Harbor Speech," the words "Pearl Harbor" never appear. Like the Last Stand and the Alamo, Japan's surprise attack needed a shorthand label that would work to rally. Roosevelt did not instantly coin the phrase that would catch on, but headline writers did. In its afternoon edition on December 9, the Portland *Oregonian* adapted the familiar "Remember the Alamo!" into a new battle cry: "Remember Pearl Harbor!" The phrase quickly caught on. The catchy song hummed by many new recruits went:

> Let's remember Pearl Harbor
> As we go to meet the foe.
> Let's remember Pearl Harbor
> As we did the Alamo.[9]

One of the earliest and most famous of the wartime propaganda posters reiterated the "remember" theme. Below a tattered but still waving American flag, set against both the blue sky of peace and the black smoke of war, emerge the words: "Remember Dec. 7th!" Above the flag appears another familiar historical reference: "we here highly resolve that these dead shall not have died in vain."[10] Many wartime films repeated the "remember" theme with lines such as "There's a date we'll always remember—and they will never forget!" (*Bombardier,* 1941). The words "Pearl Harbor" gradually became the common descriptor of what was to be remembered. They became the rhetorical shorthand for the "infamy" that would be remembered and then avenged through "righteous might."

In the wake of Roosevelt's speech, longtime interventionists stitched another theme into the Pearl Harbor symbol: the complacency and ignorance of the American people were partly to blame for the attack. Liberal columnist Walter Lippmann wrote that Americans since World War I had been under "deadly illusions" that they had no ultimate responsibilities for peace in the world. Journalist Dorothy Thompson wrote, "I accuse us. I accuse the twentieth-century American. I accuse me."[11] The United States, according to many, had been "asleep." The *Christian Science Monitor* wrote that the United States had been "too flabby and sleepy." America was not only sleepy, but also "innocent." In August 1945, the Honolulu *Advertiser* summarized: "The shame of Pearl Harbor . . . was the product of towns and villages, of big cities and big factories, of oil, copper, cotton and scrap iron that flowed to potential enemies, of 'America Firstism,' the corn and hog farmer and of the slushy societies that were sure that love and understanding were all that a sick world needed."[12]

The "sleeping" metaphor—Americans as innocent, naive, and appallingly ignorant of a dangerous world—became a common part of the infamy story, reinforced by the dawn timing of the raid and the "rising sun" symbol of Japan itself. Since the 1970s American representations of the Pacific War have made pervasive use of an alleged quotation by Japanese admiral Isoroku Yamamoto, the Harvard-educated naval strategist who planned the attack. The film *Tora! Tora! Tora!* (1970) quoted Yamamoto as leavening his victory at Pearl Harbor with the fearful prophecy that Japan had awakened a "sleeping giant" and filled him with a "terrible resolve." This quotation well carried out the basic internationalist narrative of the sleeping nation, and it illustrates how narrative structures shape what is remembered and handed down through famous quotations. Yamamoto's "sleeping" quote has become a standard anecdote that, assisted by the blood-red "rising sun" insignia, has helped structure many renditions of the Pearl Harbor story, seeming to provide special authenticity because it is presented as coming from the enemy itself.

The "sleeping" theme implicitly blamed the attack partly on the "isolationism" of Roosevelt's Republican opponents. By tilting blame onto congressional isolationists and the pressure groups who had opposed Roosevelt's cautious moves toward rearmament and involvement in the war, Roosevelt internationalists made Pearl Harbor a highly visible symbol in partisan political debates. Internationalists ridiculed Republican isolationists as ignorant and dangerous to the republic. In his nightclub act of the 1940s, comedian Zero Mostel imitated an isolationist senator decrying, "What was Hawaii doing out there in the middle of the Pacific anyway?"[13]

A narrative in which the nation suddenly loses its childlike innocence suggests that maturity and manhood, symbolized in military force, will surely follow. For most of the war, this image of a sleepy America, misled by immature, ignorant, and weak (feminized) isolationists and pacifists but awakened to military manhood by infamy, held the spotlight. Circulated in presidential proclamations and hometown journalism, the "sleeping" metaphor, too, has continued to structure the retellings and rememberings.

To motivate Americans and keep up morale during the war, the Roosevelt administration carefully directed wartime culture. Propaganda agencies, censorship, and self-censorship shaped visual and written representations of the conduct and purpose of the war. Today, the public memory of World War II resides less in personally remembered pasts than in these highly manipulated images that have been left behind. These images themselves— especially those powerfully presented on film—may even have helped shaped the "reality" that people "experienced" and "remembered."[14] Many Pearl Harbor veterans commented upon seeing the grinning faces of the Japanese bomber pilots, for example, and one wonders whether films may have helped cement these remembrances through so many similar images. Shooting film can be "the continuation of war by other means," but only the film remains behind to be recycled over and over after the war ends.[15] How was the Pearl Harbor story presented in wartime motion pictures?

Movies by two of Hollywood's most acclaimed directors, John Ford and Frank Capra, embellished the narrative of innocence awakened by infamy. Both directors were master dramatists. As in Roosevelt's speech, potentially complicated explanations about national interest, the geopolitics of natural resources, or the importance of balance of power were sublimated into a simpler representation easily grasped by all Americans: a fight of good (us) against evil (them).

John Ford's *December 7*, the first feature-length documentary film depicting the attack on Pearl Harbor, was designed to inspire Americans to sacrifice by adapting stock Hollywood formulas to the Pacific theater of World War II. Ford knew the elements of a good story and understood evocative visual imagery. *December 7* elaborated Roosevelt's infamy framework.

The film that emerged as *December 7* had a complicated birth. Colonel William B. ("Wild Bill") Donovan, head of the Office of Strategic Services (oss), put Ford in charge of a field photographic unit and proposed that he oversee the creation of a feature-length film on Pearl Harbor. Ford enlisted one of Hollywood's most talented cameramen, Gregg Toland, who went to Hawaii, fashioned a semidocumentary script, and shot 38,000 feet of film. In Washington, however, reaction to the rough cut was unanimously negative, and the project was shelved. Some argued that it was a poor picture, with flawed narrative form; some felt the government should not be in the business of feature film production; some objected to Donovan's freelancing outside of the Office of War Information (owı) structure; some charged that it left the impression that the navy was asleep and that the film was unfair to the American commanders at the Pearl Harbor base. Almost everyone agreed that it lacked a clear message. In 1943, then, the film was cut down to thirty-three minutes, its message was simplified, and it was distributed for public showing. Ford won an Academy Award for Best Short Subject. Toland, discouraged, packed up for a new assignment in Brazil, but his aerial re-creations and special effects remained the core of the recut film. The original film remained in the Smithsonian and was released on video only in the 1990s.[16]

As it appeared to the public in 1943, the shorter film contained three distinct sections: the bombing of the U.S. fleet, a memorialization of the dead (emphasizing America's class and ethnic diversity), and a promise of military victory. This structure followed that of the last-stand Western legend (indeed, of many successful dramatic forms) by presenting challenge, sacrifice, and then triumph.

The film opened with close-up shots of letters from Secretary of War Henry Stimson and Secretary of Navy Frank Knox endorsing it as a "factual presentation." With these official documents, *December 7* kicked off a technique that would become a standard feature of popular representations of Pearl Harbor: the invocation of official documents that, in some way, certified the account as "fact," ignoring what any writer or filmmaker knows—that "facts" never speak for themselves but are necessarily selected and structured into an interpretive story that is directed toward a particular audience.

The first section opened with a character portraying Uncle Sam dozing restfully in Hawaii. (This clip was from a much longer segment, present in the unedited version, showing a dialogue between a complacent [sleepy] Uncle Sam and a thoughtful realist who urges him to look beyond the beautiful scenery of Hawaii at the extreme danger posed by Japan and by the people of Japanese descent living there.) Shots of Honolulu showed the entire city similarly asleep. The base at Pearl Harbor was on alert, viewers were told, but against sabotage, not external threat. Planes were neatly lined up, the better to secure them; the base was tranquil; and a radar operator who detected incoming planes reported to an inexperienced person who disregarded his report. Into this sleepy scene (a clear metaphor for the disengagement of interwar American isolationism), a formation of airplanes swarmed in "like tiny locusts." At this "deceitful moment" Japanese diplomats were shown presenting new peace proposals. "The treachery of an empire was on the wing."

As the attack began, men dispersed to their battle stations. The USS *Arizona* and other targets were hit. Young men, shown in close-up, fired antiaircraft guns. Explosions filled the screen with fire and smoke. After a pause, the bombing attack resumed, finally to be "beaten off—yes, beaten off" by American soldiers who "showed they had only begun to fight." The Americans killed numbered 2,443. The "diabolical plan of attack" would always be remembered, the narrator promised.

Japan's bombing of Pearl Harbor in *December 7* looked so realistic that the film has come to be used as though it were actually taken at the time—the "surprise attack" amazingly captured on film from every angle! Capra's *Why We Fight* and the later award-winning documentary *Victory at Sea* both used Toland's recreations as "real." And in 2001, a CBS evening news broadcast still used these images of the incoming Japanese planes as documentary footage of the attack. (American cameramen at Pearl Harbor at the time filmed a total of only about five minutes during the attack, showing burning ships, flames, and wounded men. Japanese aerial footage became available later and is used, for example, in the movie shown at the *Arizona* Memorial Visitors' Center at Pearl Harbor.)

In the second section of *December 7*, the camera visited the graves of the fallen men, and, one by one, seven of them made a ghostly appearance to be interviewed. This visualization of the dead had the same message that would be stressed by Capra: the national unity of a diverse population. The soldiers were Irish, Jewish, African American, Mexican American (though not Japanese American). The scene assured that "we are all Americans" and ended in the singing of "America" as little flags fluttered on each grave.[17]

The third, short section promised a vigorous military rebound. The contrast with the opening scene's sleeping America could not be more stark. A twenty-four-hour salvage and repair effort, served by an armada of supply ships from the mainland, meant that the ships Tokyo declared as "lost" would soon fight again. America's "tropical suburb" of Hawaii became a garrison of citizen preparedness. A promise to General Hideki Tojo ended the film: Those who take up the sword will perish by the sword.

As the ending suggested, the promise of ultimate victory contained a justification of righteous vengeance. The theme of vengeance, justified by Pearl Harbor, became more and more pronounced as the war's brutality escalated. In countless films, journalistic pieces, and memoirs, Pearl Harbor provided the narrative beginning for the fight against Japan and, ultimately, for the U.S. firebombing and atomic attack.[18]

Frank Capra also made the attack on Pearl Harbor one of the most dramatic touchstones of his multipart *Why We Fight* series. This series, required for army trainees and then shown in theaters during the war, has become a classic. It is possible that more people today have seen Capra's films than saw them between 1943 and 1945; they may be rented in most video stores, are frequently available in cheap prints on discount tables, replay on cable television, and are often shown in high school and college history courses. (The exception is the portion called "Know Your Enemy—Japan," which was not released in the postwar period because of its racist characterizations of Japanese people.) Like so many other World War II images, these films, through recirculation, solidified Capra's images into memory. The heavily censored informational culture of World War II, shaping media and remembrance at the time, still presents powerful visual material to new generations.

Even before the war, the head of the U.S. Army's Morale Branch had reported that soldiers had no real knowledge of why they were in training and recommended soliciting cooperation from Hollywood. At that time, the Roosevelt administration was understandably reluctant to engage in any overt, prowar propaganda campaigns. But after the Pearl Harbor attack the Morale Branch placed Capra on active duty in its office and assigned him the job of making a film to show soldiers "why we fight." Although Capra had never before made a documentary, his *Mr. Deeds Goes to Town* and *Mr. Smith Goes to Washington* were said to express a kind of simple, grassroots patriotism that army officials wished to convey.

The opening film of Capra's series, *Prelude to War,* closely followed the messages that Roosevelt, General George C. Marshall, and Secretary Stimson hoped to project, and the latter two closely supervised its production. In *Prelude,* Pearl Harbor became the galvanizing act that awakened Americans to danger and united them in common purpose. Using what became a standard World War II trope, Capra showed Americans of diverse religious, class, ethnic, and regional backgrounds putting aside differences and disagreements in their embrace of the nation.

Capra framed the war within Hollywood's formula for Western and gangster films, with a clear delineation of heroes and villains. The war was a "fight between a free world and a slave world." It was, more than anything, the *character* of the enemy (militaristic and bent on conquest) and of Americans (peaceful and democratic) that defined the struggle. The owi, trying to pursue a "strategy of truth," at first objected that the film was too emotional. Nelson Poynter, head of the Hollywood office of the Bureau of Motion Pictures, characterized Capra's films as shallow. By concentrating on the evil of Axis leaders and downplaying the economic and social conditions that gave rise to them, he commented, Americans would be misled about the causes of international turmoil. Still, in April 1943 the owi finally agreed to encourage public showing of the film. The promotional release to theater owners billed it as "the greatest gangster movie ever filmed . . . the inside story of how the mobsters plotted to grab the world! More vicious . . . more diabolical . . . more horrible than any horror-movie you ever saw!"[19]

Other wartime films elaborated upon the basic structure of the Roosevelt-Ford-Capra messages and on their themes emphasizing infamous character, sleep, national unity, military revitalization, and last-stand vengeance. World War II gave rise to its own film genre—the combat film, which emerged from Hollywood's desire to make a profit by providing entertainment to a war-weary population and from the government's appeal to Hollywood to help mobilize citizens in the war effort. The combat genre had several distinctive features. It had a contemporary setting and often used a documentary-style realism to produce, in effect, a vast chronicle of the war's battles, in films such as *Wake Island* (1942), *Air Force* (1943), *Bataan* (1943), *So Proudly We Hail* (a nurse's version of the combat film, 1943), *Guadalcanal Diary* (1943), and *30 Seconds over Tokyo* (1944). It employed a good-guys-versus-bad-guys formula, despite the owi's appeal for Hollywood to deal more with "the issues" at stake in the war. It often featured a single fighting unit in a last-stand situation in the Pacific theater. Made with the military's close cooperation, it celebrated both military technology and "typical" soldiers, carefully drawn to represent the class and ethnic differences that the war had presumably rendered unimportant. Finally, the combat film often presented December 7 as a dramatic focal point for plot and character development: after this date all lives undergo change.[20]

Air Force, directed by Howard Hawks, employed a highly effective and commonly used trope to carry out the infamy theme.

As in so many World War II films, people hear the news of the Pearl Harbor attack over the radio. This device, foregrounding radio, cements a bond with an audience who probably also recalled (or perhaps was thus schooled to recall) experiencing the same shocking radio news. In this case, the crew of the bomber *Mary Ann* hears first that Japanese envoys have "assured the President that Japan's intentions are wholly peaceful." Later, they hear of the attack and, as in many films, the audience sees their faces reacting with a grim determination to retaliate. Furious, the character played by John Garfield says, "They send a couple of oily gents to Washington with an olive wreath while the boys back home clobber Uncle Sam with a crowbar!" Later the commander of forces on Wake Island underscores the theme: "I've studied all the wars of history, but I've never come across any dirtier treachery." The conventions in this realistically filmed combat genre, which moviegoers experienced sandwiched in between newsreels about the war, could easily blend into and help fix memories of how it "really" was.

In the late 1940s and 1950s, a new cycle of postwar combat films, which continued to offer a mix of entertainment and patriotic instruction, followed or referenced the conventions established during the war. U.S. citizen-soldiers continued to be represented as a melting pot of diverse ethnicities and classes, fighting on behalf of women and families at home. Although peace-loving, they maturely recognized that combat, though unwelcome, expressed manhood, duty, and patriotism. Christian G. Appy has called the sensibility of these postwar films "sentimental militarism" and points out how their themes proved consistent with America's rapidly militarizing cold war environment.[21] The postwar combat films were "sentimental" not in the sense that they sugarcoated violence and loss. Indeed, most graphically depicted the horror of combat as a backdrop for plots dramatizing the sorrows and personal psychological dilemmas of war and its aftermath. Many had love and family themes, posing the dilemma of how men and women might reconcile their personal attachments with duty to the nation. Although plots varied widely, a "truth" that helped structure most of the powerful films about World War II, such as *The Sands of Iwo Jima* (1949), *From Here to*

Eternity (1953), and *In Harm's Way* (1965), was that loyalty to personal family must, sadly, be subordinated when it conflicts with the military "family." In each of these films, the male heroes, either supported by or in conflict with their women and/or children, projected manliness as duty to nation and to comrades-in-arms above all else, even personal commitments. The symbolic identifications linking men, the military, and the rescued nation, which had been forged during the war in the invocation of the ubiquitous last-stand metaphor, continued to shape America's cold war culture—its films, its gender ideology, and its assertively masculine foreign policy.[22]

From Here to Eternity, directed by Fred Zinnemann and probably the most successful and acclaimed film that centered around the Pearl Harbor attack, presented no interpretation of the war's causes or of its larger politics. Based on James Jones's 1951 novel by the same name, several personal dramas glorified the men for whom the army became family, taking necessary precedence over love of women. Burt Lancaster and Montgomery Clift portrayed the toughest of the tough, and they were passionately committed to the other men in their units (represented by Frank Sinatra's Academy Award–winning character), so much so that they themselves eschewed both career advancement and relationships with the women they loved. Despite some bad officers and misguided policies, the army unit and the nation commanded ultimate filial devotion, a choice clarified during the dramatic and tragic attack scene, in which Clift's character was killed. The film closed with the two women whom Lancaster and Clift loved (Deborah Kerr and Donna Reed) sailing back together toward the mainland, the domestic sphere where women belong and that men must band together to protect. The film, with its iconic beach scene of the embraces and desires that must ultimately be left behind in wartime, garnered eight Oscars, tying the record set by *Gone with the Wind* in 1939.

Many of these wartime and postwar combat films, resting in Hollywood's vaults, declined in popularity during the era of the Vietnam War, and few new heroic war dramas were made from the mid-1960s into the 1990s. (One of Steven Spielberg's few box office flops was his *1941* [1979], an embarrassing attempt to turn the weeks after Pearl Harbor into a zany satire about Californians' fears of a Japanese invasion.) They would return in recycled and renewed form, however, when video and cable technology enlarged the demand for "classic" movies and Hollywood turned once again in the 1990s to patriotic themes. New entertainment technology would, in time, revive dissemination of the powerful visual remembrances of Pearl Harbor.

Did the government-influenced and -censored images affect— then and now—how Americans have viewed and remembered the war? The power of motion picture film to alter popular attitudes provokes interpretive controversy. Some scholars used to dismiss Hollywood as an unimportant entertainment medium, not worthy of study by serious historians. But twentieth-century governments have clearly operated on just the opposite premise, enlisting mass media to programs of social change and popular mobilization, particularly in times of war. Still, are audiences simply passive receptors of government messages? A recent study examining European propaganda films has concluded that films "that were positively received were almost always films that confirmed and reinforced existing ideas and attitudes," and those that tried to transform the culture failed to attract viewers. Moreover, "cinema audiences exercised considerable discrimination, both in the films that they chose to see and in the meanings that they constructed in the films."[23] Movies, in this view, must be taken seriously in their potential to reinforce established values and modes of thought and to prompt audience reactions of various kinds, but they must certainly also be seen as somewhat open and flexible texts. Films setting forth a narrative of history/memory are not "magic bullets" that simply inoculate viewers with the producer's ideology, but they must be seen in terms of their interplay with other, reinforcing or contesting, non-cinematic narratives.

In the case of representations of Pearl Harbor, the intertextuality among prior frontier legends, presidential proclamations, newspaper headlines, and wartime and postwar films provided reinforcement for what was to be remembered and how it would be structured. Moreover, governmental involvement in cultural production during World War II meant that various cultural texts probably expressed more similarity in messages about Pearl Harbor—all generally associated with the last-stand infamy theme—than would be true in times of less direct control and censorship. Still, it will be important to keep in mind that not every American received the very same messages in the very same way. Nor, as images recirculated in later generations, in other contexts, and among different audiences, would their meanings remain stable. As this book will emphasize throughout, representations of Pearl Harbor could be contested terrain, suggesting a variety of meanings.

"Remember Pearl Harbor; Keep America Alert"

During the war, the most prominent themes attached to Pearl Harbor (as noted) suggested infamy and treachery by Japan, the dangers of isolationism, unity on the home front, and the imperative of a strong and alert military. These themes were invoked to mobilize the nation and to discredit domestic dissent from isolationists or pacifists. The familiar frontier narrative structure of challenge, sacrifice, and triumph helped make Pearl Harbor a powerful metaphor for international vigilance, a large military establishment, and a need for standing tough and unified against forces that might threaten the nation.

Firmly established in wartime culture, the Pearl Harbor metaphor of vigilance became available in the postwar period to those who feared lapsing back into military or political isolationism. As communism became the new threat that might employ treachery and surprise, Pearl Harbor (like Munich) provided a rhetorical resource to support a policy of cold war containment. The United States needed to be on guard against new "Pearl Harbors" by enlarging intelligence capabilities, building new weapons, and increasing military budgets.

With the end of the war, the government disbanded its principal intelligence agency, the oss. By 1947, however, many foreign policy experts and intelligence advocates worried that threats from the Soviet Union and from local communist parties in Western Europe, especially in Italy and France, could not be countered without the kind of centralized intelligence gathering and analysis, together with counterespionage and covert action capabilities, that the oss had once offered. Avoiding surprise in the future through better intelligence collection was one concern; another was improving coordination in the use of intelligence among various military and foreign policy bureaucracies—a failure that a 1946 congressional investigation into the Pearl Harbor disaster had conveniently highlighted. George S. Petee's *The Future of American Secret Intelligence* (1946), for example, cited the inadequacy of U.S. intelligence in the 1930s in order to stress the dangers of surprise attack in the future. William L. Langer, the prominent Harvard historian who had also headed the oss's research branch during the war, likewise argued that Pearl Harbor showed the need for an ongoing intelligence agency in peacetime.[24]

Pearl Harbor thereby provided a rhetoric for advocating new and rationalized structures for the emerging cold war. When the Truman administration took to Congress the National Security Act of 1947, with its proposal for creating the Central Intelligence Agency, the congressional investigation into the Pearl Harbor attack was fresh in the news, and Pearl Harbor, even more than cold war justifications, seemed uppermost in congressional deliberations. "If we had had a strong central intelligence organization, in all probability we would never have had the attack on Pearl Harbor; there might not have been a World War II," proclaimed Representative Carter Manasco, a Democrat from Alabama.[25] Even the great number of members of Congress who were suspicious of international involvements and secret governmental agencies felt compelled to endorse an agenda to remember Pearl Harbor, an event still less than six years in the past, by striving to prevent a similar surprise attack in the future. Historian Rhodri Jeffreys-Jones has elaborated how Pearl Harbor remained an icon frequently invoked by advocates of the ever-enlarging intelligence apparatus.[26]

Even as the cold war ended in the early 1990s, Pearl Harbor could still be marshaled to support intelligence agencies, now under threat of shrinking because of the absence of a clear enemy. In a *Foreign Affairs* article in 1991 David Kahn, who had previously written books on World War II code breaking, retraced the intelligence failure prior to Pearl Harbor in order to emphasize that the CIA and the National Security Agency (NSA) provided vital protections that needed to be nurtured even in the post–cold war era. He concluded that "Pearl Harbor has taught the United States to gather more information and to evaluate it better. That unforgotten lesson of a half-century ago still matters; it is why Americans, even today, remember Pearl Harbor."[27]

Just as intelligence advocates deployed the symbolism of Pearl Harbor, so did the military, an institution that commanded immense respect and loyalty in the late 1940s but also encountered the traditional American distrust of standing armies and international entanglements. Toward the end of World War II, the newly created Joint Chiefs of Staff argued that U.S. postwar security depended on global military reach to avoid "sudden danger beyond any Pearl Harbor experience." The United States, the Joint Chiefs urged, must always be able to strike before it is hit.[28] Scientific advisers such as Vannevar Bush pressed for ongoing weapons research by arguing that new technologies might allow adversaries to deliver unexpected strikes with overwhelming power. Pearl Harbor, Bush wrote, was "only a mild warning of what might happen in the future."[29] Policymakers such as Paul H. Nitze also invoked the lessons of the Pacific War. Just after the war, the Strategic Bombing Survey report, signed by Nitze, had concluded that "the Japanese would never have attacked Pearl Harbor had they not correctly assessed the weakness of our defenses."[30] In 1950, Nitze recommended in National Security Council Document 68 (NSC-68), the top-secret blueprint for America's approach to the cold war, that the nation contain the evils of communism by a massive buildup of military strength. He relied on an alarmist, good-and-evil framework that recalled the language of frontier fighting and Frank Capra's *Why We Fight*.

To implement containment, military spending soared, the development of nuclear weapons propelled an arms race, and the United States accumulated military bases throughout the world. The historical "lesson" of Pearl Harbor, shaped within the last-stand, "infamy" metaphor of the war, provided a building block for cold war policies. Pearl Harbor "taught" that the nation should not be asleep, immature, or feminine; that negotiation could be deceit; that manly, military vigilance was always needed against people of bad character. Pearl Harbor was the "defining event for American empire," wrote historian John Lewis Gaddis, because it provided a justification for a broad and global approach to national security.[31]

Filmic reminders of Pearl Harbor reinforced this preparedness narrative. In 1952, coinciding with the Korean War buildup, the acclaimed twenty-six-part TV documentary series *Victory at Sea* encouraged Americans to relive key moments of World War II in their own living rooms. Placed on NBC's prestigious lineup of cultural programs for Sunday afternoon viewing, the series featured live footage from both Allied and Axis governments; offered a stirring musical score by Richard Rodgers; and garnered thirteen awards, including a Peabody and an Emmy. In this era, when the new medium of television provided a kind of electronic hearth around which family members gathered to share a viewing experience, *Victory at Sea* became a classic. Reminding its audience of the military struggles and victories just past, it went into syndication in May 1953 and played repeatedly on local television stations for the next ten years, showing as many as twenty times in some markets. After NBC recut the material into a ninety-minute format in 1954, United Artists distributed it in movie houses, and it again showed on prime time television in 1960 and 1963. Later, it went into video and DVD release and became a standard offering in the video collections of public libraries.

The second part of this series, "The Pacific Boils Over," presented the Pearl Harbor story. Offering visual memories of the attack and establishing the pattern for many future documentaries, it was structured by the familiar challenge-sacrifice-triumph framework. It also deemphasized the international politics of the war to concentrate primarily on military history, depicting the details of both sides' ships, planes, and maneuvers.[32] In addition, by the early 1950s the second cycle of combat films was hitting the theaters, once more commingling "realistic" Hollywood images with personal recollections of World War II. Fighting in Korea, in effect, brought flashbacks of World War II culture.

The cold war buildup, which was recommended in NSC-68, implemented during the national security emergencies of the Korean War, and surrounded by a supporting culture of preparedness, continued through each subsequent presidential administration. The metaphor of Pearl Harbor was omnipresent. President Dwight Eisenhower justified U-2 surveillance flights as preventing "another Pearl Harbor." Those who charged Eisenhower himself with presiding over a dangerous "missile gap" could warn against a "Pearl Harbor."[33] President Lyndon Johnson's secretary of state, Dean Rusk, justified American involvement in Vietnam by noting that only ten years had passed between the seizure of Manchuria and Pearl Harbor. The two words told a longer story. Treacherous others must be met by constant vigilance and the ever-present possibility of overwhelming counterforce. As Michael Sherry has written, "Pearl Harbor could justify nuclear deterrence, global intervention, peacetime conscription, and . . . preparedness."[34] In that way, the Pearl Harbor story helped structure expectations and behavior in the cold war. The Pearl Harbor Survivors' Association, formed in 1964, adopted the motto: "Remember Pearl Harbor; Keep America Alert."

The emotive words "Pearl Harbor" could become even more elastic, connoting any potential national security disaster. In 1958, Walter Lippmann called Nixon's ill-fated "goodwill" visit to Latin America a "diplomatic Pearl Harbor."[35] In 1993 conservative analyst Frank Gaffney called a declassification initiative by Energy Secretary Hazel O'Leary "the most devastating single attack on the underpinnings of the U.S. national security structure since Japan's lightning strike on the 7th Fleet."[36] Pearl Harbor served as an all-purpose cue for those wishing to trigger insecurity and a proactive response.

Pearl Harbor's persistent association with infamy, "sneak attack," and military strength arose, understandably, from the surprise that suddenly sliced through a peaceful Sunday morning and brought war to America. But other stories could and would be framed. Surprise is, after all, a common element in military strategy, and undeclared wars have been common in the twentieth century. Japan's surprise attack against the Russian fleet in 1904, prior to a declaration of war, received wide acclaim in the

West as a stunning military achievement. Nor did Japan ever formally declare war on China during the decade of military attacks that preceded December 1941. Hitler turned surprise attacks into an art. Moreover, there were no formal declarations of war associated—on either side—with any of America's major post–World War II conflicts: the wars in Korea, Vietnam, or Iraq. Was Japan's attack so uniquely "infamous"? Moreover, strong military preparedness was hardly the only lesson that could be derived from the attack. As will be developed below, some historians in both the United States and Japan constructed a history that positioned Japan as the victim of both a lopsided and exploitative global economy and unwisely provocative U.S. actions.

Nevertheless, the infamy framework has proved a resilient structuring story for Pearl Harbor history/memory. It seems to have been born as an already familiar motivational narrative in 1941 and has continued to circulate as a useful cautionary tale invoked repeatedly by advocates of strengthening the nation's intelligence and military capabilities.

American nationalism, like all nationalisms that bind political communities, is an imaginary that must be continually retaught and reconstituted in culture.[37] The Roosevelt administration fashioned the "infamy" at Pearl Harbor into a resonant and long-lasting symbol of nationalism, reinvigorating national unity and power while countering centrifugal pressures and fractures. "Infamy was the note that struck home, the word that welded the country together," wrote Walter Lord in the concluding sentence of his *Day of Infamy,* still probably the most widely read book on Pearl Harbor.[38] The basic allegory of Pearl Harbor predated the attack itself. It fit preexistent traditions, updating the Custer and Alamo motifs that held such emotional power in national memories before World War II. Throughout the war, the rallying cry of "Remember Pearl Harbor" served to remind Americans of the treacherous character of the enemy, to underscore the morality of the cause, to rally support for preparedness and for unrelenting military action if attacked, to warn against "sleeping" and isolationism, against weakness and dissent. This infamy framework expressed the causes and justifications of the war in terms of national character rather than national interest. It rooted the story of the Pacific War not in geopolitics but in a highly personalized and religiously tinged language of retribution. After the war, the term "Pearl Harbor" served as a rhetorical resource in support of building an effective intelligence capability, maintaining ongoing military preparedness, and sustaining a masculine ethos that placed loyalty to nation above personal imperatives and associated itself with military power. It assured that any defeat of the United States by outsiders would become a prelude to a glorious American victory.

Examination of the infamy framework suggests how building blocks of memory/history take shape. Familiarity of structure; memory activists who fashion compelling phrases, images, and narratives; and intertextual repetition and circulation all played a part. Infamy, in short, became the first, and perhaps most entrenched, rhetorical formulation of the events at Pearl Harbor. Others, however, quickly developed.

2 Backdoor Deceit

Contesting the New Deal

The message that the country must pull together in face of Japan's "infamy" and "treachery," though certainly dominant during the war, contended with another one. Franklin Roosevelt was one of America's most beloved—and also one of its most intensely detested—presidents. When the dedicated Roosevelt haters advanced December 7 as a day of "deceit," they were overwhelmingly concerned with proving that the deceit rested in the White House.

In his war speech, Roosevelt attributed the Pearl Harbor loss to Japan's infamy, but he did not address why American outposts were so unprepared for the attacks. As Americans struggled to understand and respond to the tragedy, questions about responsibility could hardly be avoided. As with so many other historical controversies involving blame for lives lost in war, interpretive disagreements flared.[1]

A date which will live in inquiry

Two days after Japan's planes delivered their devastating blows, Secretary of Navy Knox undertook a hasty investigation to assess the damage and the reasons for the base's lack of preparedness.

Knox, a Republican whom Roosevelt had added to the cabinet in 1940 to give his foreign policy a more bipartisan look, concluded that the attack was "a complete surprise to both the Army and Navy." It "was due to a lack of a state of readiness against such an air attack, by both branches of the service" because neither of the Pacific commanders in Oahu had "regarded such an attack as at all likely."[2]

Various anti-Roosevelt newspapers and leaders in Congress saw things differently. They suggested that officials in Washington bore more of the blame, and some, including "Mr. Republican" Senator Robert Taft, called for an independent inquiry. The attack on Pearl Harbor seemed to confirm, for many previously isolationist Republicans, that Roosevelt had manipulated the country toward war. Debates heated up in both the House and the Senate over the issue of responsibility.[3]

To avoid a popular backlash, Roosevelt ordered another official investigation to determine "whether any derelictions of duty or errors of judgments" by army or navy personnel were responsible. Headed by retired Supreme Court justice Owen J. Roberts and comprised of four high-ranking military officers (two from the navy and two from the army, three of them retired), this commission met over a five-week period and issued a report that Roosevelt approved on January 24, 1942. The secretaries of navy and war had relieved the Pacific commanders of their duties on the first day of the Roberts Commission proceedings, and the view of holding these two commanders at fault generally prevailed.

The final Roberts Commission report argued that existing emergency plans would have been adequate but that the commanders had failed to confer with each other and implement such plans. Although a false sense of security prevailed "in diplomatic, military, and naval circles, and in the public press," this widespread view did not relieve commanders of their special responsibility to protect the Pacific Fleet. In light of warnings transmitted from Washington to both commanders between November 17 and December 7, the investigation charged Admiral Kimmel and General Short with dereliction of duty due to errors of judgment. It cleared those directly in charge in Washington, General Marshall and Admiral Harold R. Stark. The wartime secrecy that shrouded U.S. ability to read the Japanese diplomatic code and other civilian-military-intelligence procedures, however, rendered the Roberts Commission report necessarily sketchy and incomplete.[4]

The Roberts Commission was only the beginning of inquiry. Although the general journalistic response to the report seems to have been favorable, many Republican critics charged that the commission had not gone far enough in moving the blame up the chain of command to include officials in Washington. Senators Robert LaFollette Jr. and Wayland Brooks, among many other isolationists, demanded a new congressional investigation focusing on Washington, a move that was beaten back by Democrats. Meanwhile, Kimmel and Short were pressured to retire, and their retirements, which would preclude full hearings through courts martial proceedings, became public in February 1942. Although Republicans gained forty-four House seats and nine in the Senate in the midterm elections of 1942, the Democrats still controlled both houses of Congress and kept the Pearl Harbor attack from becoming a major issue.[5]

Early in 1944 Secretary Knox ordered retired admiral Thomas C. Hart to gather more testimony from naval personnel who were or soon might be on dangerous assignments. The concern was that many of those with intimate and firsthand knowledge of the events surrounding the attack might be killed in battle during the brutal Pacific campaign. Hart's information gathering lasted four months, but his investigation was not made public until after the war and drew no new conclusions.

As the 1944 election approached, Republicans joined Kimmel and Short in asking for formal courts martial proceedings, which might bring forth information to embarrass the Roosevelt administration. In congressional debates over an ultimately unsuccessful resolution to force such courts martial for each commander, Republicans argued that the country deserved to discover "the truth" about Pearl Harbor while Democrats countered that any such proceeding might give "aid and comfort" to the enemy. In a compromise resolution, the Seventy-eighth Congress asked both the army and the navy to hold hearings on the Pearl Harbor attack, assess blame, and make recommendations for the future. Some Republican strategists advised that focusing on the president's poor leadership *before the war* could provide a campaign issue that skirted around Roosevelt's appeal for unity *during the war*.[6]

The army and navy reports, submitted to the president in October 1944 but not immediately made public, defended the commanders and tilted the blame toward Washington. The army's Pearl Harbor Board found that the commanders had committed errors of judgment only, not derelictions of duty. Moreover, it suggested that the army chief of staff, General Marshall, had failed to warn the Hawaiian command and that Roosevelt and Hull had set nearly impossible conditions in their negotiations with Japan. The navy's board also emphasized the lapses from Washington, faulting Admiral Stark for failing both to transmit important information and to provide sufficient aviation force to carry out reconnaissance.[7]

To undercut the conclusions of the army and navy boards, Secretary of War Stimson and Secretary of Navy James Forrestal in early 1945 announced that the boards had reached flawed, incomplete conclusions and ordered even more extensive inquiries and additional reports, coordinated by Major Henry C. Clausen and Admiral H. Kent Hewitt respectively. (Years later, in 1992, Clausen would reenter the Pearl Harbor debates by writing a book reiterating many of his conclusions.) The War Department was also taking testimony on the handling of top-secret intelligence, including the so-called Magic Intercepts, decoded versions of Japan's diplomatic correspondence. These inquiries highlighted a lack of coordination among various military and civilian units but generally supported the conclusion that the commanders at Pearl Harbor had been deficient in their preparations. President Harry S. Truman, having taken office after Roosevelt's death, announced public release of the reports on the same day that victorious U.S. troops entered Tokyo, headlining them with his own interpretation that "the country itself" shouldered the blame for the lack of preparedness.[8]

By the end of 1945, then, there had been seven inquiries, seven reports, and thousands of pages of testimony. Partisan debates framed the issues, as rival investigators asked whether officials in Washington or commanders at Pearl Harbor were the more to blame. Republicans charged that the inquiries blaming Kimmel and Short were simply partisan defenses of the Roosevelt administration, and some among them asserted a dark conspiracy—that Roosevelt had actually provoked Japan to war and deliberately withheld vital information from the Pacific command in order to generate an incident that would bring the United States into the war. Polls suggested no public consensus over the issue of blame. By the election of 1946, the war was over and Roosevelt was dead, but partisan passions remained. Anti-Roosevelt forces warned that the Truman administration was continuing to cover up misdeeds.

The spirit of inquiry, with both sides still wanting to substantiate their claims in some definitive finding, persisted. The contest, by now, was over history—how to remember and recount the disaster. Throughout 1946, a congressionally appointed ten-person committee (four Republicans) again took testimony on Pearl Harbor. It sought to fix responsibility for the lack of preparedness and, after learning lessons from this history, to ascertain whether Congress should consider new legislation to reorganize civilian-military command structures. This process would feed into the drafting of the National Security Act of 1947.

Ultimately, this joint congressional committee's five-hundred-page report, with thirty-nine volumes of comments and testimony, concluded that Kimmel and Short, though not derelict of duty, had made significant errors of judgment and coordination. The commanders remained retired in disgrace with no courts martial. The committee vote was 8 to 2, with two Republicans on each side of the vote. The majority report echoed the administration's framework emphasizing Japan's infamy, the unpreparedness of the Pacific commands, and the "sleeping," isolationist country.[9] The minority report, written by Senators Owen Brewster (Maine) and Homer Ferguson (Michigan), inverted these emphases and advanced what became popularly known as the "backdoor" interpretation. It sketched a narrative of Pearl Harbor that would circulate widely among Roosevelt's critics in the postwar era.

The history advanced in the minority report suggested that the Roosevelt administration had failed to pursue opportunities to avoid or delay a rupture with Japan because it had sought a "back door" to entering the war. Eager to steer the nation into the war in Europe and help save Britain from the German advance, the report alleged, Roosevelt pushed Japan into a spectacular attack that would convince Americans to join the Allies. At the same time that it was provoking Japan to strike, the administration failed to alert the commanders in Hawaii about clearly known dangers, couching its warnings and intelligence reports in "conflicting and imprecise language." In their relations with Kimmel and Short, officers in Washington exhibited "mismanagement, non-cooperation, unpreparedness, confusion, and negligence."[10] Although the minority report also found that the commanders had fallen short in executing their responsibilities in Hawaii, it emphasized that the president, the commander in chief, held ultimate responsibility for ensuring the high quality of the men and the informational systems that established critical defenses.

An entire section of the minority report denounced the idea that "the country" was to blame for Pearl Harbor because of its insufficient vigilance (the "sleeping" metaphor directed at former isolationists). Roosevelt, it charged, had kept Americans in the dark. "How could the American people be responsible for the warlike operations conducted from Washington . . . about which they were never informed?" "Indeed the high authorities in Washington seemed to be acting upon some long-range plan which was never disclosed to Congress or to the American people. A nation in mortal danger is entitled to know the truth about its peril."[11] If America slept, in short, it was because of Roosevelt's deception.

The minority report lashed out at the credibility of the committee itself. First, its "partisan character" had created an "iron curtain" that limited the scope of investigation. Second, the committee's inability to question high executive branch officials discredited its conclusions: Roosevelt and Knox had died earlier; Harry Hopkins, Roosevelt's closest adviser, passed away during the investigation; Stimson and Hull, in poor health, provided only limited testimony, with no chance for cross-examination. Third, the restriction on disclosing cryptanalytic information blocked adequate inquiry. (The committee, however, did force the administration to reveal its ability to read Japanese diplomatic codes, an admission that Democratic officials charged compromised existing intelligence gathering.) The minority report concluded that "there was a deliberate design to block the search for truth."[12]

Debating the backdoor interpretation

The minority report's back-door-to-war narrative became a fervent article of faith among Roosevelt's critics, especially on the Republican right. To those Republican politicians who still attempted to make Pearl Harbor an issue in the 1948 election, the attack symbolized how Roosevelt had deceived the American people by manipulating them into war and then made military officers the scapegoats. The backdoor interpretation warned against the dangers of the powerful and deceitful central government that Roosevelt's New Deal had built.

The rhetorical contours of the arguments in each interpretation seemed partly shaped by those of the opposing other. The "asleep" framework (which emphasized the country's generalized innocence and unpreparedness, usually blaming the Hawaii commanders for a specific lack of vigilance) and the "deliberate design" framework (which blamed Washington officials for a backdoor provocation) constituted opposing interpretive poles that helped organize partisan views and subsequent contests over history/memory. Moreover, the controversy over locating blame with the commanders in Hawaii or with the commander in chief in the White House refracted a larger dispute about the big-government legacy of the New Deal.

These political disputes became a feature of postwar journalism. The conservative McCormick newspaper chain, owner of the Chicago *Tribune* and advocate for an isolationist stance before Pearl Harbor, championed pro-Kimmel, backdoor views. A month after the end of the war, an article for the *Tribune* by John T. Flynn (later expanded into a book called *The Truth about Pearl Harbor*) prefigured the argument of the minority report by sketching out the backdoor theory. Flynn became a widely read critic of globalism and New Deal–style centralized government. A stalwart voice for the old right, he sold four million copies, in *Reader's Digest* condensation, of his 1949 *The Road Ahead,* which warned against an omnipotent government.[13] George Morgenstern, another Chicago *Tribune* reporter, also detailed a backdoor conspiracy carried out by Roosevelt and his compliant "pets" in the military's high echelon in Washington.[14]

A spate of books, some by professional historians and some by journalists or participants, buttressed the backdoor argument. These works, which the more dominant pro-Roosevelt historians called "revisionism," elaborated the idea that Roosevelt deliberately provoked Japan. Within that common thesis, several variations emerged. William Henry Chamberlin, for example, criticized Roosevelt for undertaking an anti-Axis policy that allied the United States with the Soviet Union. He believed that communism represented a greater threat to the United States than fascism and promoted the Republican charge that the Roosevelt administration harbored procommunist sympathizers. A related, but even more extreme, view suggested an international Jewish conspiracy. FDR's former son-in-law, Curtis B. Dall, publicly and privately alleged that "international financiers and Zionist leaders"—especially Bernard Baruch and Felix Frankfurter—controlled Roosevelt's policies and misdirected the president into a war against Germany and Japan.[15]

Charles Beard, one of the age's preeminent historians, also charged that Roosevelt had maneuvered the United States into war. His critique came from the political left. A social justice progressive who had lost his academic position at Columbia University by protesting against U.S. entry into World War I, Beard believed that war would spell the death of reform at home and strengthen a moneyed oligarchy. Although he did not directly charge that FDR had plotted the Pearl Harbor attack in advance, he implied that the president deliberately allowed it to come without opposition. Oddly, Beard became so intent on showing Roosevelt's *personal* responsibility for bringing the war that he minimized the broader economic perspective with which he had long been associated.[16] The view that economic interest lay behind the dangerous U.S. bullying of other nations, a general position Beard had forcefully argued in his earlier book, *The Idea of Na-*

tional Interest, would be elaborated by Beard's leftist followers in the 1960s and 1970s.

Charles C. Tansil and Harry Elmer Barnes became the most influential of all backdoor proponents. Tansil's book, *Back Door to War,* helped popularize the phrase. Barnes had consistently opposed U.S. economic expansion abroad, which he thought inevitably led to conflicts with other nations and then to war. Their books elaborated the classic backdoor charges: the president and his advisers had schemed to provoke Japan, deliberately withheld any warning, and orchestrated a massive cover-up.[17]

On the other side, in a 1947 *Saturday Evening Post* article called "Why We Were Caught Napping at Pearl Harbor," Seth Richardson, a Republican from North Dakota who had served as general counsel for the joint congressional committee, rejected the backdoor perspective. Drawing from the majority report and invoking the familiar "sleeping" metaphor, Richardson asked why virtually no one in Washington or Hawaii considered an attack on Pearl Harbor a possibility. Although he showed that a joint army and navy report in March 1941 had warned that a dawn air attack from the northwest sector would be the most likely form of a Japanese surprise against Hawaii, most officials in both Hawaii and Washington testified that they believed Japan would make its move elsewhere. Nearly everyone, Richardson concluded, assumed that the Japanese navy and aviators lacked the technical skill to mount such a distant and complex attack. They all committed the "unpardonable mistake of underestimating one's adversary."[18] Such arguments, emerging from the majority report and now headlined in America's most popular magazine by a prominent former isolationist Republican, indirectly challenged any claim of backdoor, deliberate design while supporting the case for better intelligence and preparedness in a new national security state. The argument that explained America's ill preparedness by emphasizing an unfounded disdain for Japanese military skill also fit with the cold war's new emphasis on building respect for Japan as an ally in the fight against communism.

In a *New York Times* Sunday magazine article on Pearl Harbor's tenth anniversary in 1951, liberal correspondent Cabell Philipps rehashed the thirty-nine volumes of the congressional Pearl Harbor report, again underscoring the lesson of America's general unpreparedness. A barrage of letters to the editor followed, blaming officials in Washington instead. For decades to come, the histories/memories of one side stimulated counterhistories/ memories from the other side, perpetuating a cycle of partisan controversy that was sometimes thinly, and sometimes not too thinly, veiled. Each side invoked the authority of historical truth and saw the other view as revisionism or falsification.[19]

Some naval personnel or strongly pro-navy writers added to the anti-Roosevelt argument. If Roosevelt could be shown at fault, then military officers of the U.S. Pacific Fleet could not be held responsible. Restoring the navy's good name became a sidebar to the backdoor critique, as Rear Admiral Robert A. Theobald's *The Final Secret of Pearl Harbor* (1954) and Admiral Kimmel's own book, *Admiral Kimmel's Story* (1955), illustrated. Theobald stressed that the Magic Intercepts, read in Washington, showed that Tokyo had sent several requests to its consul in Hawaii for detailed reports on the position of ships in the harbor. Was this not evidence of a forthcoming Japanese attack? Theobald concluded that "we were unready at Pearl Harbor because President Roosevelt's plans required that no word be sent to alert the Fleet in Hawaii. . . . The individuals in high position in Washington who willfully refrained from alerting our forces at Pearl Harbor should never be excused." Admiral William F. Halsey's introduction to the book stated that Kimmel and Short "were thrown to the wolves as scapegoats."[20] Theobald's and Kimmel's books were widely excerpted and reviewed in popular magazines during the mid-1950s, often with rejoinders or discussions alongside.[21] All of this attention kept the backdoor controversy alive and familiar to a broad public.

Among many professional historians, however, these backdoor charges gained little credibility. Samuel Eliot Morison (whom backdoor theorists dismissed as a "court historian"), writing in the *Saturday Evening Post* on the twentieth anniversary of Pearl Harbor in December 1961, implicitly answered Theobald by pointing out that "scores of such orders [for intelligence on ship positions] . . . for over a year had been sent to Japanese consuls in major seaports of the non-Axis world." Echoing the 1946 con-

gressional report and Richardson's 1947 article, Morison concluded that officials in Washington and Pearl Harbor had been
caught by surprise because of "their inability to imagine that Japan
would do anything so suicidal." He also emphasized that officials
had sent a generalized war warning to the commanders. Endorsing a yet unpublished manuscript by Roberta Wohlstetter, he
claimed that the specific timing and locale of Japan's attack were
impossible to ascertain due to the confusion and fragmentation in
intelligence gathering.[22]

Wohlstetter's book appeared the next year and quickly became
one of the most influential studies of American decision making
on the eve of the Japanese attack.[23] Wohlstetter argued that indica-
tions of an attack had been lost amid the clutter and noise of so
much incoming intelligence. Implicitly, her thesis backed post–
Bay of Pigs proposals for a more active, better funded intelligence
agency, an agenda that her husband, security analyst Albert Wohlstetter, advocated over the next decade as he warned against underestimating the Soviet threat.

Morison and Wohlstetter provided an authoritative historical
analysis that became embedded in most subsequent history textbooks. A typical amount from one of the most widely used textbooks of the cold war era, for example, read: "The administration
thought an attack upon American territory unlikely. The commanders in Hawaii were routinely warned. Negligence there and
in Washington, not diabolical plotting as was later charged, led to
the disaster ahead."[24]

While both sides had accumulated a shelf of books and articles
to cite as authority for their views, disputes over blame for Pearl
Harbor generally received little magazine space from the mid-
1960s into the early 1970s. As Americans became involved in controversies related to Vietnam, interest in Pearl Harbor lagged.
Even on the political right, backdoor accounts of World War II
went into eclipse. At the twenty-fifth anniversary of Pearl Harbor,
for example, the conservative magazine *National Review* published a backdoor spread by Harry Elmer Barnes. In the next issue,
however, it carried a sharp retort by William Rickenbacker protesting what he considered the provincialism and anti-intellectualism
of the backdoor "clique": "There is a persecution complex thinly

concealed beneath the surface of this I'm-right-and-all-the-rest-are-wrong line; and persecution complexes are death on clear thinking."[25]

During the 1980s there seemed to be a resurgence of new work—and renewed controversy. Gordon Prange, with Donald Goldstein and Katherine Dillon, authored a series of widely read books on the Pacific War, two of which dealt with Pearl Harbor: *At Dawn We Slept* (1981) and *Pearl Harbor: The Verdict of History* (1986). Prange popularized views that were consistent with the dominant wartime narrative and with Wohlstetter. In his rendering, policymakers could not realistically have avoided war with expansionist Japan; they understandably believed the attack would come elsewhere, and no convincing evidence showed credible forewarning of the danger to Hawaii; the Congress (under sway of isolationism) showed indifference to Japan's threat; the country was too complacent (asleep); and there were deficiencies in coordination and communication of information. Although Prange's books concluded that "no one was without blame—all made mistakes" leading up to Pearl Harbor, Prange assigned Kimmel and Short very substantial responsibility and, invoking a now-familiar structure, presented their deficiencies as a larger metaphor for the country's complacency. Prange's books became perhaps the most widely cited works on Pearl Harbor and brought renewed authority to the dominant cold war view that the primary lesson of Pearl Harbor was the need for alertness, adequate armed forces, and—above all—an effective intelligence system.[26]

Prange and others argued that the backdoor interpretations lacked logic. If a provocation was to have been plotted as a back door to war, it hardly made sense to sacrifice much of the Pacific Fleet. An attack against a fully prepared base could have been just as inflammatory as an attack against an unprepared one—and could have spared the losses. There were many ways that FDR could have maneuvered Japan into firing the first shot, if that were his goal, but only a madman would have dreamed up the Pearl Harbor debacle. Moreover, what if Hitler had not stupidly declared war on the United States? The United States would have directed all of its military might toward Japan, leaving Britain even more vulnerable to Hitler's forces. Prange and others charged backdoor advocates not only with flawed logic, but also with a "disregard for the laws of evidence."[27] As Morison had argued, any Rooseveltian conspiracy would have to have been impossibly broad based, needing the connivance of Hull, Stimson, Knox, Marshall, Stark, and others—"all loyal and honorable men who would never have lent themselves to such monstrous deception."[28]

Still, the blame for Pearl Harbor remained highly contested. If the Wohlstetter-Prange view dominated textbooks, other works came to the defense of the Pearl Harbor commanders. Rear Admiral Edwin T. Layton and Admiral James O. Richardson wrote anti-Roosevelt memoirs, desiring to "set the record straight" before they died. Historian John Toland's *Infamy* concluded that the "comedy of errors" on December 6 and 7 "appears incredible. It only makes sense if it was a charade, and Roosevelt and the inner circle had known about the attack."[29] In 1991, with the fiftieth anniversary celebrations piquing greater interest, yet another inflammatory revisionist account, by James Rusbridger and Eric Nave, attracted widespread attention.[30] The day of infamy would live on in ever-renewing controversy over Roosevelt's responsibility.

Blame the government!

The conclusions of the 1946 inquiry, refined and popularized in magazines, in scholarly work by Wohlstetter, and in Prange's best-sellers, provided the most visible narrative of the disaster at Pearl Harbor. Yet the story that Roosevelt had planned a back door to war continued to circulate widely. Donald Goldstein, Prange's co-author, reported how frequently the question of the president's machinations arose whenever he spoke on Pearl Harbor.[31] College teachers have for years reported that the question of Roosevelt's deceit is one of the few historical controversies already familiar to incoming students. Apparently the controversy is well entrenched in folk and popular culture. Why? Certainly the propaganda frameworks and films of World War II had not articulated a backdoor view. And probably very few Americans actively engaged the intricacies of the controversies raised in the many pro- and anti-Roosevelt books. How might the persistence of backdoor theories and the distrust of government that they represent be understood?

Initially, of course, many of those who hated Roosevelt and the New Deal adopted backdoor views. There may, however, be explanations beyond simple partisanship. Journalist Thurston Clarke's *Pearl Harbor Ghosts* links the persistence of conspiracy theories to overconfidence and injured pride. "There is no greater disgrace than to be defeated by an opponent you have previously denigrated."[32] Emphasizing your own side's errors—even treachery—implicitly helps preserve a continued sense of personal superiority over the enemy. America's racism and sense of superiority, in this view, worked on behalf of a backdoor formulation. This logic might help explain why the most extreme nationalists—America Firsters, for example—would provide the most congenial ground for backdoor conspiracy theories.

Another explanation might relate to the narrative imperatives of dramatic representation. In this regard, it will be helpful to turn to the most popular and influential film representation of Pearl Harbor during the cold war era: *Tora! Tora! Tora!* During the war itself, films that featured the Pearl Harbor attack had largely employed the infamy/last-stand framework, seeking to motivate Americans toward retribution. *Tora!*, however, told a far different story. In its dramatization of the events leading up to the attack, this movie did not overtly promote a backdoor interpretation or make any specific charge against Roosevelt, who never appeared on screen. In fact, opening credits cited Gordon Prange's work. Nonetheless, an examination of *Tora!* may help illuminate how the workings of its dramatic narrative remained open to a backdoor interpretation.

This film was unusual in its evenhanded presentation of the two now allied principals in the conflict, the United States and Japan. With the preliminary script and shooting done collaboratively between Americans and Japanese, this Hollywood product violated many standard movie-making conventions. First, half of the film dramatized Japanese decision making and action, and much of the film employed Japanese-language dialogue and English subtitles. (Most other Pacific theater films only briefly presented Japanese characters, and they used English so that American audiences would not be put off by unpopular subtitles.) Second, because no central "star" organized the perspective and the drama, the film projected a decentered point of view that was unusual in Hollywood productions. Although this important movie will be dealt with below in terms of U.S.-Japan relations, for now the focus will be on its treatment of foreign policy decisions made on the American side.

In crucial and lengthy scenes, put together from historical research, the film depicts top officials in Washington as inexplicably unconcerned about alarming reports from Asia and even as reluctant to report them to the president. In one key scene, army and navy intelligence officers in Washington receive decoded Japanese diplomatic messages that alarm them. Lieutenant Commander Alvin Kramer of Naval Intelligence (played by Wesley Addey) hurries to the White House to deliver the top-secret Magic decrypts to the president himself, only to find that the president is out. He then rushes the material to Secretary Marshall, only to be told that the secretary has gone to bed. Finally, he gets the messages to Admiral Stark, who seems rather unconcerned and says soothingly that the president has sent a personal message to the emperor. Then, on the morning of December 7 (Washington time) intelligence decodes a message instructing the Japanese embassy to destroy its codebooks and decrypting machinery. Clearly, this instruction seems a prelude to war with the United States. Intelligence officers again rush to alert top officials. Again, Kramer goes to Admiral Stark, recommending that he call Kimmel in Hawaii. Stark says he must call the president first and asks everyone to leave the room. The scene closes with Stark looking at his telephones but not reaching for them. No explanation for his inaction is provided. Meanwhile, Colonel Rufus Bratton, the other intelligence officer in the film (played by E. G. Marshall), goes to warn Secretary Marshall. The secretary is unavailable; he is out riding his horse. Only later, one and one-half hours before the attack, does Marshall reappear and order an alert telegraphed to Pearl Harbor—a message that goes out without an "urgent" label and is received in Hawaii after the attack.

These scenes might imply the poor communication and coordination that Wohlstetter and Prange stressed. They might also suggest that the president did not welcome receiving alarming information and his subordinates knew why. In any case (whether by ill coordination or by design), Washington seems to be a rather detached place where people go horseback riding and seem generally unavailable but do not pay attention to urgent matters of war and peace. Admiral Kimmel (played by Martin Balsam) is scripted as a competent, if not particularly strong, commander who does his best for a government that keeps him in the dark. The film leaves open whether FDR's top administration was incompetent or participating in some backdoor deceit.

Tora! may provide insight into the resilience of backdoor views in popular memory. Like any narrative representing "real life," it has to focus a story through a process of simplification and filtering. In real life, a thousand things happen simultaneously; in historical representation, a single story is often stripped down to the theme at hand—in this case Pearl Harbor.[33] Thus, those attentive to the possibility of a Japanese attack at Pearl Harbor are portrayed favorably; those less attentive may be variously interpreted as unengaged, negligent, perhaps even duplicitous. Since most concerns other than Pearl Harbor are eliminated for narrative coherence, it is hard to imagine that anyone *not* thinking about the possibility of this particular attack was truly doing his job. In this hindsighted and necessarily single-focused projection, constructing a narrative of "what happened at Pearl Harbor" implicitly suggests "blame" in those not focused upon that particular issue. *What were all those people doing when they should have been preparing for attack?* Through its structure, which implicitly foregrounds the issue of blame, *Tora!* may reinforce backdoor interpretations among viewers who are already predisposed to an anti-Roosevelt or antigovernment persuasion.

Somewhat the same process may be at work in the more general creation and circulation of history/memory. Most Americans "remember" Pearl Harbor as part of a narrative: the Japanese attacked; Americans were surprised and unprepared; they took huge losses; the war began. From this simple, dramatic story line, the concurrent things that are not to be remembered fall away, and the issue of blame emerges as a necessary accompaniment to the dramatic structure. Stripping off all of the contingent possibilities of what might have happened but did not, memory simplifies by remembering some aspects of the past and forgetting others. The dramatic form of this memory-narrative helps guide the selection of what will remain as content and what will be discarded (forgotten) as irrelevant to the story.

Ironically, it may be the very mode of cause-and-effect narrative structures, which, by promoting a habit of mind that insists on locating cause, can often breed conspiracy theory.[34] The official "blame" for Pearl Harbor always seemed somewhat unsatisfying because it was so diffuse. A complex mix of disunited commanders, inadequate intelligence, bureaucratic disorganization in both Hawaii and Washington, poor (or unlucky) decisions, and underestimation of the enemy produced a highly abstract "cause." How much more satisfying to believe that some powerful *person*, rather than complicated and intertwining circumstances, was at fault. Pearl Harbor was only the first of many postwar disasters that were followed with inquiries whose reports then became controversial as possible "cover-ups" for allegedly darker conspiracies.

Timothy Melley's *Empire of Conspiracy* further suggests that a pervasive postwar fear about the disappearance of individual agency may have provided fertile cultural ground for interpretations that, in effect, imagined that *people* were in control after all. It is hardly surprising that, faced with the emotion of such a devastating blow, many Americans wished to assign blame to those who failed to prevent the action. As Melley writes, conspiracy theories "grossly oversimplify the causal origins of complex events. They hinge upon a fantasy of individual autonomy," and ironically grow stronger when feelings of personal powerlessness increase.[35]

Still, if personal blame is a structuring attribute of the backdoor story, why blame people in high authority? Why not accept the disciplinary actions against the commanders and the inquiries that cleared top officials? In America, conspiracy theories supporting a distrust of the central government have been popular at least as far back as the revolutionary movement's campaigns against King George III. Since the American Revolution, powerful presidents have regularly been targeted as power abusers. Roosevelt, of course, was one such powerful president, and his enlargement of the role of the federal government in American life, to fight depression and then war, became interlaced into larger narratives of distrust for a distant central authority.[36]

From this perspective, it is not surprising to find that backdoor, distrust-the-government themes grew right along with the post-war expansion of federal power. Truman's Fair Deal, Kennedy's New Frontier, Johnson's Great Society, and Nixon's Watergate-related secrecy marked the trajectory of larger government against which conservatives on the right, sometimes joined by radicals on the left, mounted an ever more visible critique. By the post-Watergate era, deep public cynicism about the federal government had become mainstream. The assumption that governmental officials lie, keep secrets, and engage in cover-ups was widespread. A film like *Tora!* may have credited Prange at the start, but its interpretations are open to many readings and seem potentially congenial to early 1970s audiences, who were steeped in reports of executive branch abuse of power.

The prevalence and popularity of the backdoor interpretation, in short, emerges from a larger cultural context that seeks to identify a clear, even personalized, cause and fits into a pervasive cultural narrative of backlash against power wielders in Washington. *Tora!*'s compatibility with backdoor views also illustrates how the dramatic simplifications required by narrative, along with these contemporary contexts, may have worked together to make Roosevelt's "deceit" seem eminently plausible to large numbers of Americans.

At the same time that Pearl Harbor became a nationalistic rallying cry against infamy, it also could be a code word for critiquing Roosevelt's New Deal. Roosevelt, charged some of the old isolationists, intentionally plotted the Pearl Harbor debacle to provide a back door to war. The central tenets of this backdoor critique maintained that the Roosevelt administration provoked Japan to war, withheld vital information about Japan's intentions from the commanders in Hawaii, and covered up its misdeeds with partisan inquiries. This view became an article of faith among Roosevelt haters, especially within the right wing of the Republican Party and among some defenders of the navy's (and especially Admiral Kimmel's) honor. Although the backdoor interpretation gained little support in most academic history or in commonly used textbooks (where Wohlstetter's and Prange's formulations stressing intelligence failures and the unreadiness of commanders dominated), it persisted in memory, probably fed by culturally familiar discourses of governmental distrust that had long circulated in American life. Dark fears of the central government waxed strongly among anti–New Deal groups during the immediate postwar period. In the aftermath of Vietnam and Watergate, such antigovernment rhetoric became fairly mainstream, shaping a great deal of the political discourse of a growing conservative movement. For many people, even if they had enthusiastically supported World War II out of patriotic duty and hatred of fascism, Pearl Harbor seemed an available metaphor for expressing distrust of the Democratic Roosevelt and his New Deal social agenda and/or the federal government's growing power and capacity for secrecy and manipulation. As a narrative of blame, Pearl Harbor provided a continuing rhetorical resource for expressing distrust of those in power in Washington.

3 Representations of Race

and Japanese-American

Relations

The story of Pearl Harbor also assumed an important role in shaping contesting images of U.S.-Japanese relations. Through the icon of Pearl Harbor, Japan could be positioned as a treacherous and subhuman enemy or as an industrious potential ally.

Americans' views of Japan drew upon a century of contact between the two countries. Since Commodore Matthew Perry's arrival in Tokyo harbor in 1853, traditions of both Japanophobia and Japanophilia had circulated widely. These negative and positive formulations provided rhetorical traditions that could be drawn upon to demonize Japan during the war and then to transform an arch-enemy into a close friend during the cold war that followed. Different versions of the Japanese-American relationship could be plotted by selecting (remembering and forgetting) different contexts within which to set the Pearl Harbor story.

"We were back to primitive days of
fighting Indians on the American frontier;
no holds barred and no quarter."

During the war, Pearl Harbor became the central American symbol to justify retribution and righteous vengeance against a "sneak
attack" by a treacherous foe. Japan's racial and national character
was commonly associated with treachery, and the infamy-and-
retribution narrative, like its last-stand predecessors, drew upon
racial ideologies that marked "Americans" as white and superior
and Japanese as animalistic, undifferentiated, cruel, and deceitful.
Samuel Eliot Morison explained that the war was not "civilized"
but recalled the "primitive days of fighting Indians."[1]

The tradition that demonized Japan as both a strategic and racial threat had roots not only in America's own frontier rhetoric,
but also in various historical antagonisms. Geopolitical rivalry,
particularly related to the ambitions of both countries in Manchuria and China, had flared periodically for the previous half century.
Aggravating strategic competition, racism by American whites
against Japanese immigrants, especially in the West, had shaped
turn-of-the-century immigrant exclusion acts, justified alien land
laws that prevented Japanese immigrants from owning land, and
prompted various other anti-Japanese measures throughout the
early twentieth century. Domestic sentiment against Japanese immigrants flowed into foreign policy, where it aggravated Japan's
nationalism and hostility toward the United States and heightened Americans' anger against Japan's "infamy" at Pearl Harbor.[2] (A section below will investigate the special place that Japanese Americans have occupied in relationship to Pearl Harbor
memories.)

During the war, animalistic imagery (especially of insects and
monkeys) became a standard trope that became increasingly vicious. In Ford's *December 7,* Japanese planes were "tiny locusts."
On the first anniversary of Pearl Harbor, the cover of the mass-
marketed *Collier's* magazine showed a bloody-toothed vampire
bat ready to drop bombs in the harbor.[3] After ordering the use of
atomic bombs on Japan, President Harry Truman connected the

act to the "unwarranted attack by the Japanese on Pearl Harbor. . . . When you have to deal with a beast you have to treat him as a beast."⁴ The animalistic imagery projected Japanese people as undifferentiated. Capra's *Know Your Enemy—Japan,* part of the *Why We Fight* series, included the controversial (even then) scene that asserted Japanese people were like "photographic prints off the same negative."⁵

Wartime representations of Japan's culture decried a lack of openness and forthright honesty that led to deceit. Some anthropologists who wrote wartime studies of Japan's "national character" drew a picture of collective pathology—compulsive, suspicious, and devious. Magazines popularized these themes. *Time,* for example, published an illustrated article on how Americans could tell their friends, the Chinese, from their foes, the Japanese. The differences ran from the trivial ("most Chinese avoid horn-rimmed spectacles") to the absurd ("Japanese are dogmatic and arrogant while the Chinese expression is kindly and placid").⁶ Wartime "experts" on Japan explained the "topsy-turvy mind of the Jap" and described how "With His Trick Mind, the Japanese Fools Himself."⁷ *Life* did a feature in 1942 on the Japanese language, which was "perfect for hiding facts or saying what you don't mean." The article, which was subsequently reprinted in the widely read *Reader's Digest,* quoted OWI head Archibald MacLeish as stating that only three Americans had full command of the Japanese language. It was so complicated, the article explained, that Japanese diplomats conveniently "insist that it is impossible to make the correct translations of many documents and statements," thus making it possible for them to assign various meanings to their texts, depending on convenience. "Even native Japs have a hard time understanding each other," it asserted.⁸

Wartime portrayals also accentuated the cruelty of the Japanese war effort. Even before 1941, harrowing newsreel images of the Japanese invasion of China and especially of the mass killings in Nanjing highlighted Japanese soldiers' barbaric acts. Capra's *Why We Fight* recirculated these newsreel scenes, and other wartime films added to the available visual repertoire of hideous images. In *Air Force,* a grinning Japanese fighter pilot shoots a helpless young American after he bails out and opens his parachute. John

Garfield, on the ground, retaliates by shooting down the plane, and the audience sees the Japanese pilot's body subsequently burning in flames (hell? firebombing?). *Destination Tokyo* (1944) offered a similar scene, again featuring Garfield.

The owi worried about such images. Its manual advised Hollywood to avoid images of the "little buck-toothed treacherous Jap" because they might promote racism rather than antifascism. owi liberals wanted to fight "a system" not "a race." They were also pragmatists who realized that portraying America's cause as a race war might be problematic for enlisting support from people of color at home or in the colonized countries of Asia.[9]

Still, Hollywood's demonization of the Japanese generally remained only slightly tempered during the war. *Air Force, Eagle Squadron* (1942), *Destination Tokyo,* and many other films referred to Japan's "stab in the back" treachery. Ironically, because Japanese Americans were rounded up in internment camps, a small boom in Hollywood demand for *Chinese* actors developed. The famous Chinese American actor Richard Loo specialized in playing the character of the evil Japanese.[10] In 1945 an owi poll showed that 73 percent of Americans selected the word "treacherous" to describe the Japanese character.[11] In the future, these familiar negative tropes about Japan, tied to strategic or economic threats, could be summoned anytime that relationships between the two countries deteriorated.

A worthy ally

The position of Japan in U.S. foreign policy shifted dramatically in the late 1940s. With the triumph of the Communist Party in China in 1949 and Kim Il Sung's bid to unify Korea under communist rule in 1951, U.S. policymakers saw Japan as the principal bulwark against communism in Asia. U.S. occupation officials tried to forge a postoccupation government in Japan that would subdue communist influence internally and become a strong capitalist ally. During the military buildup of the Korean War, Japan became not only a vital supplier of materiel, but also a friendly location for the rest and relaxation of American troops. U.S. policymakers considered the Japanese alliance, embodied in the Security Treaty signed in 1951, one of their major cold war assets. The postwar generation of Japanese leaders likewise embraced American capitalism and security guarantees.[12]

This new Japanese-American partnership, in full bloom within only half a dozen years after the end of an unspeakably brutal, racialized war, might be seen as quite remarkable. It was certainly a testimony to how perceived geopolitical necessity (in this case anticommunism and the preservation of capitalism) could help reshape cultural attitudes. However, viewing the emergent Japanese alliance only against the antagonistic rhetoric of the war years would be misleading.

A tradition of more positive attitudes about Japan had also circulated in America before the war and was culturally available to contest wartime discourses of demonization. The Philadelphia Exhibition of 1877, the first of the American world fairs to feature an exhibit from Japan, had touched off a broad fascination with Japanese culture and attracted a wide respect for the skill and refinement of its artistic traditions. A vogue of Japan swept both America and Europe at the turn of the century, as Western interpreters, enchanted by "eastern" traditions, filled books, magazines, and museums with paeans to Japanese civilization. Much of this Japanophilic literature was filled with Orientalist and highly gendered tropes, in which Japan stood for the esthetic, feminized East who waited to become the perfect consort to an industrial, masculinized West. Still, this Japanophilic tradition certainly did *not* portray the country as an uncivilized, unreliable demon nation. The vogue of Japan that had swept the art and design world at the turn of the century returned after 1950, coinciding with the Security Treaty and the growing cold war alliance. In the early 1950s, as anticommunist fears swept through American culture, Japan could rather easily be revised into America's friend—a country whose admirable skills, industriousness, and sense of duty and harmony could, when properly channeled, complement the virtues of the West.[13] Many of the histories told in journalism, films, and books reversed wartime imagery and represented the enemy-turned-ally in positive terms.

Magazines paid little attention to the tenth anniversary of Pearl Harbor in 1951, which came in the context of the new Security Treaty and the Korean War. The few accounts that were published, however, suggested the new friendship that was being established with Japan. *Time*'s foreign correspondent in Tokyo found Japan to be a "rising sun once more" because of its "dynamic, aggressive and industrialized people." The magazine called for a "full and equal partnership as the basis for mutual long-term friendship in the face of a common enemy" and celebrated that "Japanese have taken to Christmas as enthusiastically as they took to baseball half a century ago."[14] *Flying* magazine carried a memoir from a sub-lieutenant who had bombed Pearl Harbor, its tone signaling no rancor on either side but, rather, a fascination with firsthand stories.[15] Ten years after the "infamy," the former enemy could now have a human face.

American historians increasingly wrote of Pearl Harbor less as an expression of treacherous "character" than as a failure of *American* diplomacy. Backdoor adherents, with their insistence that Roosevelt had intentionally provoked Japan to war, implied that Japanese leaders were rather innocent of ultimate responsibility for the attack. Tansill, Barnes, and Toland, for example, all portrayed Japan as sincerely trying to negotiate a peaceful understanding with an obdurate Roosevelt administration during the late 1930s. This view, by implying that the United States could (and perhaps should) have negotiated some accommodation for Japan's hold over China, took a decidedly pro-Japanese stance at a time when China's turn toward communism gave its plight a less sympathetic sounding.

More surprising, perhaps, was that scholars writing from other interpretive perspectives also embraced views sympathetic to Japan. George Kennan, the architect of cold war containment and a leading foreign policy "realist," published his widely influential *American Diplomacy* in 1951. Ridiculing America's early-twentieth-century pro-China policy as based on misguided moralism, Kennan advanced a history through which he made clear his advocacy for a pro-Japan stance. "I cannot say that Pearl Harbor might have been avoided had we been over a long period of time more circumspect in our attitudes toward the Japanese, more considerate of the requirements of their positions, more ready to discuss their problems. . . . [But] the course of events might have been altered by . . . a recognition of power realities in the Orient."[16] By "power realities," Kennan meant a pragmatic acceptance of Japan's strength and China's weakness and a consequent effort to cooperate with Japan.

America's foremost specialist on Japan, Edwin Reischauer, held a similar view. As ambassador to Japan during the height of the cold war, the highly respected Reischauer extolled the new U.S.-Japan alliance, writing that the "real meaning of Pearl Harbor" was as a dramatic turning point in world history. The attack, he claimed, diverted the "river of history" onto a new course that, by linking together the security interests of America and Japan, would transcend "the racial and cultural divisions that defined the international system of the nineteenth century."[17]

If Kennan and Reischauer represented establishment viewpoints, historian William A. Williams offered a more radical reading of the past. Williams's influential work, *The Tragedy of American Diplomacy* (1959), drew on the interpretive stance of Charles Beard, who saw the pursuit of economic interest behind America's globalist posture. Williams placed considerable blame for Pearl Harbor on the United States. He argued that the attack, a "combination of American arrogance and negligence and of Japanese brilliance," stemmed from the expansionist pressures of "America's corporate economic system."[18]

The so-called "Williams school" (also termed the "new left" or cold war "revisionism") pushed critiques of U.S. policy even farther during the 1960s and 1970s, as perspectives became influenced by antinuclear activism and opposition to the war in Vietnam. Left-leaning and antiwar interpretations highlighted Japan's position as a nuclear victim. Photos of the aftermath of the atomic bombing of 1945 had become public after the end of the occupation and the lifting of censorship in 1952. Images of burned children, scorched landscapes, and suffering families strengthened Japan's moral claims as a victim, somewhat effacing America's own claim to victimhood at Pearl Harbor. This evidence of the horror that Americans had wrought in Japan also served as a warning about the dangers of conflict in a nuclear age (now even more frightful after the Soviets had the bomb). Antinuclear activists memorialized the bombing of Hiroshima and Nagasaki as a symbol of the near-genocidal consequences of a war culture that they worried was developing in the context of the arms race with the Soviet Union.[19] The Vietnam war augmented fears about militarization, bringing many more scholars and activists into the antinuclear and antiwar movements. Some, by emphasizing the role of "American empire" and American-led global capitalism, portrayed the Pearl Harbor attack as one of Japanese self-defense; others advanced a broader critique of militarism—in Japan as well as in America.[20] In accounts that highlighted the atomic bombings as the focal event in the war, Japan's attack at Pearl Harbor moved away from center stage.[21]

As popular articles and diverse academic traditions in the Unites States became more sympathetic to Japan, some of their messages dovetailed with historiographical trends in Japan. Immediately after the war, a group of distinguished Japanese historians had shaped their accounts of the war to repudiate the disastrous consequences of Japanese fascism, militarism, and empire building. This group had cast Japan's defeat into what Yoshikuni Igarashi calls the "foundational narrative" of postwar U.S.-Japan relations: a "drama of rescue and conversion" in which "the United States rescued Japan from the menace of its militarists, and Japan was converted into a peaceful, democratic country under U.S. tutelage." Revising the idea of a premeditated "sneak attack," this view held that Admiral Yamamoto had intended, slightly before the attack, to notify the Americans of Japan's intention to go to war. An unfortunate error in the timing of the typing and translation had prevented this more honorable procedure. By questioning the account of an intentional stab in the back, this portrayal showed Japanese character in a far better light. The emperor, in this narrative, also seemed hesitant about the bellicose course the army was taking and now, cooperating with Americans, could be represented as a force for reconciliation and reform. Revised representations of the emperor's role in the attack generally followed the interpretation of benign imperial leadership that General Douglas MacArthur had developed during the postwar, U.S. occupation.[22]

Meanwhile, other Japanese scholars and activists on the anticapitalist left and, increasingly, on the emerging nationalist right, promoted alternative views that stressed Japanese (and Asian)

victimization at the hands of Western imperialists. The anti–
Security Treaty movement that grew during the late 1950s and
1960s, for example, embraced the view that America's determination to dominate Asia and FDR's provocations had pushed
Japan toward war. At the same time, Japan's status as a victim of
atomic bombing underscored memories of victimhood that led to
a neglect of Japan's own aggressions. Although not without challenge in Japanese society, views that privileged a "victim consciousness" served multiple agendas and became widespread
during the 1950s.[23]

Thus, the shifting structures of histories in both countries
tipped more blame for the war toward the United States and advanced more sympathetic views of Japan and some of its leaders.
Hardly the animalistic fanatics who were "photographic prints
off the same negative," Japanese leaders could be differentiated
and Yamamoto accorded more respect than the more militaristic
army faction. Moreover, an emphasis on the capable planning
and exquisite execution by Japanese pilots permitted even Japanese soldiers, depicted as patriots who had been misled by militarism, to become sympathetic characters. In this historical moment, the backdoor conservatives, the cold war "realists," and the
antinuclear/antiwar new left, together with Japanese scholars
and activists who promoted both the embrace of and the resistance to Americanization, all advanced narratives that, although
written from widely different ideological perspectives, complicated the infamy framework. New interpretations allowed some
U.S. culpability in U.S. Pacific policy and highlighted Japan's victimization by the West, by its own militarists, or by atomic power.

Drawing on earlier Japanophilic traditions and circulating
along with sympathetic discourses linked to the cold war alliance
or to antinuclear and antimilitarist activism, favorable views of
Japan appeared widely in American popular culture. Readapting
the old gendered formula of an alliance between a feminized,
submissive Japan and a masculine, dominant America, films of
the 1950s presented love stories that conflated gender and nation.
Although their story lines and resolutions differed, films such as
Teahouse of the August Moon (1956), *Sayonara* (1957), and *The
Barbarian and the Geisha* (1958) all wrote narratives of East/West

reconciliation in terms of romance between Japanese women and American men. After examining popular films of the era, Gina Marchetti writes that "the geisha was Hollywood's chief emblem of postwar reconciliation. . . . Metaphorically, a bellicose Japan, through the figure of the geisha, became a yielding and dependent nation."[24] Through such representations, the rancor of the war years all but disappeared from view.

Walter Lord's *Day of Infamy* also took a long step away from the wartime "infamy" narrative. The book provided an account of December 7 based on eyewitness reactions, by both Japanese fighters and Americans, as remembered and recounted to Lord in 464 interviews. Lord seemed uninterested in blame and portrayed no one negatively. *Day of Infamy* was a collection of many personal stories that made up that one fateful day—stories from officers, crews on warships and aircraft, townspeople, and rescue workers. In relatively nonjudgmental language, Lord forgivingly chronicled the U.S. Hawaiian command's missed warnings, which he helped make into standard features of the Pearl Harbor story. General Short's alert against sabotage, for example, explained his order to closely line up planes so that they could be guarded. Admiral Kimmel, Lord recounted, understood that Japan's fleet had changed its naval codes, that Japan's diplomats had been ordered to burn their diplomatic codebooks, that Japan's carriers had disappeared from the view of American intelligence, and that Washington had warned about imminent hostile action. Still, Lord explained, Kimmel failed to go on highest alert because he shared the widespread belief that another location in Southeast Asia would be Japan's target. He detailed how Lieutenant William Outerbridge's report to his Naval District Headquarters—that he had fired upon a submarine (one of Japan's minisubmarines, launched just before the air attack) in the defensive sea area—was met by incredulity and delays. He observed how Private Joseph Lockard's report that radar showed a large number of planes approaching at 137 miles north, 3 degrees east, was answered by the explanation that they were probably friendly planes so he should not worry. General Marshall's cable to Kimmel, warning that Japan would present an ultimatum at 1:00 P.M. (Washington time) and that Kimmel should be on the alert was sent by Western

Union and delivered after the attack. All of these "what ifs" provided drama, giving the Pearl Harbor story the form of classic tragedy, but the focus remained on human error on the American side, rather than on larger explanations related to Japanese character or to international or domestic politics.[25]

Many other representations from the cold war era went much farther than Lord's in recasting the older wartime infamy and retribution narrative. Several influential films that retold the Pearl Harbor story during this era, which we have already considered in a different context of meaning, exemplified the revised messages.

The highly popular television series *Victory at Sea,* in its twenty-five-minute section on Pearl Harbor called "The Pacific Boils Over," presented a bare-bones interpretation of events leading up to the attack and concentrated, instead, on Japan's skillful execution. The film gave a quick introductory context: Japan was "on the march" in Asia, pursuing the glory of conquest and a vision of its divine mission (with few details about, for example, aggression in China). Because Japan needed oil and the U.S. Pacific Fleet was a main obstacle, Japanese leaders made a careful strategic decision to sink the fleet. With this very brief opening, the film went on to show Japanese leaders devising a plan: well-informed intelligence services pinpointed all targets, and training drills "perfectly" prepared the fliers. It described at length all aircraft in the 360-strong striking force. Yamamoto, it claimed, ordered the striking force *after* the war message to the United States had been delivered, but the message was unfortunately delayed. The scenes of destruction, some taken from *December 7,* comprised most of the film and unfolded against the backdrop of Richard Rodgers's stirring musical score.

Victory At Sea did not completely overthrow the negative wartime images of Japan. It suggested that Japan had a split culture: both Orientalist and traditional yet also modern. As Tojo and his flag-waving followers are shown foolishly celebrating their "victory" at Pearl Harbor, the tonal configurations of the musical score accentuate the idea that these militarists were an "Oriental" throwback from which Japan needed to be rescued. True to the structure of the "foundational narrative," however, the film reminded viewers that Japan was a modern and powerful nation whose pilots were well-trained patriots and whose Harvard-educated admiral did not intend the treachery of a sneak attack. Japan was shown to be a worthy enemy (and implicitly, now, ally).[26]

Two feature films of this cold war era manifested the new Japanese-American cooperation by being collaborative presentations of the Pearl Harbor story. *I Bombed Pearl Harbor,* a 1960 Japanese production directed by Shuei Matsubayashi and starring Toshiro Mifune, used both Japanese and American writers and tried to employ Hollywood-style blockbuster effects to portray the period from Japan's success at Pearl Harbor to its defeat at Midway. It was released in the United States variously named *Attack Squadron, Storm over the Pacific,* and *Kamikaze.* No matter what the name, the film flopped in both countries and received little critical attention—and almost no audience—at the time or in subsequent years.

If *I Bombed* bombed, however, *Tora! Tora! Tora!* became a classic in both countries and deserves consideration in this context. Both governments supported the making of *Tora!,* it gained a wide audience among Americans, and its documentary-like style boosted its status as a reliable historical presentation. It was widely acclaimed for its background historical research and collaborative mode of production.[27]

Finally released in 1970, *Tora!* stemmed from negotiations that had begun many years earlier. Twentieth Century–Fox had initially tried to make two films: one showing the American side of the Pearl Harbor story, the other depicting the Japanese side. Richard Fleischer directed the American portion. Akira Kurosawa, the Japanese director best known in the West for *Rashomon* (1951) and *The Seven Samurai* (1954), began working on the Japanese portion. After concerns about cost and timing, however, the Hollywood studio replaced Kurosawa with Toshio Masuda and Kinji Fukasaku. Finally, the two films were spliced together to make one film, though two slightly different versions were issued for the separate audiences. Following the pattern of so many Pearl Harbor representations, the film began with a written text promising the viewer that "all of the events and characters depicted are true to historical fact."

Like *Victory at Sea, Tora!* provided little explanation of the coming of the war. One brief opening scene showed Tojo arguing that now was the time to strike because the United States had leveled embargoes against Japan. Japan, he explained, consequently needed sources of supply in Southeast Asia, and the movement of the U.S. Pacific Fleet from San Diego to Pearl Harbor represented a "knife aimed at our throat." The next scene showed Japan joining the Tripartite Pact with Germany and Italy. *Tora!* presented no context of the Japanese invasion of China and no sense of what was at stake in the negotiations between Japan and the United States. The very brief and undeveloped suggestion that Japanese policy was a *response* to U.S. economic provocations, as suggested above, was consistent with the emphasis in much of the cold war historical scholarship in both the United States and Japan at the time.

The film portrayed Admiral Yamamoto as a very reluctant belligerent pressured by the militaristic army faction. Early in the film he was shown worrying about the army "hotheads" who might take the country into war. Later, he warned war enthusiasts not to assume that the United States was so soft and isolationist that it could be pushed around. "I studied at Harvard," he remarked, "and I know that Americans are proud and just." According to the film, Yamamoto insisted that the final ultimatum be delivered to Washington an hour before the attack, and this interpretation was underscored by shots of a painfully slow typist. When Yamamoto discovered that the message was delivered nearly an hour *after* the attack, he wisely warned that the bombing of Pearl Harbor might not be the success that Japan imagined. The movie ended with the Yamamoto prophecy that would become a standard "fact" of many later Pearl Harbor representations: "To awaken a sleeping giant and fill him with a terrible resolve is sowing the seed for certain disaster."

With the exception of the "sleeping" emphasis, the contrast between the *Tora!* story and the wartime "infamy" narrative is striking. The portrayal of Yamamoto as reluctant, honorable, and prescient was a far cry from the wartime images of fanaticism and "sneak attack." The depiction of a split within the Japanese government differed dramatically from the wartime view of identical "prints off the same negative." And the careful planning and execution of the attack inspired respect for the dedication and skill of Japanese planners and fighters. The audience was taken through the thoughtful planning of the attack; introduced to the charismatic and enthusiastic pilot, Fuchida; and allowed to approached Pearl Harbor from inside the Japanese bomber. The perspective of the camera suggested elation when the mission was seen to be a complete surprise![28]

Thus the themes of *Tora!* fit the framework of the cold war alliance. In a treatment similar to Walter Lord's, America was shown as a somewhat inefficient (and thus not threatening) global power. Japan was drawn as a worthy ally. As the film "forgot" the wartime theme of infamy ("sneak attack" became a typing mistake), it nevertheless ended by reinforcing the preparedness discourse (the "sleeping" metaphor) that cold war policymakers now invoked against communism. It emphasized the importance of honing military skill by favorably showing the Japanese planners and pilots. China, then a victim of Japanese aggression but now a cold war geopolitical and ideological enemy of the United States, remained completely outside the film. With these themes, *Tora!* marked a high water of bilateral cooperation between the United States and Japan in the context of the cold war and the Vietnam War.[29]

An economic Pearl Harbor!

The 1980s saw a widespread revival of negative images of Japan. It was not that cold war discourses of respect and friendship disappeared; pro- and anti-Japanese images had long coexisted in American life and have continued to do so. During the 1970s and 1980s, however, the Japanese economy seemed to be outperforming that of other nations in the world, and the U.S. economy was struggling with inflation, deficits, and high unemployment. The Pearl Harbor metaphor became a convenient way of blaming the Japanese for many of America's woes. "America has needed an economic Pearl Harbor to wake us up," said the president of an American engineering school, invoking the familiar "sleeping" metaphor.[30]

The infamy narrative, with all its images of "sneak attack," treachery, and racism, again provided a rhetorical resource that many Americans seized upon to formulate their understanding of America's supposed economic decline in the world. Japan had again launched an attack upon a complacent, innocent, and inept (asleep) America. This time, so the story went, Japan did not bomb Hawaii; its businesses simply began to buy it. And an economic offensive was targeting the U.S. mainland as well. Japan's new economic muscle was cast as especially treacherous because Americans themselves had generously helped boost Japanese prosperity and had even paid the bill for Japan's "free security" during the cold war.[31]

Several groups helped develop the idea of an "economic Pearl Harbor." Protectionists, especially within the American labor movement, found that the term successfully rallied nationalism in support of their trade agenda. As Japan captured growing shares of the American steel, textile, automotive, and electronics markets in the early 1970s, the metaphor of Pearl Harbor began to appear in calls to protect American jobs. Similarly, experts— from business, labor, and various think tanks—who had been calling for some kind of new "industrial policy," by which government should provide more support for American business, also highlighted the threat of Japan's economic prowess. The peril emanating from Japan, they claimed, should prompt changes in industrial policy at home in emulation of what Ezra Vogel called *Japan as Number One.*[32] Vogel denounced mindless Japan bashing and called on Americans to learn from the way that the Japanese government and businesses cooperated and to revamp their institutions in a similar manner. The structure of these industrial policy arguments, though laudatory of the Japanese political economy, nevertheless reinforced the idea that Japan was America's archrival in world trade and investment.

Fears of Japanese economic dominance accelerated during the late 1980s. Japan had become the largest net capital exporter and largest creditor in the world, while the United States had become the largest net capital importer and debtor. In 1987, one-third of America's yawning trade deficit was with Japan. Japanese investors owned two-thirds of the hotels on Hawaii's Waikiki Beach, and many people suggested that this state was becoming an economic colony of Japan. Japanese companies began to dominate the semiconductor, automobile, and consumer electronics industries. In 1989 Sony bought Columbia Pictures in a $3.4 billion deal, and in 1992 Mitsubishi purchased a substantial interest in Rockefeller Center, the famed home of Radio City Music Hall's Rockettes. In 1992 polls reported that 60 percent of Americans deemed Japan the most critical threat to the United States.[33]

An anti-Japanese feeding frenzy gathered momentum, and publishers stocked their shelves with both sober and sensational books. "Not since Pearl Harbor," wrote Vincent Canby of the *New York Times*, "has Japan-bashing been such big and popular business."[34] Daniel Burstein's *Yen!* (1988) predicted that Japan might force the United States into a financial receivership and then demand the state of California. Michael Crichton's *Rising Sun* (1993), a book and then a movie, reworked old images of shifty Japanese characters, now in business suits. And there were many, many others.[35]

Meanwhile, the Japanese threat became a reliable theme for jokes and cartoons. One *Newsday* cartoon showed a bomber dropping investment dollars while pilots yelled "Tora Tora Tora." A spokesman for the Soviet Foreign Ministry in Washington quipped, "The cold war is over, and Japan won." On April Fools' Day of 1991 a popular radio program in Honolulu pretended that Japanese investors had purchased the station, and it made racially offensive jokes about needing to lower microphones by several feet and giving bags of rice as prizes.[36]

The reaction in Japan to the sudden "economic Pearl Harbor" uproar in the United States did not help soothe relations. In a spate of anti-Americanism that paralleled and fed off of America's new suspicions, Japanese officials made a series of disparaging comments about the disintegration of values and work ethic in the United States. One complained that having followed the American advice to be diligent, the Japanese were now criticized for their virtue.[37] Books proclaiming Japan's superiority, such as Shintaro Ishihara's *The Japan That Can Say No* (1990), became best-sellers in Japan and subjects of commentary in the United States.[38] Americans' hostile reactions to Japanese insults reinforced a nationalistic discourse that was now becoming broadly cultural as well as economic. On the eve of the fiftieth anniversary of Pearl Harbor in 1991, relations reached a low not seen since the end of World War II. A book called *The Coming War with Japan* garnered substantial sales in both the United States and Japan.[39]

The economic Pearl Harbor metaphor—embraced by labor, advocates of a new "industrial policy," and various writers and humorists—was not without its challengers. Robert B. Reich, just before entering President Bill Clinton's cabinet in 1993, wrote that the Pearl Harbor metaphor was dangerous because it reflected an obsolete and inaccurate image of U.S.-Japan relations. "Metaphors are powerful because they shape the way we think," he wrote, and "war metaphors are among the most powerful of all." To combat the power of this injurious metaphor, Reich confronted the anti-Japanese critique point by point. British and German importers and investors had also gained substantial positions in U.S. markets, but only the Japanese had become symbols of American loss. (The British, he pointed out, owned twice as much in America as did the Japanese.) In addition, because one of every ten Americans worked for a non-American company, it made no sense to imply that foreign ownership was unwelcome. And if Japanese businesses shifted production into less costly countries, the practice was hardly different from what U.S. businesses had also been doing for years. Moreover, although many Americans believed that Japan was a nearly closed market and wanted to demand that Japan open up, Reich explained that the average Japanese citizen purchased only slightly less from the United States than the average American bought from Japan. Germans purchased far less.[40] Reich, along with others, countered the new Japanophobia and tried to reemphasize the value of extending the Japanese-American friendship that had characterized the cold war era.

In various invocations of the icon of Pearl Harbor after 1941, representations of Japan swung wildly in the contexts of different geopolitical and economic circumstances. As Maurice Halbwachs and subsequent scholars of memory have shown, the remembering of the past is necessarily refracted through perspectives rooted in different groups of people existing in different presents.[41] The treacherous Japanese of World War II morphed into the exacting and honor-bound allies who co-anchored the cold war system in Asia and morphed once more into devious rivals who threatened to buy what they had not won in battle. Both negative and positive views of the Japanese people, embedded in variously framed renditions of the histories/memories of Pearl Harbor, provided rhetorical resources for structuring very different stories of U.S.-Japan relationships.

4 Commemoration of Sacrifice

Pearl Harbor was not just an icon whose various meanings circulated in films, books, articles, and speeches. It was also a physical place in Hawaii, a major military base that increasingly served as a location for remembrance and as a monument to commemorate the wartime sacrifice of lives. Unlike the "sacred ground" holding most other war monuments, the harbor was a place of actual burial, and it developed visibility as one of the most important symbolic locations in American culture.

Commemoration on hallowed ground, such as Pearl Harbor's waters, is rarely a static practice but often involves battles over meaning. Memory work can be highly political, and contests over representation and signification erupt easily. Who frames the histories to be remembered and the lessons to be drawn? Semiotic stakes seem especially high when meanings cost so many lives.[1]

A weeping tomb

The sunken hull of the battleship *Arizona* became the central focus of commemoration at Pearl Harbor. At 8:10 A.M., in the first wave of the Japanese attack, a 1,760-pound bomb tore through the deck of the *Arizona* and ignited the forward ammunition magazine. Commander Mitsuo Fuchida later recalled that "a huge column of dark red smoke rose to 1000 ft, and a stiff shock wave rocked [his] plane. . . . It was a hateful, mean-looking flame. . . . Terrible indeed."[2] The ship sank in less than nine minutes. Aboard were 1,177 crewmen, the largest single loss ever incurred in U.S. military history. The bodies of 1,102 of these servicemen were never recovered and remain entombed in the ship. To this day, the ship still weeps oil, giving its surrounding waters a murky, slightly rainbow cast that makes the disaster seem ongoing, even somewhat miraculous—like a Virgin's image that cries or a stone from which water flows.

The first few years after the end of the war, the *Arizona* remained a relatively neglected war ruin in the midst of a still active naval base. Many visitors to Pearl Harbor, however, complained about the neglect of this entombment. In 1949 the Territory of Hawaii established a Pacific War Memorial Commission (PWMC) to raise funds for commemorative sites on the island. The navy began running a shuttle boat to the *Arizona* ruins in 1950 and raised and lowered the American flag each day. A few years later, at the request of naval officers, the PWMC decided to focus on building a memorial over the sunken ship, but efforts proceeded slowly. Although Congress authorized building a memorial to the *Arizona* in 1958, it approved no funding. The PWMC approached private donors and successfully lobbied for a contribution from Hawaii's territorial legislature. Hawaiian officials had been energetically building a tourism industry that they hoped would bolster their bid for statehood (which succeeded in August 1959). War memorials, especially the *Arizona,* seemed a sure-fire attraction. The navy's desire to commemorate its dead and Hawaiian leaders' plans to promote tourism neatly dovetailed.[3]

High-profile celebrity benefits became part of public-private fund-raising efforts to erect an *Arizona* memorial. On March 25, 1961, Elvis Presley swaggered onto the stage at Pearl Harbor's Bloch Arena for a sold-out concert. Minnie Pearl, a favorite of the Grand Ole Opry radio shows, joined Elvis in a guest appearance. The packed house raised the then substantial sum of $64,000. A special program of the popular television series *This Is Your Life,* hosted by Ralph Edwards, brought in $95,000. Meanwhile, another fund-raising group tapped into the model-building fad, a current rage among young boys. A campaign to sell model kits of the *Arizona* raised another $40,000.⁴

As these efforts stimulated public interest, the PWMC commissioned a design. The first architectural concept would have lowered visitors into a submerged enclosure and allowed viewing of the *Arizona* through portholes. The navy rejected this plan. The second concept drew more enthusiasm. The memorial was to be a 184-foot white structure suspended over, but not touching, the *Arizona*. It would feature wide openings to allow the sunlight and the serenity of the sea to be visible. The architect explained that it would sag in the center but appear strong at the ends, a metaphor for "initial defeat and ultimate victory." Inside, a marble wall would list the names of those killed. After strong lobbying in Congress, President John Kennedy signed into law a bill that authorized sufficient funds for the project, and the official dedication took place on Memorial Day, 1962. In 1965 the naval base at Pearl Harbor was designated a National Historic Landmark.⁵

The *Arizona* Memorial slowly became a tourist attraction, and the numbers of people visiting the memorial by tour or naval boats increased steadily. Within a decade, the memorial was hosting thousands of visitors a year, despite hours of waiting in long, outdoor lines. The National Park Service and the navy both lobbied to build a visitors' center, which finally opened in 1980. The Park Service began to hold two official ceremonies each year: on Memorial Day and on December 7. In 1989, the *Arizona* and the *Utah*, a target ship torpedoed when it was mistakenly identified as an aircraft carrier, both received landmark designation.⁶

One function of any war memorial is to serve the psychological and cultural needs of postwar situations. The experience of war, both on the homefront and in combat, disrupts familiar patterns and meanings. War-related anxiety and trauma affect groups (even nations), as well as individuals, and war's sociological as well as psychological effects are well documented. Experiencing the fragility of everyday life, the loss of stability, and an alteration in "normal" morality, people in war face an anxiety that mixes fear, anger, and sadness. This painful feeling of loss for a world that has slipped away deepens what Pierre Nora calls a "commemorative consciousness" that seems to demand "sites of memory" to impart solace through remembrance.[7]

Commemoration gives memory a performative dimension, offering social rituals and common experiences that, presumably, bind together the participants and reestablish meaning, fixity, and sanity.[8] Commemorative sites and rituals honor the sacrifices that were endured. They soothe displacement by establishing explanatory narratives imparting meaning to loss. They provide hope and purpose by memorializing heroes and establishing cautionary tales for future generations. For the Pacific theater of World War II, the *Arizona* Memorial gradually became Americans' central commemorative site.

As an antidote to pain and loss, the *Arizona* Memorial became a national declaration that the war had a noble purpose and that the dead did not die in vain. In this sense, memorialization drew upon practices that had become widespread in Europe after World War I, when the body of the dead soldier increasingly became a symbol of transcendence achieved through patriotic nationalism. During the 1920s, nation-states asserted claims to memory of the war dead; fallen soldiers memorialized in monuments, cemeteries, and holidays became shrines to the nation and its state-organized memories.[9] Against these representations, artists of the interwar years had advanced a literary genre stressing the trauma and disillusionment arising from the war, in effect challenging the nationalistic memory embodied in state monuments. Though never explicit, the *Arizona* Memorial asserted itself against the revival of this tradition of postwar trauma literature, exemplified in the United States by bleak works such as Norman Mailer's *The Naked and the Dead*, Kurt Vonnegut's *Slaughterhouse Five*, and Arthur Miller's *All My Sons*. These writings, like their interwar counterparts, linked worldwide war to the irrepressibility of evil, to moral randomness, and to pain for no redeeming reason. The memorial, as post–World War I memorials had done, competed with such dark rememberings, countering narratives of hopelessness and moral abandonment. At Pearl Harbor, the war deaths were given purpose.

The memorial also counteracted unsettling memories by advancing representative images of individuals who became heroic through their innocence and sacrifice. Inside the *Arizona* Memorial the marble wall with the 1,177 names of the dead crew members provided a central focus, and the documentary film made to precede the boat trip to the memorial opened with a slow shot of these names. Displays in the museum's Visitors' Center also celebrated individual lives. The reference to these ordinary heroes sought to assure the viewer of the willingness of their sacrifice and emphasized the theme of national unity that had been so visible in wartime culture. Accentuating the individual merged into one nation recalled John Ford's *December 7*, in which one after the other of the Pearl Harbor dead, all from diverse backgrounds, rose to speak about their common hopes for the future.

In addition, the memorial aimed at providing reassurance of eventual triumph. Meticulous maps and displays of artifacts underscored the enormity of the loss, but this loss was made bittersweet by the assurance of eventual transcendence in victory. By commemorating defeat followed by victory, the memorial expressed its redemptive message within the familiar narrative structures of tragedy/triumph (the Alamo and Custer stories rewritten as Pearl Harbor); of religious sacrifice and rebirth; and of the natural, seasonal metaphor of death and renewal. The commemoration commingled sacred and patriotic themes.[10]

Yet if the memorial addressed the trauma of war by stressing purpose, representative heroes, and a reassuringly redemptive formula, it also raised controversy. Who should control remembrance, and how should remembrance of the past speak to the shape of possible futures? Because public commemorative spaces often suggest a future that should evolve from the memorialized past, they are, in the words of David Chidester and Edward T. Linenthal, "always highly charged sites for contested negotiations over the ownership of the symbolic capital (or symbolic real estate)."[11] At Pearl Harbor, struggles developed over how the sacred patriotic space should be ritualized and interpreted.

The memorial was established, physically and figuratively, at a number of crossroads. It began, for example, as both a military and a tourist site, developed in conjunction with the diverse objectives of both the U.S. military and Hawaiian political and economic elites. Moreover, it lay within a highly multicultural territory located halfway between the mainland United States and Japan, attracting tourists from both East and West. (Of course, in Hawaii "West" is east and "East" is west.) The memorial also took shape in the shadow of the Vietnam War, a struggle that divided Americans over foreign policy goals, military intervention, and definitions of patriotism. As conflicting policy agendas played out and as the World War II–era culture fragmented, the sacred symbol of Pearl Harbor became a center of controversy, with every side seeking to invoke its view. A messy intersection of purposes, nationalities, and diverse generational perspectives, the site was necessarily marked by ambiguity, conflicted messages, and cultural negotiation. People flocked to the commemoration site at Pearl Harbor to learn about American heritage, but, as Barbara Kirshenblatt-Gimblett writes, "the world imagined under the banner of heritage is a battlefield."[12] As memories of the past took shape among different groups in the ever-changing and always political present, conflicts emerged over the possible messages symbolized at Pearl Harbor.

"All monuments are efforts to stop time.
History, of course, moves relentlessly to mock any such beliefs."

Which narratives about heritage would this literal and figurative battlefield advance and which would it silence? What were the themes and conflicts of public commemoration that emerged at the *Arizona* Memorial and Visitors' Center?[13]

For many, the story of Pearl Harbor buttressed a hawkish stance on Vietnam, suggesting the need for maintaining a strong military and fighting through to victory. In the contentious year of 1968, for example, Admiral Harold G. Bowen Jr. used a Memorial Day speech at the *Arizona* to decry America's declining nationalism and to warn that Americans must be willing to keep fighting, as a way of honoring the sacrifice made there.[14] The Confederate Air Force (CAF), an organization chartered in 1961, began ritual reenactments of Pearl Harbor at air shows in 1974. Clearly directed to combat the so-called "Vietnam syndrome," which warned against military involvements abroad, the CAF's "WWII

Airpower Demonstration" proclaimed its message: "We must never be caught asleep again as we were on December 7, 1941." In promising to see to it that Americans did not forget Pearl Harbor, the CAF also darkly warned that other nations should likewise "not forget what made it necessary to drop that bomb on Hiroshima and Nagasaki."[15]

The film produced by the navy and shown in the *Arizona* Memorial Visitors' Center after it opened in 1980 became the focus of substantial controversy. The film provided an initial interpretive introduction, after which viewers would take a short navy shuttle boat ride to enter the memorial that lay over the ship. This film echoed much of the standard wartime Pearl Harbor narrative and even used some of the battle recreations from *December 7*. It glorified the navy's recovery—"like the mythical phoenix the fleet would rise"—and ended by pinning down a single meaning: "The lesson of Pearl Harbor is that we must never be unprepared again."[16] As in *December 7*, commemoration went hand in hand with the commonly invoked preparedness theme.

The film, however, departed from the wartime narrative in how it represented the Japanese enemy. Written in the context of the cold war security alliance, it borrowed themes from *Victory at Sea* and *Tora! Tora! Tora!* by placing the attack in the context of America's oil embargo, giving little visibility to Japan's invasion of China or its empire in Korea and borrowing Admiral Kimmel's description of Japan's raid as "one of the most brilliantly planned and executed attacks ever achieved."[17]

Structured by the narrative conventions of both World War II and the cold war and then refracted through the social divisions of the Vietnam War era, the film was assailed from many sides. The chief historian at the memorial noted that his office received more complaints and comments on this film than on all of the National Park Service's other historical sites combined.[18]

One group directed its wrath at what it considered a lack of patriotism and a favorable view of Japan. These critics usually denounced the film's mention of America's oil embargo as the cause of Japan's attack and the description of the attack as "brilliant." One viewer claimed that he had suffered a heart attack from his anger at the film. Retired Rear Admiral Victor Dybdal regarded the film as "a damned movie that gives the impression it was all our fault." These critics, generally coming from the political right, attacked the Park Service for using tax money to propagate an anti-American tone at a national shrine.[19] Some demanded that the navy take over total management of the site and its messages, apparently unaware that the navy itself had produced the film. Protest over the so-called anti-American tone of the film became something of a *cause célèbre* on the political right. "People who are squeamish about telling the truth and apologetic about being Americans are the last people to be left in charge of a national shrine like that at Pearl Harbor," proclaimed columnist Thomas Sowell.[20] Reflecting the growing political activism of veterans' groups, the American Ex-Prisoners of War asked members to write their representatives to protest the film.[21] An organized letter-writing campaign began.

The "economic Pearl Harbor" Japan bashing of the 1980s augmented these complaints. Some visiting Americans expressed shock at the growing number of Japanese tourists in Hawaii. Finding that the hotel in which they may have been staying was now Japanese owned probably accentuated their anger. Americans frequently complained to museum staff and their congressional representatives about what they saw as the defilement of their sacred site by the Japanese presence; many registered special displeasure that some souvenir items for sale in the gift shop bore "Made in Japan" labels. In 1991, the Rusbridger and Nave book linked its anti-Roosevelt, backdoor-to-war interpretation to a critique of the memorial's film. The film was "sanitized" and pro-Japanese, the authors charged, because of the "economics of Japanese tourism."[22]

Other, less numerous, complaints leveled a very different charge against the film: that it perpetuated the nationalistic and even racist discourses of the war. Park Service personnel themselves expressed concern that the aggressive theme of military preparedness could work against a reverential tone of remembrance. They reported that some Americans would accost visitors whom they took to be of Japanese descent (even if they were Chinese or Asian American) with hostile words. The sacred site, in this view, needed to soften its promilitary, propreparedness tone and concentrate on a message stressing the horror of war and the need for peaceful settlement of disputes.[23]

Some of the controversy over the commemorative message at Pearl Harbor (not nationalistic enough or too nationalistic) undoubtedly intersected with the simultaneous public discussions surrounding the memorialization of the Vietnam War. Sculptor Maya Lin proposed a minimalist-inspired monument consisting of two ten-foot-high, 250-foot-long black walls inscribed with the names of the nearly sixty thousand soldiers who had died or were missing in action in Vietnam. Although the Vietnam monument would eventually become admired by most Americans of all political persuasions (a testament to the pliancy of minimalist sculpture and to the power of honoring individual names), the selection of Lin's design initially provoked opposition from those who felt that the stark black gash across the landscape seemed too grim and even too antiwar to be a proper commemoration. The detractors, led by Texas businessman Ross Perot and President Ronald Reagan's interior secretary James Watt, successfully crusaded to erect nearby a more conventional, representational memorial showing three soldiers shadowed by an American flag. This effort was later augmented by another representational memorial honoring women veterans.[24] The fight over how to commemorate the Vietnam War and the fear of some leading conservatives that antiwar perspectives endangered America's war memorials heightened sensitivity to the politics of commemoration at Pearl Harbor.

The controversy over the navy's Pearl Harbor film—and the conflicting demands placed upon it—led the Park Service to begin scripting a new one. Facing the prospect of the fiftieth anniversary spotlight in 1991, the Park Service, as will be discussed below, would aim "to eliminate elements of racism and inappropriate rhetoric that distorts or makes history too simplistic."[25]

Although the visible controversies over the commemorative site revolved around attitudes toward Japan, nationalism versus internationalism, and which policies might lead to war or peace, the site raised more subtle, if less contentious, questions as well. What does it mean to construct national monuments—as reminders of national identity and history—largely around military sites? A huge body of scholarship has examined monument building in the United States after the Civil War and in Europe after both world wars, movements that promoted the identification of national history with war commemoration.[26] This identification remains firmly entrenched in popular history, as military histories and histories of wars remain by far the most salable genre of history writing.

Such an identification—embodying the nation's history in the imagery of fallen male soldiers—promotes powerful gender messages. Men, because of their ultimate sacrifice, become symbolic carriers of the nation, while women serve only indirectly and invisibly. Women, of course, also experience war, but not generally in a monumental way and, therefore, not in a way that comes to figure significantly in the circulation of history/memory. To the extent that public war memorials honor and stage history around one of the most gender-segregated activities in society (soldiering), they naturalize a particular vision of difference: men appear as primary custodians of the state and of its political affairs. Michel Foucault has emphasized that the most powerful discourses governing human behavior in any society come not from those arenas where controversy reigns but from "regimes of truth" that project messages that seem so obvious and natural as to remain almost unnoticed.[27] The public reteaching of seemingly natural gender divisions through war monuments (and who would want to question the appropriateness of commemorating soldiers who paid the ultimate sacrifice?) is not written explicitly into monuments but is exemplified by their very existence and by their sheer *monumental* status.

Pearl Harbor served as an available icon and rhetorical resource in many cultural contexts. It figured in arguments for military preparedness, in discussions of executive branch power and partisan politics, in bilateral relations with Japan, and in variously interpreted acts of commemoration. The term "Pearl Harbor" served rhetorically as shorthand for diverse narratives and lessons that various groups of Americans selectively invoked and fought over. Still, popular attention to the event of December 7, 1941, seemed to dim somewhat as the years passed. The Pearl Harbor anniversaries were small-scale affairs, barely noticed in the national media. The dedication of the *Arizona* Memorial on May 30, 1962, attracted little media attention; the opening of the Visitors' Center in 1980 also had little coverage; and the tourists to Pearl Harbor were still relatively small in number.[28] All that changed in the 1990s, when Pearl Harbor as a cultural icon rapidly gained visibility.

1. Overview of Pearl Harbor, May 3, 1940. This photograph, taken at 17,200 feet, looks down on the U.S. Pacific Fleet and the fleet air base on Ford Island. Official U.S. Navy photograph, now in the collections of the National Archives.

2. USS *Arizona* bombed, December 7, 1941. The forward
magazines explode and burn after the Japanese raid.
Official U.S. Navy photograph, from the collection of
the U.S. Naval Historical Center.

3. USS *Shaw* explodes, December 7, 1941. Photographed from Ford Island, the second wave of the Japanese attack turned the skies black with fire. U.S. Naval Historical Center.

DRAFT No. 1   December 7, 1941.

PROPOSED MESSAGE TO THE CONGRESS

Yesterday, December 7, 1941, a date which will live in ~~world history~~ *infamy*

the United States of America was ~~simultaneously~~ *suddenly* and deliberately attacked

by naval and air forces of the Empire of Japan.

The United States was at the moment at peace with that nation and was

~~continuing the~~ *still in* conversation with its Government and its Emperor looking

toward the maintenance of peace in the Pacific. Indeed, one hour after

Japanese air squadrons had commenced bombing in ~~Hawaii and the Philippines~~ *Oahu*

the Japanese Ambassador to the United States and his colleague delivered

to the Secretary of State a formal reply to a ~~former~~ *recent American* message. ~~from the~~

~~Secretary.~~ *While* This reply ~~contained a statement~~ *stated* *it seemed useless* that diplomatic negotiations

~~must be considered at an end, but~~ *it* contained no threat ~~and no~~ hint of *war or* ~~an~~

armed attack.

It will be recorded that the distance ~~of Hawaii, and especially~~ of

Hawaii from Japan make it obvious that the attack ~~were~~ *was* deliberately

planned many days ago *or years weeks*. During the intervening time the Japanese Govern-

ment has deliberately sought to deceive the United States by false

statements and expressions of hope for continued peace.

DRAFT NO. 1

The attack yesterday on ~~Manila and on the Island of Oahu have~~ *the Hawaiian Islands* HAS

caused severe damage to American naval and military forces. Very

many American lives have been lost. In addition American ~~████~~ ships

have been torpedoed on the high seas between San Francisco and

Honolulu.

Yesterday the Japanese Government also launched an attack

against Malaya.

Q Last night Japanese forces attacked Guam.

~~A~~ Japan has, therefore, undertaken a surprise offensive extending *The Philippine Islands*

throughout the Pacific area. The facts of yesterday speak for

themselves. The people of the United States have already formed

their opinions and well understand the implications ~~of the attacks~~

~~even on~~ *to very* the safety of our nation.

As Commander-in-Chief of the Army and Navy I have, ~~of course,~~

directed that all measures be taken for our defense.

Long will we remember the character of the onslaught against

us.

(A) *No matter how long it may take us to overcome this premeditated invasion the American people will in their righteous might win through to absolute victory.*

5. and 6. "Work-Fight-Sacrifice." The attack on Pearl Harbor became the central rallying symbol of the war, as in these posters created for the War Production Board. National Archives.

They Shall Not Have Died in Vain

1941 Dec. 7th. 1942

Remember PEARL HARBOR

WORK
FIGHT
SACRIFICE

Let's get it over with!

COME ON, C-H....DO MORE!
THIS ISN'T PEACE-IT'S WAR!!

7. "REMEMBER DEC. 7th!" This famous poster, designed
by Allen Sandburg and issued by the Office of War
Information in 1942, featured a quotation from
Abraham Lincoln's *Gettysburg Address*. U.S. Naval
Historical Center.

8. "Treachery." This 1943 poster from the Office of War Information drew upon the view that Japanese diplomats had negotiated for peace while planning for war. National Archives.

9. "We'll Remember—and, by God, You Won't Forget!"
This 1943 poster, drawn by Charles Alston, drew upon
familiar Pearl Harbor themes. National Archives.

10. Labor Pool, 1942. "Remember Pearl Harbor" signs
were ubiquitous, here rallying workers to sign up for war
work. Robert Ryan, photographer, courtesy of Minnesota
Historical Society.

11. "I AM AN AMERICAN." On December 8, 1941, the
owner of this store, a Japanese American and University
of California graduate, placed this sign in front. The
photographer, Dorothea Lange, took many photos
sympathetic to the plight of Japanese Americans, who
were interned during the war. Credit: Courtesy of the
Bancroft Library, University of California, Berkeley.

12. Pearl Harbor flag returned to the Capitol. The U.S. flag that flew over the Capitol on December 7, 1941, had been raised over Rome, Berlin, and Tokyo to signal the defeat of the Axis powers. On April 6, 1948, it was returned to Washington, D.C., in an Army Day ceremony. Photograph from the Army Signal Corps Collection in the National Archives.

13. *Arizona* Memorial. Dedicated in May 1962, this white, open-air memorial has space for 250 people and spans the sunken ship USS *Arizona*. Official U.S. Navy photograph.

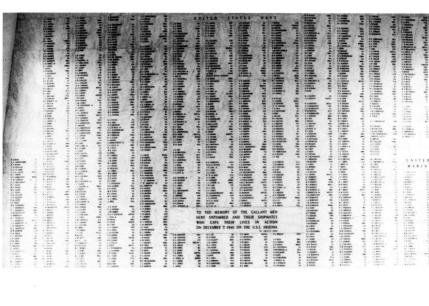

14. Interior of the *Arizona* Memorial. The marble wall
contains the names of the men who died in the attack.
Official U.S. Navy photograph.

1941- PEARL HARBOR 30TH ANNIVERSARY -1971

15. Thirtieth anniversary, December 7, 1971. This photographic montage, prepared for the anniversary, depicts images of the attack and its remembrance. Official U.S. Navy photograph.

II

Reviving Pearl Harbor after 1991

Toward the end of the twentieth century, cultural references to the "date which will live" proliferated exponentially. In part, the Pearl Harbor revival began in the context of the fiftieth-anniversary commemorations and a fresh interest in every aspect of World War II. But much more was involved. Why did the symbolism of Pearl Harbor take on renewed visibility nearly two generations after the attack had occurred?

Sociologists and historians have tried to understand the processes by which some things in the past become forgotten and others become vivid "secondary memories" for new generations. I argue that the key to successful visibility in memory, in (post)modern America, is mutually reenforcing circulation in the variety of modern media—books, journalism, television, film, Internet—that refresh and reassemble images to feel "real" and that shape memory into familiar (and hence even more memorable) stories. Memory activists promote particular, often diverse, perspectives on the past, simultaneously producing understandings of both the present and of history/memory.

This section examines the various international, cultural, and political contexts that during the 1990s contributed to the reemergence and renewed prominence of the Pearl Harbor stories and images that had taken shape over the half century after 1941. Specifically, it examines Pearl Harbor representations in six contexts: bilateral between the United States and Japan; the growing memory boom that honored the aged veterans of World War II as the "greatest generation"; the politics of the "history wars," including the often partisan crusade to restore rank, posthumously, to the commanders in charge at Pearl Harbor in 1941; the intricate cultural politics of memory among Japanese Americans; the extravagant hype associated with the blockbuster film *Pearl Harbor* during the spring and summer of 2001; and the post–cold war national security warnings, capped by a new "day of infamy"—September 11, 2001.

5 Bilateral Relations

Pearl Harbor's Half-Century Anniversary

and the Apology Controversies

Given the deterioration of U.S.-Japanese relations and the use of Pearl Harbor metaphors in the Japan bashing in the late 1980s, some people feared that the fiftieth anniversary of the attack in 1991 would further inflame American hostility. "Hatred toward Japan Is about to Explode!" headlined one of the many articles predicting that an outpouring of anti-Japanese sentiment would accompany Pearl Harbor's memorialization in the United States.[1] But the anniversary, although not without its bilateral tensions, took a different turn. Commemoration, rather than confrontation, set the memorial tone.

"Heroes of the harbor"

On the eve of the fiftieth anniversary of the attack, many irritants disturbed relations between the United States and Japan. The strength of the yen and Japan's favorable trade balance during most of 1991 continued to feed talk of an "economic Pearl Harbor." Japanese ownership of the headquarters hotel at which the

Pearl Harbor veterans would stay during the ceremony in Honolulu symbolized the perceived threat. On the other side, many in
Japan angrily charged Americans with "cultural imperialism"
and with "scapegoating" Japan to evade dealing with America's
own economic weaknesses. The recent Persian Gulf War accentuated such disputes, as the United States urged Japan to play a
more significant role in bankrolling this and other post–cold war
"peacekeeping" efforts. Moreover, the planning for the fiftieth
anniversary revealed different understandings of the history of
World War II: dominant views on each side still saw the other as
the principal aggressor leading up to the attack of 1941. Although
most Americans continued to assume that Pearl Harbor stood for
aggression on the part of Japan, many Japanese leaders propounded the view that the attack had been a necessary strategic
measure in a defensive war that had been pushed upon Japan.[2]

The issue of clashing popular memories about how to interpret
World War II was itself a sign of the times. The emergence of
strong identity politics during the 1980s and 1990s, together with
broad activism on behalf of international human rights and the
end of the cold war, placed new emphasis on assigning blame and
on sorting out victims from perpetrators. As the World War II
generation inexorably aged, many old antagonisms resurfaced.
Chinese, Korean, and American POWs stepped up their demands
for greater recognition of their wartime suffering at the hands of
Japan. In this context, the memorialization of the American victims at Pearl Harbor highlighted Japanese culpability and provided a cultural antidote to the visibility that had often been
accorded to the Japanese victims of the atomic bombing at Hiroshima and Nagasaki.[3]

In this contentious atmosphere, several proposals to use the
1991 ceremonies as a symbol of reconciliation proved unsuccessful. The superintendent of the *Arizona* Memorial had once
broached such an idea, but the acting director of the National Park
Service deemed the suggestion "inappropriate, possibly offensive."[4] The president of the PHSA in Atlanta, Jack Westerman, also
advanced a plan for reconciliation. With the support of his membership, he proposed a reunion in which old enemies could become friends. Japanese pilot Zenji Abe and other respondents

established a Japan Friends of Pearl Harbor Association to become the counterpart group for a projected reunion to take place in October 1991. When the president of the national PHSA, Gerald A. Glaubitz, heard of the plan, however, he denounced it, stating that "99.99%" of the membership would not approve. "We did not invite the Japanese 50 years ago, and we don't want them now," said Glaubitz.[5] The reunion was canceled. Attempting to avoid any criticism from veterans' groups, President George H. W. Bush announced definitively that the commemoration would be a "national" ceremony, for Americans only. When Honolulu mayor Frank Fasi suggested inviting Japan if its government apologized for Pearl Harbor, officials in Tokyo replied that the United States should apologize for its atomic bombing. This suggestion, along with other irritants, so infuriated President Bush that he canceled a trip to Asia and declared that "this president" would not issue an apology. This apology controversy boiled right up to the days of the commemorative ceremonies.[6]

Still, despite the predictions and indicators of rising tension, the opposite also occurred. A Japanese television crew that came to the United States to document surging Japan bashing reportedly found so little that it changed the focus of its report. In some places, images of reconciliation prevailed. After the formal ceremonies, a diverse group of American and Japanese survivors, historians, underwater archaeologists, and others attended a symposium in Honolulu that accentuated themes of reconciliation; at the concluding banquet Glaubitz embraced Zenji Abe. The American Airpower Heritage Museum in Midland, Texas, held a seminar during the week of the anniversary, inviting both U.S. and Japanese veterans of the conflict, and *People* magazine did a spread featuring photos and interviews of individuals from both groups, labeling them "survivors from both sides" and alternating the coverage to emphasize the commonalities in personal experiences rather than the national polarity of the conflict.[7]

In the end, the books, articles, television programs, and speeches during the commemorative year of 1991 drew lessons to suit every persuasion. Barry Hillenbrand and James Walsh in *Time* used the commemoration to underscore current U.S.-Japanese tensions over economics, textbook coverage of the war, and strategic interests. McGeorge Bundy in *Newsweek,* by contrast, lauded the long American-Japanese alliance, arguing that "in the end, the attack was good for both" because it led to the "victory that made lasting peace possible." Ralph Kinney Bennet in *Reader's Digest* used Pearl Harbor to advance a triumphalist version of the cold war's end: Pearl Harbor had taught the lesson of vigilance that, in turn, led to the defeat of the Soviet Union. Alexander Cockburn in *The Nation* suggested that memories of Pearl Harbor should not ignore U.S. diplomatic and trade "offensives" against Japan in the 1930s, or eclipse the memory of U.S. guilt for dropping atomic bombs, or demand Japanese apologies when the United States had not apologized to Vietnam for its suffering in the 1960s. Histories advancing the backdoor-to-war thesis, blaming Roosevelt for pushing Japan into striking first, vied with pro-Roosevelt interpretations, which stressed poor coordination of intelligence and laxity on the part of the base commanders. The vcr also re-introduced the "sentimental militarism" of the late 1940s and 1950s, as motion pictures from those decades were rereleased in the new, small-screen format. Fox Video, for example, released "The Pearl Harbor Collection," ten films of "raw courage, bravery, and heroism in the face of combat." Americans were exhorted, from many sides, to remember Pearl Harbor, but that memory was invoked to substantiate many different narratives and history lessons.[8]

The commemoration ceremonies both at Pearl Harbor and around the country, while not free of anti-Japanese sentiment, generally accentuated themes other than bilateral relations with Japan. They focused on patriotism, unity, and the singular virtues of the now elderly World War II veterans. Honoring a passing generation, which became a symbol of dedication and common purpose, was part of a broad memory boom that was sweeping through American life. The day before the major speeches, a large parade honored the Pearl Harbor veterans. Members of the phsa walked behind banners that identified their ships or phsa chapters. The men behind the banners were themselves monuments of a sort. Having enlisted as mostly poor boys in depression-ridden America, they now paraded as prosperous retirees, symbols of America's postwar affluence and upward mobility. The Sons and Daughters of the Pearl Harbor Survivors (SDPHS), wearing red and white, also marched, a testament to intergenerational solidarity. Reflection and personal memory, rather than vengeance and acrimonious relations with Japan, set the dominant tone.[9]

On Saturday, December 7, President George H. W. Bush, himself a World War II navy pilot who had been shot down by the Japanese, delivered two speeches in Hawaii. At the Punchbowl, a memorial to war dead, he apologized for the internment of Japanese Americans. Later, he delivered a moving speech in front of Pearl Harbor survivors at the *Arizona* Memorial, prefaced by airplanes flying the "missing man" formation. Although Japan's parliament had failed to agree on any resolution of apology (the foreign minister instead expressed "deep remorse"), the president did not bring up the recent apology controversy. He commented that he had "no rancor in my heart" toward the Japanese and then hardly mentioned Japan at all. In the formal speech, he honored the "heroes of the harbor," who had instinctively rushed to their posts and "did not panic." Choking up on the second to last paragraph as he remarked that the harbor's water had carried the "finest sons any nation could ever have" to a "better world," he moved the audience to tears. It was a speech of shared memories, celebrating the achievements and sacrifices of the World War II generation. For the individuals in the audience and for the nation as a whole, the message looked inward, a testament to an American generation drawn to stand for old-fashioned virtues—a bulwark against the changing present.[10]

"The USS Arizona stands as a call of peace to every nation on the planet"

At the time of the 1991 anniversary, the National Park Service was making significant changes to the film that introduced the *Arizona* Memorial. The older film had become much too controversial, catching the Park Service in a political crossfire. In addition, the demography of Hawaii and the changing composition of tourists to the monument prompted a reconsideration of the film.

Originally seen primarily as American sacred space, Pearl Harbor increasingly attracted tourists from all over the world. Honolulu itself, of course, was a highly international city, with a mixture of people who had moved from the mainland, native Hawaiians, and those of Japanese, Chinese, Filipino, Korean, and Vietnamese descent. Within this multicultural milieu, the mission of the *Arizona* Memorial shifted somewhat to emphasize a general commemoration of all the World War II dead and a vaguely defined hope for peace.[11]

The new introductory film, finished in 1992 after two years and seventeen scripts, was still structured around the basic narrative of *December 7* and the first memorial film: it projected visions of Hawaiian somnolence (with the surprise attack depicted in newly available Japanese-shot film rather than the recycled *December 7* re-creations), the massive efforts to recover and mobilize, and the somber commemoration of war dead. It provided little historical context for explaining Japan's actions, as such explanation might appear to be justification.[12]

Unlike the previous film, however, this new film did not end with the lesson of national preparedness but, instead, specifically invited each member of the audience to find his or her own meanings related to war, death, and remembrance. "How shall we remember them, those who died? Mourn the dead. Remember the battle. Understand the tragedy. Honor the memory."[13] There was little overt nationalism or militarism in the accompanying music. National Park Service historians suggested that one of the main messages of the *Arizona* site was the "futility of war."[14] The superintendent of the site remarked that "For older veterans . . . the lesson really is that America must never be unprepared again. Younger Americans see it as a peace memorial. Because of Vietnam they believe that war is not the answer to international disputes—that there have to be other lessons."[15] Park personnel and viewer surveys reported that pride and sadness, rather than militancy and anger, were the predominant emotions that people reported feeling after viewing the film.[16]

The memorial itself offered a very general lesson: the men died for a better future and in the promotion of a more lasting peace. Individual people could read a variety of messages into the injunction to "Remember Pearl Harbor." The potentially incompatible discourses of nationalistic military might and internationalist tourism were blended together; controversy and blame remained muted. As anthropologist Geoffrey White put it in his account of the complex negotiations among constituencies that shaped the successfully received film, "the Pearl Harbor film does not so much tell a single story as mediate diverse readings among multiple publics."[17]

The emphasis on commemoration and the availability of multiple messages were compatible with Hawaii's two largest sources of employment, the military and tourism, and both anchored themselves in gendered imagery. In so many film and written renditions of the Pearl Harbor narrative, a sleepy, feminized Hawaii beckoned to Uncle Sam's boys; grass-skirted sirens offered leis to distract men who came on the (male) nation's business. During the military and tourist booms of the cold war, these images were carefully cultivated so that America's dominant image of Hawaii became that of a pleasant young woman waiting to embrace (male) visitors on military "rest and recreation" or on business. Met on their incoming flights with leis, Americans would feel hosted, in effect, by the women of the house, who stood ready to assist and make comfortable. The new film at the memorial, for example, abandoned the authoritative male voice of the previous, more controversial, film and now featured a woman's voice (Stockard Channing's) as narrator. Soft and sometimes ever so slightly cracking with emotion, the voice offered to soothe visitors no matter what interpretations or meanings they reached. Potential clashes of interpretation between the United States and Japan or between nationalism and internationalism were muted by an open text and a feminine voice.

During the 1990s, Pearl Harbor remained a negotiated site, encompassing diverse messages. Public tours of a docked submarine became an added attraction, and in 1999 the battleship *Missouri,* upon which Japan had signed formal documents of surrender in Tokyo Bay on September 2, 1945, also opened to the public in an area adjacent to the memorial. The arrival of the *Missouri* linked the end of the war to its beginning. These additions provoked some controversy. The navy, eager to heighten

tourist interest in military prowess, welcomed the USS *Missouri;*
the National Park Service worried about avoiding a theme park
atmosphere and may have had qualms about politicizing the site
anew with end-of-the-war memories.[18] Other elements of the
commemorative displays also underwent revision. The Visitors'
Center assigned a prominent place to Doris (Dorie) Miller, the African American mess attendant on the USS *Arizona* who grabbed
an antiaircraft gun and let loose a barrage of fire. The OWI's
wartime poster displaying Miller's picture was placed on the sight
line from the entry, near an interactive computer display offering
details on Miller's life and deeds. Meanwhile, the solemnity of the
site grew as the *Arizona* became the final resting place for other
veterans, survivors of the disaster who requested that their remains be interred in the No. 4 turret's barbette, close to their
former shipmates.[19]

As multiple meanings and varied purposes attached themselves to the memorial site at Pearl Harbor, the numbers of visitors grew exponentially. Hawaii's tourism boom, of course, both
augmented and drew from the fame of Pearl Harbor. A relatively
minor monument site for years, even after the Park Service
opened its Visitors' Center in 1980, by 2000 the *Arizona* Memorial hosted over 1.5 million visitors a year and the staff began
planning a major expansion.[20]

More apology controversies

The new, less controversial film at the *Arizona* Memorial coincided with renewed attempts at reunion and reconciliation on the
part of U.S. and Japanese veterans. Jack Westerman had canceled
his reconciliation plans in 1991, but interest on both sides of the
Pacific prompted him to reschedule. Held in October 1992 at
Pearl Harbor, the meeting included a few Japanese veterans and
over a dozen Pearl Harbor survivors from the mainland. Arriving
at the *Arizona* Memorial by special ferry, the group joined hands
as Westerman expressed the hope that their "act of friendship"
would "ensure a spirit of peace for the world" and as Zenji Abe
expressed "heartfelt condolences."[21] Attendance at such joint cer-

emonies would, like visits to the *Arizona* Memorial itself, grow throughout the decade.

By December 1995, the World War II American and Japanese Veterans Friendship Program, sponsored by the East-West Center and the Matsunaga Institute for Peace at the University of Hawaii, attracted veterans from both countries and more than eighty people who volunteered to assist with translation and logistics. Still controversial, the reunion began only after the main events commemorating December 7 had ended. The participants, according to one of the volunteers, comprised "two rather specific factions of veterans within each nation." American veterans who had themselves experienced the Pearl Harbor attack came largely from the Georgia or Hawaii chapters of the PHSA, which had veered away from the still rancorous views of the larger membership. The Japanese "were almost exclusively members of the Unabarakai, veterans who were student pilot trainees from the elite high school naval academies." Only a few of them had been present at Pearl Harbor in 1941, and they were slightly younger than the American cohort. Both groups seemed to share a bond of having loyally served their countries and of having broader hopes that world peace would prevail in the future. Some deep friendships developed.[22]

Such ceremonies, however, had different meanings in each country. In the United States, reconcilers often spoke of tolerance and even antimilitarism. In Japan, meanings could be more complicated. Like their American counterparts, some Japanese stressed friendship with the United States and expressed regret for the war. But the reconciliation movement could also help accord new honor to Japan's World War II veterans, who had been culturally disdained for years. In this way, the veterans' movement in Japan might fit with a rising tide of Japanese nationalism and help to silence victims of Japanese aggression, who wanted a Japanese apology before any reconciliation. If the "friendship programs" could suggest narratives of peace, then they could also suggest a revival of Japan's discredited militaristic tradition with its refusal to acknowledge wartime abuses. As in so much else, the symbolisms associated with Pearl Harbor were always complicated and context specific.[23]

After the fiftieth anniversary of Pearl Harbor, newly visible concerns shaped the symbolic politics of U.S.-Japan relations. During the 1990s, a large body of scholarship on the Holocaust against the Jews in Europe raised issues related to trauma, memory, history writing, and meaning. Scholars and others adapted these Holocaust themes in examining the horrors of the atomic bombing of the citizens of Hiroshima and Nagasaki, underscoring their status as victims.[24] At the same time, well-publicized investigations and awards of compensation to Holocaust victims and their families helped focus attention on those who had been victimized by Japan. A growing movement throughout Asia and among Americans of Asian ancestry demanded that the Japanese government make a full disclosure of its World War II crimes, provide reparations to victims, and place this history in its official textbooks. Activist groups promoted Iris Chang's widely read (and also widely criticized) *Rape of Nanking* (1997) and publicized interviews with now aged "comfort women," who had been held in sexual slavery for Japanese troops. A new museum, which opened in Los Angeles, highlighted Japan's atrocities in Asia. Activist groups increasingly referred to an "Asian Holocaust" and countered any memorializations related to Hiroshima with exhibitions or memorials about Japan's victims, especially in China.[25]

Which groups of victims should have priority in the remembering of the Pacific War—Japanese atomic victims or Asian and POW victims of Japan? Issues of respective victimization became highlighted during the fiftieth anniversary of the atomic bombing in August 1945. Those Americans emphasizing reconciliation asked their country to remember the horrors of the atomic attack; those demanding Japanese apologies cautioned Americans to remember Pearl Harbor and other aggressions. Pearl Harbor and Hiroshima anchored larger historical narratives that positioned Japan primarily as perpetrator or as victim.[26]

In February 2001 the USS *Greeneville,* a nuclear submarine, accidentally rammed and sank a Japanese fishing boat, the *Enhime Maru,* off the coast of Honolulu. Nine people, mostly students, were lost at sea, and many in Japan demanded an official apology and compensation. For many Americans, the location of the sinking highlighted controversies over apologies. Although

the sinking actually occurred off Diamond Head, U.S. media
nearly always gave its location as Pearl Harbor, an identification
that heightened audience interest because of its symbolic association with U.S.-Japanese conflict. The U.S. government agreed to
raise the vessel and pay compensation and the submarine commander, Scott Waddle, offered numerous personal apologies, but
many Americans bristled at Japanese suggestions that an *official*
apology for the sinking should be forthcoming. Japan, as many
American commentators quickly pointed out, had never officially
apologized for its 1941 attack. Dan Rather, on the *CBS Evening
News*, for example, overtly linked a discussion of blame in the
submarine incident with World War II issues. He noted the failure of Japan to apologize for brutality against Chinese people, sex
slaves, and POWs during World War II. Showing the stock footage
of the Pearl Harbor attack (not identified as the recreation done
for *December 7*), he also criticized a Japanese politician's recent
implication that the United States—not Japan—was to blame for
the 1941 attack at Pearl Harbor because of the embargoes it had
leveled against Japan.[27]

The USS *Greeneville* dispute came amid other apology-related
disputes. In the late 1990s, in the shadow of several settlements
on Holocaust claims and rising demands for similar recognition
of wrongdoing by Japan, American POWs began to organize.
Linda Goetz Holmes published *Unjust Enrichment*, the research
for which informed a landmark class-action suit brought in 1999
by five hundred former POWs against five Japanese companies.
Former POW Lester Tenney mounted a parallel campaign to demand Japan's formal apology and compensation for forcing thousands of U.S. soldiers into slave labor for businesses such as the
Mitsubishi Corporation. Taking his case before the U.S. Congress
and the American media, Tenney clashed with the State Department. The U.S. and Japanese governments both took the position
that the San Francisco Peace Treaty of 1951, which officially ended
World War II and restored Japan to full sovereignty, resolved all
postwar settlement issues and closed the book on claims for compensation.[28] In April 2001, more controversy mounted when the
Japanese Education Ministry approved a book developed by the
right-wing Japanese Society for History Textbook Reform and
published by Fusosha Publishing, a group known for justifying

Japan's colonial past. Americans of Chinese, Korean, Filipino, and Okinawan ancestry demonstrated in front of the Japanese consulate in Los Angeles against the omissions in the textbook related to Japan's aggression in World War II and called for Japan's apology.[29] On September 8, 2001, when Japan's foreign minister, Makiko Tanaka, and U.S. Secretary of State Colin Powell joined to celebrate the fiftieth anniversary of the San Francisco peace treaty and to formally renew the strategic partnership between the two countries, protesters gathered outside of the San Francisco Opera House to demand formal apologies and reparations for Japanese atrocities against Asians and American POWs. Although Japan's foreign minister admitted that her country had "caused tremendous damage and suffering to the people of many countries" and, for the first time, singled out "former prisoners of war" among the sufferers, protesters dismissed the gesture because it fell short of an official apology.[30]

The *Greeneville* incident, coinciding with these other apology controversies, showed how easily any irritant between the United States and Japan could quickly devolve into a revival of Pearl Harbor memories. The Japanese writer Shin'ya Fujiwara, in an editorial in the *New York Times,* wrote of his "strange feeling" when he noticed that the *Greeneville* incident was located "off Pearl Harbor" in the United States but "off Hawaii" in Japan, a small difference of emphasis that cast the event in very different political and historical contexts in the two countries.[31]

Despite all of the public issues related to reconciliation and discord between the United States and Japan, it is perhaps surprising how *small* a role representations of Japan played in most of the renewed attention and media circulation related to Pearl Harbor after 1991. The revival of Pearl Harbor as a site of historical memory in American culture, as the commemorative events of 1991 had suggested, said much more about issues internal to America than about bilateral relations. The "date which will live" provoked controversies, narratives, and images related to what seemed to interest Americans the most in the 1990s, and relations with Japan, while important, had less cultural visibility than many other concerns that will be subsequently examined.

6 The Memory Boom

and the "Greatest Generation"

From the 1970s on, a memory boom reverberated through American life, proliferating and blurring forms of history, heritage, and commemoration. Set amid this engagement with the past, the fiftieth anniversaries that began in 1991 riveted media attention on the meanings and experiences of World War II, including the war's most prominent icon—Pearl Harbor. After years of reticence, members of an older generation grew anxious to tell their wartime stories—to get them into the nation's memory/history before passing from the scene. Their children, baby boomers of the Vietnam generation, seemed eager to honor and commemorate their parents and to rediscover a more glorious, less ambiguous time. The much discussed "generation gap" that had divided World War II parents from their Vietnam-era children rendered the sudden outpouring of memory and reconciliation more poignant.

Voices from "the good war"

Even before the commemorative events of 1991, Studs Terkel's *"The Good War"* (1984), a collection of remembrances about World War II gathered from interviews with a wide range of

Americans, won a Pulitzer Prize and topped the best-seller list. This book followed on the success of his *Hard Times,* a similar collection about life during the Great Depression. " '*The Good War,*'" Terkel wrote, was "a memory book, rather than one of hard fact," designed to counter the "disturbingly profound dis-remembrance of World War Two." It presented highly readable stories, carefully selected by a master at listening and editing. The theme of the book subtly invoked a comparison with the Vietnam War, opening with a verse of Tom Paxton's bitterly antiwar song "What Did You Learn in School Today?" ("I learned that war is not so bad; I learned about the great ones we have had; We fought in Germany and in France; And I am someday to get my chance.") By invoking Paxton and the "bad war" that had divided Ameri-cans and ravaged Indochina, Terkel reminded readers of the ear-lier "good" and unifying war, but he also put "the good war" in quotation marks, both advancing and also subverting the term.[1]

Terkel's book dovetailed with a rising interest in "oral history." Collecting oral testimony grew out of a new emphasis on social history—the history not just of great (largely male) leaders, but also of common people who left few written records of their own. The call to do "history from the bottom up" was closely linked to the ideological insurgency that marked the antiwar protests of the 1960s and early 1970s. The new social historians frequently con-centrated on collecting the "voices" of women, African Ameri-cans, and others whose views had previously been underrepre-sented in historical texts. Sherna Berger Gluck's *Rosie the Riveter* (1988), for example, presented interviews with working women during World War II within a discourse of feminism. A film by the same name, featuring interviews with five women whose lives were shaped by the gain—and subsequent loss—of homefront job opportunities during the war became widely used in college American history courses. Wallace Terry's *Bloods* (1984), a collec-tion of oral histories from African American soldiers serving in Vietnam, focused attention on this particular group. The em-phasis on such "authentic" voices implicitly advanced the idea that individual memory, especially if taken from "below," might provide a more direct path to understanding the past than the more traditional accounts of professional historians, who had centered their work on written sources and the elites who left them. Frequently, the turn by social historians toward collecting oral histories exuded a kind of redemptive aura, as though some precious part of the past was being "recovered" in some unmediated and "authentic" form.

Oral history's emphasis on "authentic" voices and the "experience" of ordinary folks was not without criticism. Conservatives and many traditional political historians chafed at the diminished prestige of great narratives and the emphasis on individualized, often insurgent, perspectives. Cultural historians raised a host of quite different, theoretical objections. Who selects oral testimonies that are recorded and edited, and by what criteria and process? Can "experience" be a foundational category, or is not memory of experience itself subject to construction and reconstruction over time? Critics derided the idea that collecting people's stories was somehow less filtered than other kinds of history.[2]

Oral history, however, became undeniably popular, and Americans appeared to be increasingly fascinated with personal stories of travail and triumph. Oral history *seemed* to provide access to an unmediated "truth" of the past and *seemed* to democratize the elite-based practice of doing and writing history. As Studs Terkel discovered, stories told by common people about big events could have a ready popular market that thrived on the appearance of "authenticity."

Terkel's best-seller, perhaps, helped generate some of the enthusiasm that accompanied the fiftieth-anniversary commemorations of Pearl Harbor in 1991. The political disagreements and ideological wars related to Vietnam had long eclipsed the memory of World War II. But, suddenly, "the good war" seemed to be rediscovered, and the new fascination with oral history fed an urgency about preserving the fading memories of those days. Radio broadcasts featured interviews with veterans; television documentaries took new interest in ordinary people who had lived through the war years; magazines ran features; museums and universities developed oral history collections; and more and more books of World War II recollections rolled off the presses.[3] The interview format, quickly embraced by publishers, offered a kind of popular history that avoided the complicated interpretive questions of grand politics and, instead, highlighted specific detail, personal feelings, and the element of chance. In oral histories of the Pearl Harbor attack, the descriptions of first reactions, of explosion and death, and of panic and response could rivet audience attention. Whereas some of Terkel's interviews had suggested an ironic twist to "the good war," the 1991 celebratory mood generally highlighted individual courage and heroism.

Capping the media attention sparked by the commemorations of the December 7 attack, Congress established a new Pearl Harbor Survivor's Medal. The medal, included in the Defense Authorization Act for 1991, honored those who had been at Pearl Harbor during the Japanese raid, including civilian employees of the army or navy if they were present and either killed or wounded. The inscription on one side of the bronze, one-and-one-half-inch medallion read, "Remember Pearl Harbor"; the other side read, "A Day Which Will Live in Infamy" and "For Those Who Served." One side featured a battle scene; the other side showed an eagle clutching an olive branch.[4]

Memory boom

The new visibility of memories of World War II—in books, radio and television programs, print journalism, and commemorative acts—was part of what Jay Winter has called a "memory boom" and Michael Kammen has termed a "heritage phenomenon" in American culture. During the closing decades of the twentieth century there seemed to be an upsurge of public historical pageants, new museums, flea markets, "living history" displays, historical preservation, and re-enactors. Americans embraced time-travel fantasies, collected memorabilia, and visited the antique malls that mushroomed throughout the country. New strip mall specialty stores devoted to remembrance guided people in preserving their personal memories in albums, videos, and digital files. *Antiques Roadshow* surprised public television producers by becoming an overnight sensation. Assisted by new Internet technology, researching genealogy became a popular pastime, as American families sought to identify their roots. One of the few successful new Internet companies, eBay, provided a virtual marketplace linking sellers with collectors of anything and everything. There seemed to be a new emphasis on "witnessing," as historians, writers, artists, and others experimented with ways to record experience so that it would be remembered in art and history.[5]

What might explain this upsurge? Michael Kammen sees it as a "response to postwar anxiety and the sense of sharp discontinuity." Change propels nostalgia, a quest for timelessness, which then offers commercial opportunities to sell repackaged, imagined versions of the past.[6] David Lowenthal similarly analyzes four principal psychological and sociological "uses" for "wistful memories of imagined idealism and heroic sacrifice": *validation* of present attitudes and actions through an affirmation of their resemblance to the past; *guidance* that supports current decisions and values; solidification of personal and national *identity*; and *escape* into an imagined time, free of modernizing change.[7] In a related explanation, cultural critic Andreas Huyssen ties the late twentieth century's preoccupation with historical memory to consumer capitalism's destabilization of identity. Huyssen argues that the remarkable upsurge of "memory practices" in today's "memory culture" seeks to invoke the past as a space of stable relationships, known boundaries, and sense of place—those attributes construed to be absent from contemporary life.[8]

Another line of analysis links the memory boom to globalization. As the global scale of travel, media, diasporic populations, and consciousness expands—what travel writer Pico Iyer has called the "global soul" and anthropologist Arjun Appadurai has termed "modernity at large"—the yearning for localized roots and more fixed identities also grows. History/memory helps provide structures for embraceable pasts that may buttress ever-tenuous identities. Memory thus takes shape within the identity politics that has grown stronger, not weaker, in a cosmopolitan age.[9] In this sense, the popular embrace of the past may be understood less as a reaction against consumer capitalism than as another consumerist, identity-defining site that is very functional in terms of capitalism. If the memory boom seemed to be everywhere, after all, there was more of *every* kind of consumer diversion—

more sports, more fashion, more television channels, more travel, more business, more amusement parks. Heritage, commemoration, and history, like hamburgers or stereo equipment, stimulated additional consumption and brought profits. A concern with historical identity ran parallel with, say, maintaining a fashionable wardrobe or a youthful-looking body. One mainspring of consumerism, after all, is the elusive promise of self-realized identity.

Foreign policy theorists talk of a syndrome called the "security dilemma": the tendency of hegemonic powers to feel less, rather than more, secure as they become more dominant and generate oppositional forces. The dilemma is that the more a nation builds programs to support national security, the more insecure it may feel, and the more it then promotes additional programs. One might similarly describe an "identity dilemma" in American culture: the more one worries over building an identity, the more it seems lacking. The "identity dilemma" may fuel the memory boom, as people seek their roots, their "people," their "histories," and the memories of "experiences" recounted within their communities of identification. The cultural saturation of memory products, then, seems part of a larger trend of the baby boom generation's ethic of avid consumption, with the past offering one more consumerist arena.

Building on all of these explanations of the memory boom and summarizing others, Jay Winter has suggested that the memory boom stems from the interplay among identity politics, affluence, higher educational attainment, comfort with public expression of the "interior discourse of psychoanalysis," updated artistic narratives of traumatic memory, and the "cultural turn," with its emphasis on practices of signification and representation. Winter suggests that the term "memory," invoked within varied discursive traditions, has become the "historical signature of our own generation."[10]

One irony of the memory boom is that it failed to elevate the role of academic historians. In fact, as Americans became more and more interested in the past, academic history seemed to lose its status and much of its audience. During 1993 and 1994 David Thelan, the editor of the *Journal of American History*, and Roy

Rosenzweig conducted a survey of 1,500 Americans in order to explore "the presence of the past" in their everyday lives. They found that most respondents engaged the past to grapple with personal and familial issues and with questions of identity and legacy. They trusted firsthand accounts and museums with "authentic artifacts." But they felt little connection to history as taught in textbooks or classrooms. History that seemed real and compelling, people reported, bore a personal connection to themselves and came with little perceived mediation from professionals who, in the view of many, only distorted "authentic" voices and "real experience."[11] As much of the new interest in history moved outside of educational institutions, the circulation of history/memory crisscrossed over a variety of occupational and media boundaries, blurring old distinctions between what was professional and popular, what was history and nostalgia, and what was "high" and "low" culture.

"A life-changing experience"

Borrowing from the interview format popularized by Studs Terkel and buoyed by the pervasive memory boom, NBC news anchor Tom Brokaw's *The Greatest Generation* became a cultural phenomenon. It presented a collection of stories from some fifty Americans—men and women, ordinary and now famous—who had fought in World War II. Brokaw was not interested in the international politics of the war. He took as a given that it was a just cause fought against "maniacs" and said no more about larger international causes or consequences.[12] His focus instead was on the *individuals* involved: their memories of the way they experienced the war, their everyday qualities of courage and achievement. Though certainly patriotic in its overall message, the book was primarily philiopietistic, a testimonial in praise of our "fathers."

Brokaw related how he traveled to Normandy in the spring of 1984 to work on an NBC documentary about the fortieth anniversary of D-Day. "There, I underwent a life-changing experience." He realized that veterans had been all around him as he was growing up, but he had failed to appreciate what they had experienced and accomplished. They had undertaken the task of building a better world; they had stayed true to their values. But they hardly talked of their achievements. He was "deeply moved and profoundly grateful."[13]

Ten years later, Brokaw returned for the fiftieth anniversary of D-Day, and by then he had come to understand that this was the "greatest generation any society has ever produced." Its members came of age during the Great Depression, won World War II without expecting any special thanks, and then built modern America. He wanted to extol their "common values"—duty, honor, economy, courage, service, love of family and country, and above all, responsibility for oneself." He sought to preserve their memories, but their stories, long silent, did not come easily. He appealed to other Americans to "begin to ask the questions and hear the stories that have been locked in memory for too long."[14] Indeed, World War II veterans had seemed especially reticent to talk about the war. Those who had seen combat seemed especially silent. Perhaps the most powerful memoir of the Pacific War, E. B. Sledge's *With the Old Breed,* did not appear until 1981. In a painful recollection of battlefield horror and brutality, Sledge found honor and uplift through his close relationships with comrades (his "brothers") but not through any belief in larger abstractions. Sledge, like others, hardly presented himself as a hero. Brokaw helped break the silence, but he also elevated this "greatest generation" into a heroic mold that it had hardly claimed for itself.

Suddenly, Brokaw and the trope of "the greatest generation" seemed to be everywhere. Brokaw himself expressed surprise at the outpouring of interest and suggested that he had tapped some very great desire in American culture to commemorate the deeds of the past generation. Stephen Ambrose's *D-Day: June 6, 1944* (1994) and *Citizen Soldiers* (1997) augmented the rediscovery of World War II, and Steven Spielberg's *Schindler's List* (1993) and *Saving Private Ryan* (1998) provided vivid screen images. World War II became a producer's bonanza and a national pastime. A second Brokaw book in 1998, *The Greatest Generation Speaks,* sounded a note of urgency. Now in their seventies and eighties,

Brokaw reported, World War II veterans were dying at the rate of 3,200 a month, according to the Department of Veterans' Affairs. A third book, *An Album of Memories* (2001), focused on the transference of memory to the second generation. Other books also offered the stories of fathers, now represented by sons. James Bradley's *Flags of Our Fathers* (2001), for example, told the stories of the six flag raisers on Iwo Jima (one being Bradley's father). Earlier, twenty-seven publishers had rejected Bradley's book proposal; in 2001 it climbed the best-seller lists. Americans seemed unable to get enough of World War II memory products.[15]

With the technological innovations of video and cable television, World War II also gained a renewed presence in visual images. In honor of the fiftieth anniversary, Fox Video reissued films bundled as "The Pearl Harbor Collection." "With this tribute," the promotions stated, "Pearl Harbor lives on."[16] Cable television, a relatively new phenomenon in American culture, also turned to film archives, and classic motion pictures became a staple of television viewing. Arts and Entertainment Network moguls noticed that "the American public was having a growing love affair with history," according to Dan Davids, a senior vice president for marketing. In 1994 the network decided to create a twenty-four hour history channel for cable subscription, and Davids, who was born on December 7 (1950), became its general manager. The "H-Channel" was an instant hit. In its early years, the viewer growth rate exceeded that of any other niche provider. Documentaries about the World War II era proved so popular and pervasive on the H-Channel that some channel surfers satirically dubbed it the "Hitler-Channel." The H-Channel "brand" quickly expanded from the living room to the classroom, pulled by student interest in visual learning and pushed by its manager's involvement with an organization called Cable in the Classroom.[17] The History Channel, like the Brokaw and Ambrose best-sellers, erased the boundaries between entertainment and education and between memory and history—boundaries that academic historians had often tried to delineate and uphold but that held little meaning in the arena of mass media. Americans, young and old, began to hear reminiscences and to see long-archived wartime images in abundance.

World War II veterans themselves began to seek greater recognition. Throughout the country, spearheaded by the PHSA, veterans and veterans' groups pressed local legislatures and councils for honorific resolutions. The New Jersey state legislature created a "Pearl Harbor Remembrance Day," calling on the governor to fly the flag at half-staff and to issue an annual proclamation requesting people to undertake appropriate ceremonies and activities.[18] Similar bills passed in other states. In 1996, the fifty-fifth anniversary of the attack, President Clinton proclaimed December 7 "National Pearl Harbor Remembrance Day," but some veterans lobbied for more. In March 1999 veterans from Buffalo, New York, backed Republican representative Jack Quinn in sponsoring legislation that would designate December 7 as a federal holiday on the same plane as Veterans' Day. A member of the Veterans' Affairs Committee in the House, Quinn proclaimed that Pearl Harbor deserved its special day because "it put the U.S. into World War II and as a result of America's involvement in the war, it established our country as a dominant world power." This day would give Pearl Harbor veterans "the admiration and respect they're due" and "keep their bravery remembered in years to come and their memory alive."[19] Confronted by arguments, presented especially by small business interests, that there were already too many federal holidays, Senator Quinn replied, "If the United States hadn't responded to events at Pearl Harbor, there wouldn't be any other holidays for us to talk about."[20] The idea, however, found little support, even among veterans, many of whom argued that the sacrifices made at D-Day or the Battle of the Bulge made such an enduring emphasis on Pearl Harbor inappropriate.

Despite the failure to designate December 7 a federal holiday, the commemorative mood still spread. One of the leaders of the holiday movement turned his sights, more successfully, to changing the name of a bridge over the Schuylkill River near Philadelphia to the "Pearl Harbor Memorial Bridge." The navy withdrew its long objection to naming a ship the *Pearl Harbor;* Colorado's Interstate 70 and an extension of the Pennsylvania Turnpike were both designated "Pearl Harbor Memorial Highway." Thurston Clarke reported that "Pearl Harbor continues to haunt its survivors, as well as their descendants," and he noted how many had become committed to documenting every moment, every detail, every relic.[21]

Relics, in fact, often took on a kind of sacred quality, just as did the commemorative site itself. A piece of anything related to the Pearl Harbor attack could become a treasured artifact of material culture, to be carefully preserved in a public museum or private collection. A bell from the USS *Arizona* became enshrined in the student union of the University of Arizona; the ship's anchor stood as the center of a memorial on the capitol grounds in Phoenix. The Texas Parks and Wildlife Department's National Museum of the Pacific War at the Admiral Nimitz Historical Center in Fredericksburg, the only museum dedicated entirely to the Pacific theater of the war, opened a new, 23,000-square-foot gallery named in honor of President George H. W. Bush and containing a thousand artifacts from the war, many related to Pearl Harbor.[22]

In memory boom fashion, collectors of Pearl Harbor memorabilia seemed everywhere. In Bloomington, Minnesota, for example, a retired army captain who had flown Pearl Harbor reenactments for air shows during the mid-1970s began preserving posters, letters, newspaper stories, and photos. As his scrapbooks bulged and his walls filled up, he augmented his collection with short biographies of all Pearl Harbor survivors from Minnesota. In 2001 his collection, outgrowing his home, became a Pearl Harbor history display at the Minnesota Military Museum at Camp Ripley.[23] Material memories of Pearl Harbor, especially among veterans and their families, often functioned as tangible commemoration in the "greatest generation" tradition.

In many cases, it was less the veterans themselves than their baby boomer children who propelled the World War II memory boom. Generational politics—first rebellion and then reconciliation—set agendas for memory. The phenomenon of a generational shift often profoundly affects ways in which groups of people solidify common memories and create identities. In the late nineteenth century, when the generation that had fought the Civil War began to die in huge numbers, the next generation sensed the urgency to honor and preserve. Memorializing the dead of the

Civil War and honoring its veterans served, for white Americans at least, to reunite the divided nation and heal national wounds. In 1892 the "Pledge of Allegiance" gained adoption, and the War of 1898 occasioned a celebration of a supposedly rebonded nationalism.[24] Similarly, honoring the sacrifices of World War II seemed a balm for the divisions that had come with the Vietnam War. The Vietnam generation, now middle-aged, seemed to embrace the previous generation, which it had once ignored or rebelled against. Aged fathers, perhaps once taken for granted, could now be recognized. Remembrance of the unifying "good war" might sublimate the divisions of the Vietnam era.

Congress responded to the growing public interest in commemoration with an effort to build a new war memorial on the Mall in Washington, D.C. Although the Vietnam and Korean Wars had monuments on the Mall, World War II had no significant commemorative presence in the nation's capital. In 1993, Congress approved planning for a memorial, and discussions regarding location and design began. Private donations poured in, especially after former senator and 1996 Republican presidential candidate Robert Dole and Tom Hanks, the star of *Saving Private Ryan*, made a series of television appeals. Although few people opposed a monument, differences over location and design sparked a battle royal. The project that emerged from a much criticized planning process envisioned a huge, 7.4-acre site in the middle of the Mall, containing a sunken stone plaza, a reduced rainbow pool, fifty-six commemorative pillars standing seventeen feet high, two four-story triumphal arches, and assorted star, eagle, wreath, and fountain decorations. Most architectural critics scoffed at the $160 million plan, and one called it "high kitsch style ironically reminiscent of fascist displays." A *Los Angeles Times* cartoon showed Willie and Joe, the GIS of Bill Mauldin's famous wartime cartoons, standing in the midst of the monument and commenting, "Looks like an officers' club . . . a German officers' club."[25] Pressure to memorialize World War II on the Mall, however, overwhelmed the critics. In May 2001, Congress fast-tracked the project by nullifying any further lawsuits designed to delay or deliberate. President George W. Bush signed the bill on Memorial Day, 2001 (also the debut of the blockbuster film *Pearl Harbor*), and projected a completion date in the election year of 2004.[26]

A less controversial commemorative effort grew directly from the kind of oral history that Terkel and Brokaw had helped popularize. Representatives Ron Kind and Amo Houghton and Senators Max Cleland and Charles Hagel sponsored bipartisan bills to create a Veterans' Oral History Project. Signed into law by President Clinton in October 2000, it directed the American Folklife Center at the Library of Congress to enlist the public in collecting personal stories of America's war veterans and to place the collection in the Internet. Noting how many veterans were dying each day, the center's director endorsed this effort to "preserve these folks histories of our everyday war heroes from every corner of the nation and offer selections from their stories back to the American people over the Internet."[27] Started in 1928, the Folklife Center had collected ex-slave narratives and folk songs and even "man on the street" interviews taped by folklorists on December 8, 1941.[28] Some of these folk collections had a populist, and often a left-leaning, slant. But documenting "folk" heroes from World War II united the left's championing of "history from the bottom up" with the broader interest in commemorating the sacrifices of America's "greatest generation." This bipartisan project seemed to bridge the partisan culture wars of the 1990s, a subject that will next be examined.

The persistent reiteration of World War II themes in the memory boom culture of the late 1990s transferred the memories of the war to generations that had not lived through it. With so many cultural and political institutions circulating its history/memory, World War II became, according to the noted war historian Paul Fussell, "an immense national neurosis."[29] Although World War II had seemed rather distant to many members of the baby boom generation as they grew up, by the end of the twentieth century, narratives about "the good war" had come into such prominence in America's media culture that the war, as secondary memory, became fresh again. These new rememberings reinvigorated the old debates over how to understand the meaning of one of the war's central symbols, Pearl Harbor.

7 The Kimmel Crusade,

the History Wars, and the Republican Revival

In the fiftieth year after the Pearl Harbor attack, Admiral Husband Kimmel's son Edward (Ned) turned seventy years old. He and his brother Thomas had both served in the navy during World War II; another brother, Manning, died when the submarine he commanded struck a mine in the South China Sea in July 1944. A successful lawyer for the DuPont Company in Delaware, Edward had retired in 1984 to pursue a new career: working forty hours a week to restore his father's reputation.[1] Edward's efforts, joined in by Edward's own son, Manning, and Thomas's two sons (all of whom were navy men), reactivated controversy over the issue of assigning blame for Pearl Harbor. Coinciding with popular interest in the remembrance of World War II and with several high-profile controversies over the public presentation of history, the Kimmel crusade became part of a larger, conservative movement that, after 1992, focused its wrath on President Clinton, the popular Democrat who had a group of Clinton haters that recalled the Roosevelt haters of the 1940s.

Scapegoats

Admiral Kimmel and Lieutenant General Short had been relieved of their commands immediately following the attack on Pearl Harbor and were retired at lower ranks. Short died in 1949 and Kimmel in 1968. They and many others felt Roosevelt administration officials had unfairly scapegoated them to divert blame from themselves and had blocked full and fair inquiries.

In 1987 Edward and Thomas Kimmel had petitioned President George H. W. Bush's secretary of navy, James H. Webb Sr., to restore posthumously their father's full rank. Pacific War historian Ronald H. Spector, the director of naval history in the Navy Department, did not support the petition. Spector cited Gordon Prange's influential studies, which had argued that Kimmel was aware that a Japanese attack might come from the north and that he should consequently have been more prepared and proactive. The petition was denied.[2]

Rebuffed by the Navy Department in Washington, Edward Kimmel nonetheless found a more than sympathetic hearing among some navy personnel, many of whom themselves had spent years denouncing the unfair treatment of Admiral Kimmel and General Short. (General Short's wife and son had died, so the discussions of injustice tended to emphasize Kimmel, although General Short's grandson, Walter Short, also joined into the effort.) The officers and trustees of the U.S. Naval Academy Alumni Association at Annapolis unanimously resolved in October 1990 that the navy should restore posthumously Kimmel's four-star rank. Two months later, the PHSA similarly adopted a resolution in favor of restoring rank to both Kimmel and Short. Next, thirty-six retired flag-rank officers—mostly four-star admirals—wrote President Bush, urging him to use his authority to direct "remedial action" on Kimmel's behalf.[3]

Officials in Washington rather than the military commanders at Pearl Harbor, claimed the Kimmel family and its supporters, were to blame for the lack of preparedness in late 1941. Washington, they contended, received information that an attack was imminent, yet the warnings sent to the base were so vague that the commanders believed that the target would be elsewhere or the attack might be some form of sabotage. The Kimmels themselves did not allege a full-fledged backdoor conspiracy, but by placing the blame in Washington, they implicitly bolstered that anti-FDR narrative. The Kimmel controversy also reverberated with an undercurrent of rivalry between civilian and military authorities. This rivalry had developed something of a partisan character in the contexts of both the Korean and Vietnam wars, when some military officials had charged that civilian authorities had tied their hands and thus prevented a more vigorous war fought through to conclusive victory.

The Kimmel crusade played a part in shaping the context for historical rememberings during the fiftieth anniversary of the Pearl Harbor attack. During the commemorative year of 1991, as noted, a wave of books, articles, and television shows presented an array of stories about Pearl Harbor. Just before the celebrations, the *New York Times* reported the publication of eleven new books on the subject, all with conflicting views. The *Wall Street Journal* discussed four television shows that, again, projected different interpretations, including one that portrayed the Japanese as victims of Roosevelt's maneuvering and presented a strong backdoor viewpoint.[4] Although the arguments advanced by Wohlstetter and Prange remained authoritative in most academic circles and were inscribed into most school textbooks, the backdoor, blame-the-Roosevelt-administration perspective remained very much alive in American popular culture. With another controversial Democrat, Bill Clinton, elected to the White House in 1992, these views circulated ever more prominently, especially among Republicans.

A rush of new books defending Kimmel and Short dusted off the old backdoor arguments and also advanced some new twists. Some argued the full-blown backdoor conspiracy theory; others provided a brief for Kimmel and Short that blamed Washington's miscalculations and strategic shortsightedness but fell short of charging intentionality or conspiracy. Rusbridger and Nave's *Betrayal at Pearl Harbor,* among the most extreme, alleged that intercepted naval signals intelligence offered substantial forewarning of Pearl Harbor separately to both London and Washington and that several related conspiracies suppressed this information.[5] The book broadened the backdoor conspiracy charges, blaming not just Roosevelt, but also his ally, Winston Churchill, who was maneuvering to bring the United States into the war. John Costello similarly argued that Kimmel and Short had been scapegoats and blamed FDR and Churchill, but he charged them with "miscalculation" rather than outright conspiracy. Costello also raised the question of why Kimmel and Short, but not General MacArthur, the U.S. commander in the Philippines, had taken the fall for the Japanese surprise. MacArthur, who emerged from the war with his reputation unscathed, Costello suggested, should have shouldered the blame for his "incredible" failures. His appalling inaction, Costello conjectures, may have been linked to his acceptance of half a million dollars from the Filipino president, who wanted to remain neutral in any new war.[6] In 1994 historian Michael Gannon challenged Prange and Spector's contention that Kimmel had been warned of an attack from the north and denied that, given his shortage of planes, he could possibly have conducted effective air reconnaissance to the north.[7] In 1995 retired U.S. navy captain Edward L. Beach issued an emotional backdoor, pro-Kimmel brief called *Scapegoats*.[8] Beach, a highly decorated officer, had been a naval aide to President Eisenhower.

History wars

The reignited controversy over assigning blame for Pearl Harbor coincided with another historical controversy that temporarily gained an even higher public profile. In 1993 a dispute broke out over a proposed Smithsonian Museum exhibit focused on the *Enola Gay*, the plane that dropped the first atomic bomb on Japan. The initial impetus for such an exhibit had come from air force lobbyists. The Smithsonian Institution brought in academic historians to prepare an interpretive script. As drafts began to circulate, an increasingly politicized conflict, which eventually reached the halls of Congress, erupted.

The curators and historical advisers who wrote the initial script for the interpretive panels that would accompany the *Enola Gay* display emphasized a narrative about atomic destruction and sought to raise some of the dilemmas of nuclear strategy. In this view, the Pacific War, with its escalating racial hatreds, became the context for the American decision to use the bomb, an action that inaugurated the age of atomic threats and turned Japanese victims of the bombing into symbols of the age's new perils. The *Enola Gay,* in short, became the focus for an exhibit centering on the complicated context surrounding the advent and use of nuclear weapons.

The Air Force Association and other pro-military lobbying groups, however, had expected the *Enola Gay* to highlight a narrative addressing Japanese aggression and atrocity and providing a commemorative tone for the sacrifice, and ultimate triumph, of American veterans. Oversimplifying the interpretive complexities of the draft script, they charged that it marginalized Japanese brutality and suggested an outrageous "moral equivalency" between the two sides in the war. Veterans' lobbying groups, some already mobilized in protest against the film at the *Arizona* Memorial, took the *Enola Gay* script as another sign that the "truths" of their history were under siege by the professional custodians of historical memory, people who were generally of the Vietnam generation, at the country's museums and sacred sites. The *Enola Gay,* in their view, should have anchored a story about the sacrifices of Americans during World War II and projected an appreciating, commemorative tone.

At stake was how a public museum should remember the history of the Pacific theater, and the controversy grew increasingly ugly during 1994. Many of the country's most distinguished historians generally defended the draft script, insisting that museums should aim for education and complexity rather than for commemoration. Diverse promilitary and conservative groups, by contrast, charged curators and historians with "distorting" history according to the dictates of "political correctness" and turning America's foremost museum into an unpatriotic institution. As the script underwent revision, the Air Force Association, joined by the American Legion, mounted a vigorous media offensive against the museum and its historians; it also appealed to sympathetic members of Congress, where Republicans became dominant after the midterm elections of November 1994. Reprinting often highly exaggerated charges from the Air Force Association's media campaign, newspapers throughout the country, large and small, framed the *Enola Gay* issue into a simple struggle in which patriotism and the "authentic" views of the greatest generation's veterans were being trammeled by Vietnam-era historians who warped history and sympathized with the nation's enemies. The Speaker of the House, Republican Newt Gingrich, himself a Ph.D. in history, contended that the *Enola Gay* fight represented "a reassertion by most Americans that they are sick and tired of being told by some cultural elite that they ought to be ashamed of their country."[9] The pressure—with future congressional funding as the ultimate lever—became so strong that the script was abandoned altogether, the curator of the exhibit, Martin Harwit, resigned, and the plane was displayed with minimal interpretation.[10]

The issues, splits, and multiple understandings involved in narrating the history of World War II, which had emerged in reactions to the *Arizona* Memorial in the late 1980s, became greatly magnified during the *Enola Gay* dispute. This dispute, in turn, provided a focal point for an even larger array of "history wars" during the mid-1990s.

The *Enola Gay* controversy, raising issues of history and memorialization to high political visibility, was one of many disputes that revealed the emotional contests over representation of the past. Karal Ann Marling and John Wetenhall, whose *Iwo Jima: Monuments, Memories, and the American Hero* (1991) examined the way in which the famous Joe Rosenthal photo of the raising of "Old Glory" had become an icon, suffered withering public attacks. They had examined how, despite the fact that the men in that photo had not been the same fighters who had originally endured the fight and raised a flag, the public had come to accept the photo's fighters as the original heroes. Their book's message about the power of photography and celebrity, however, became widely seen as a claim that the beloved photo was a "fraud" that somehow besmirched the popular memory of that most bloody battle. A barrage of letters to newspapers that had reviewed the book blasted "leftists" for tampering with sacred national memories.[11]

More monumental disputes followed. In 1996 a new superintendent of the Little Bighorn Battlefield National Monument announced controversial changes to accommodate American Indian
points of view. Two Smithsonian exhibits, one on the American
West and one on Columbus's "encounter" with the New World,
sparked fierce public debate over representations of American
Indians and the process of white settlement. In 1997 a fight broke
out over whether or not the new Franklin D. Roosevelt Memorial
in Washington, D.C., should depict Roosevelt in a wheelchair.
Controversy erupted about whether to place an old memorial to
women's suffrage, which honored three white women but no
African American women, in the Capitol Rotunda. The Disney
Company touched off another dispute when it proposed building a
historical theme park in Virginia. (How, for example, would Disney depict slavery?) Dozens of local quarrels in the South flared
over whether use of the confederate flag and memorials to the
Confederacy could constitute symbols of regional pride without at
the same time representing a tacit endorsement of slavery and
racism.[12] During 1995, historians who had drawn up what they
called "national history standards" in an attempt to improve history teaching in the kindergarten through twelfth grade curricu-
lum came under intense fire from cultural conservatives led by
Lynne Cheney. Cheney, who had begun a crusade against supposedly liberal academics when she headed the National Endow-
ment for the Humanities under President Reagan, charged the
history standard historians with "distorting" the past, purveying
anti-Americanism and "revisionism," and bowing to "political
correctness."[13]

While these diverse controversies crisscrossed lines of identity
and culture, the most heated debates generally pitted the country's associations of academic historians against groups of political and cultural conservatives, which often included World War II
veterans who had become increasingly mobilized into the history
wars by the disputes over the *Arizona* Memorial, the *Enola Gay*
exhibit, and the history standards. At heart was the question of
who had the right (and the power) to claim privileged knowledge
of the past. Pro-military lobbying groups, cultural conservatives,
and congressional critics railed that historians were "revising"

history to suit current agendas; many historians railed back that partisan pressure groups were seeking to "revise" history into popular oversimplifications. The dirty word of "revisionism" was slung liberally by both sides, and all the would-be custodians of history/memory went on the alert over the politics of historical representation.

In this climate, the narrower issue of Kimmel's posthumous status and the larger issue of blame for Pearl Harbor grew more visible and became entangled in political maneuvering, even involving appeals that Congress should get involved in settling the "truth" of history.

Searching for a "final judgement"

Amid the many skirmishes in the history wars of the 1990s, the Kimmel controversy remained small yet significant. Partisan sparks that had flown in the 1940s flared again fifty years later as some participants wanted to have their last say before they died or as those who had loved and admired them assumed the burden of converting their narratives to historical "truth." The fulcrum of this debate remained warring narratives (one pro- and one anti-FDR) about the strong Democratic president who had cast the blame for Pearl Harbor on local military commanders. Under President Clinton, who was generally distrusted by the military and despised by conservative Republicans, the Kimmel controversy gained political legs. The blame for Pearl Harbor took on more emotion than ever.

One partisan in the refreshed pro- and anti-FDR debates was Henry C. Clausen. Upset by the campaign mounted by Kimmel's family, Clausen decided to write a book that he called the "final judgement" on Pearl Harbor. Working with Bruce Lee, who had also collaborated with Gordon Prange, Clausen wrote that he was "totally shocked" by the "outpouring of misinformation that surrounded the fiftieth anniversary of Pearl Harbor." He detailed the continued prevalence of backdoor views and expressed special outrage at a *New York Times* letter to the editor of September 24, 1991, asserting that evidence proved the United States had broken the Japanese code, knew of the attack, and failed to alert the commanding officers at Pearl Harbor.[14]

If Edward Kimmel and prominent naval advocates sought to clear the memory of the Pearl Harbor commanders, Clausen was devoted to the memory of Stimson—"one of the greatest men who had ever served in government."[15] Clausen did not hold FDR entirely blameless, but he reemphasized the conclusions reached by Stimson's report to Congress in early March 1946 (a report that Clausen himself had researched nearly fifty years earlier), later generally supported in the influential books by Wohlstetter and Prange.[16] Kimmel and Short had been warned in careful but clear language that hostile action was possible at any moment, and it was their job to have taken all precautions. In addition, again echoing the 1946 report and the Wohlstetter-Prange view, Clausen assigned responsibility to faulty intelligence systems. "The proximate cause or guilt for the disaster at Pearl Harbor was an unworkable system of military intelligence, including the fact that the Navy withheld from the Army vital intelligence information that called for Army action." Dissemination and coordination of information were flawed; people were too concerned with protecting evidence of America's code breaking to use effectively the intelligence gained. Intelligence had not been sufficiently appreciated or coordinated by either the army or navy, and intelligence specialists had not received enough support or respect. Clausen concluded, however, that on a scale of blame where 10 was high both Kimmel and Short deserved a 10.[17] Still, he could no more finalize acceptance of his particular "final judgement" than could the Kimmel family.

The pro-Kimmel campaign stepped up its efforts in the mid-1990s. Arguments in favor of Kimmel began to appear more frequently, apparently gaining momentum from the campaigns that conservative and promilitary organizations had mounted against the proposed *Enola Gay* exhibit and from other history wars. In addition, Webb, now out of office and mentioning "new" findings from Gannon's study, reversed his position and supported another review of the case, joining the retired flag officers who had already endorsed such a request. Kimmel's grandson Manning Kimmel IV chastised the top military establishment in

Washington, charging that "at no time has the military shown any genuine interest in finding the truth. Instead, you have perpetuated the largest cover-up in U.S. history."[18] The dispute festered.

" 'Remember Pearl Harbor' now calls to mind the Kimmel-Short controversy as much as the Japanese surprise attack"

After the Republicans gained control of Congress in the midterm elections of 1994 (the first time in forty years), Kimmel's forces pushed for another hearing on Pearl Harbor. In December 1994, at the height of the *Enola Gay* controversy, the National Archives hosted a conference to air the conflicting interpretations. The mostly pro-Kimmel crowd heard arguments from Costello, Gannon, and Beach and also listened approvingly as Beach endorsed the idea of turning to Congress to set the historical record straight. Before a U.S. Naval Institute gathering a few months later, Beach explained that a person would be "nutty" to believe that officials in Washington (President Roosevelt, General Marshall, and Admiral Stark) could have gone "to bed [on December 6] not expecting anything to happen." He claimed that, by contrast with procedures in Washington, the navy at Pearl Harbor was *so* well trained and ready that men got to their battle stations "pretty damned fast for a Sunday morning in peacetime." Emotionally, Beach appealed for a public apology from the national government. "In addition to the Kimmel family's honor, I am thinking of my own honor, of the Navy's honor, and of the nation's honor." The next day, Senator Strom Thurmond carried the request to the Senate Armed Services Committee, which subsequently convened a hearing. Historians Beach, Costello, and Gannon testified, along with Kimmel family members and other military supporters. On the other side, the Departments of Defense and Navy reiterated the conclusions of the 1946 congressional report, which had held Kimmel and Short responsible for the unreadiness of U.S. defenses at Pearl Harbor. "The historical record," the Navy Department's general counsel stated, shows no evidence that Roosevelt and his subordinates withheld information from the commanders "as part of a plan for a conspiracy to expose Pearl Harbor to an attack to thrust America into a war."[19] After the hearing, the senators asked the Pentagon to conduct a new review of the controversy.

The Pentagon review, submitted by Undersecretary of Defense Edwin Dorn to the Congress on December 15, 1995, rejected the case advanced by the Kimmel crusade. The Dorn report supported the Defense and Navy Department arguments that responsibility for the attack "should be broadly shared" but that "the intelligence available to Admiral Kimmel and General Short was sufficient to justify a higher level of vigilance than they chose to maintain."[20] The finding, however, only further inflamed the pro-Kimmel advocates.

The crusade to restore Kimmel's reputation intensified. It used the new medium of the Internet, developing a website that presented the case and laid out its benchmarks.[21] Edward Kimmel also adopted a different congressional strategy. In 1998 he enlisted support from Delaware's two senators, Republican William V. Roth Jr. and Democrat Joseph R. Biden, for a resolution, to be attached to a military spending bill, clearing the names and restoring the ranks of Kimmel and Short. The amendment was backed by the Veterans of Foreign Wars, the Naval Academy Alumni Association, the Pearl Harbor Commemorative Committee, the Admiral Nimitz Foundation, the PHSA, and many high-ranking military officials.[22] Senator Roth stated that "Pearl Harbor was a systemic failure in which the gravest mistakes were made by the Washington authorities."[23] Some senators may have remained only dimly aware of the various backdoor, anti-FDR theories to which such a statement gave support, but the partisan splits were still apparent: Republican veterans Jesse Helms, Strom Thurmond, and Roth supported the amendment (though so did some powerful Democrats such as Biden and Edward Kennedy).

Meanwhile, historians lined up on various sides. On December 7, 1999, the Naval Historical Foundation hosted a symposium at the Navy Memorial in Washington, D.C., to air the divergent views. Proponents for exoneration or for maintaining the status quo all presented their views to a panel of naval historians composed of David Rosenberg, John Prados, and Norman Polmar. Naval officers and civilians comprised the audience, and the substance of the symposium was subsequently published in a book called *Pearl Harbor and the Kimmel Controversy*.[24] Of the two presenters for maintaining the status quo, historians Sarandis Popadopoulos and Robert Love, the first argued that the controversy pitted "historians," who generally endorsed the work of Gordon Prange, against "popular memory," shaped by powerful conservative journalists with political motives. Both Popadopoulos and Love implied that various personal and social pathologies, rather than historical evidence, kept the pro-Kimmel/anti-Roosevelt stories alive. Speakers on the other side reversed the roles of historical truth and political motives. Vice Admiral David Richardson endorsed the idea that Kimmel and Short took the fall so that Americans would not lose confidence in their government in Washington. Such distortion, he argued, had been justified during the war but should at long last be corrected. Captain Beach reiterated the case from his book, *Scapegoats,* and denounced how "political correctness was trumping the "history of what actually happened" and justice "based on facts." He grandly asserted that "historians the world over agree with this," ignoring Popadopoulos's earlier claim that historians all supported the other side.

The panel of naval historians tended to agree with the "status quo" side, stressing the general lack of operational readiness at Pearl Harbor and questioning the logic of backdoor arguments. Admiral Hank Chiles, in a judicious closing summation of salient issues, concluded, "Admiral Kimmel did not have all the available intelligence at his disposal that was available in Washington. At the same time . . . commanders are today, and must always be, accountable and responsible for their actions and for their commands."[25]

Congress, approaching the 2000 election, made a different call. The Biden-Roth resolution passed narrowly and became part of the defense bill of October 30, 2000. By this action, Congress called on President Clinton to exculpate the commanders at Pearl Harbor of responsibility, stating that they "were not provided necessary and critical intelligence that would have alerted them to prepare for the attack."[26]

Several historians who had long been challenging claims of executive branch culpability expressed amazement and outrage at the Senate's entry into the history business. Donald Goldstein denounced the Senate for "rewriting history." Kimmel and Short had enough information, and "they really bungled it," he said.[27] Stephen Ambrose wrote a scathing editorial about the cultural importance of people accepting personal responsibility for their mistakes. Others, such as Richard Snow of *American Heritage* magazine and William J. vanden Heuvel of the Franklin and Eleanor Roosevelt Institute, joined in. Gerald Posner, whose 1998 book had debunked conspiracy theories about the assassinations of John F. Kennedy and Martin Luther King Jr., declared it "a perversion of history to pass a resolution that effectively endorses an Oliver Stone-type conspiracy about . . . Pearl Harbor." He, too, denounced "our national obsession to absolve anyone of any responsibility for their actions" and to blame the president.[28]

Meanwhile, Robert B. Stinnett, who had served under Lieutenant George H. W. Bush in the navy during World War II and was the author of *George Bush: His World War II Years,* entered the controversy with a new backdoor polemic. His *Day of Deceit* (2000), to be addressed in chapter 9, charged President Roosevelt with provoking Japan, having full knowledge of its plan to attack Pearl Harbor, and then conspiring to hide the evidence.[29] Reaction to Stinnett's book—applause from backdoor true believers and criticism from their adversaries—showed that the history/memory of Pearl Harbor remained as bitterly contested as ever.

The various history wars of the 1990s, which blurred together historical scholarship, media campaigns, website accumulations, and political crusades, were both a product of and a contributor to the decade's bitter partisanship. As "the good war" became ever more sacred ground in memory and secondary memory, old and new controversies became more visible and acrimonious. Partisans in the Kimmel dispute all claimed that history marched on their side and charged their adversaries with politically motivated distortions. And this controversy—blaming the Democratic president in Washington versus blaming the military commanders in the field—held special resonance in 1999 and 2000, amid the Senate's impeachment hearings against Bill Clinton and on the eve of what promised to be a close presidential election. Vice

Admiral Robert F. Dunn commented that " 'Remember Pearl Harbor' now calls to mind the Kimmel-Short controversy as much as the Japanese surprise attack."[30] For a variety of memory activists, remembering Pearl Harbor played a galvanizing role in conservative politics.

Under siege and at the end of his term, President Clinton did not act on the congressional request to restore rank to Kimmel and Short, and after the uncertain and bitter election of 2000 the Kimmel crusade looked hopefully toward the new Republican in the White House, George W. Bush. Many of Kimmel's most vocal supporters, after all, were Republicans, and the general refrain that true history needed to be rescued from Democratic-leaning academics and from "political correctness" had been orchestrated by no less a figure than the new vice president's wife, Lynne Cheney.

It was not the Kimmel crusade, however, that would put issues related to Pearl Harbor front and center in the new administration. The pro-Kimmel argument, with its implication of executive branch failure (or even conspiracy) to prevent a surprise attack in order to maneuver the country into war, was hardly a narrative that the new Bush administration wanted to embrace after September 11, 2001. Congress's recommendation for presidential action remained unheeded by the White House, and the visibility of the Kimmel issue declined as the political constellation changed. "I think events of 9/11 have put [the recommendation] at the bottom of the pile," Edward Kimmel told a reporter.[31] After September 11 a Republican president had to confront another "day of infamy" and answer questions about intelligence capabilities and why America "slept."

8 Japanese Americans

Identity and Memory Culture

In April 2000, newspapers reported that the new orientation film shown at the *Arizona* Memorial was revised after the Japanese American community in Hawaii had expressed concern.[1] The film had contained a segment depicting a suspicious looking Japanese sugarcane field worker glancing at a moving ship in Pearl Harbor. The accompanying audio narrative said, "General Short believed the great danger was not air attack, but saboteurs amid Hawaii's large Japanese population." Retired U.S. Army Colonel Iwao Yokooji, a member of the highly decorated Japanese-American 442d Regimental Combat Team who had served in Europe during World War II, contended that there were no acts of sabotage or espionage by Japanese Americans and that the film "perpetuated the myth that local Japanese were going to commit sabotage." The staff at the memorial responded. After digitally erasing the field worker and excising the accompanying narration, the memorial superintendent, Kathleen Billings, said that she welcomed the opportunity to "resolve a difference of perception." After all, she added, "It's our job to keep and tell America's history. America's history is interpreted many different ways. We learned from the people we serve."[2]

During the hype over the film *Pearl Harbor,* a dilemma surfaced in newspaper editorial boards, particularly on the West Coast. In stories about the film and the event, would the common World War II–era phrase "sneak attack" be used? "This era in our history is particularly painful," explained a copy desk editor for the *Los Angeles Times.* To Japanese Americans, she said, "sneak" conjures up images of racial hatred and subsequent internment, still sensitive topics in the West. To describe the events at Pearl Harbor, the *Los Angeles Times* and others dropped any use of the word "sneak" and officially adopted the phrase "surprise attack."[3]

As these incidents suggest, the memory culture of Japanese Americans occupies a special place in American memories of Pearl Harbor. Like the war narratives recounted in more dominant representations, those of Japanese Americans usually begin with the news of the attack at Pearl Harbor. But where the infamy narrative steeled "Americans" to exact retribution, Japanese Americans found themselves cast as the racialized representatives of "infamy." Both in the continental United States, where people of Japanese heritage were forcibly relocated to internment camps, and in Hawaii, where most were not, Japanese Americans struggled with how to fit into American nationalism while so often being targeted as its opponents.

Many wartime images presented Japanese Americans as a possible fifth-column threat. President Roosevelt's Executive Order 9066 of February 19, 1942, which authorized the dispatch of over 110,000 Japanese Americans from the West Coast to interior camps, projected the fear that members of this immigrant group might be enlisted as spies or saboteurs for the enemy.[4] Not until December 17, 1944, did the government allow these internees to begin returning home. The last camp was finally closed in November of 1945. The original version of *December 7* contained a long and disturbing segment depicting people of Japanese ancestry in Hawaii as being dangerous and disloyal. In the final, shorter cut of the film, this scene was eliminated except for one small clip in which a Japanese Hawaiian denied that the planes bombing Pearl Harbor were Japanese. The scene left vague whether the denial stemmed from disloyalty or simply from ignorance of the morning's events; officials in charge of information had decided that it was a poor idea to further inflame viewers with the portrayal of disloyalty. Moreover, Japanese Americans were so vital to the economy of the territory of Hawaii that they were not systematically interned there, as in the states. Most wartime productions from Hollywood, however, were less circumspect. *Across the Pacific* (1942) showed a Japanese American traitor. In *Purple Heart* (1944) and *God Is My Co-Pilot* (1945), Richard Loo played a deceitful villain who lived in California in the 1930s and spied for Japan. *Air Force* showed "local Japs" attacking a crew that landed in Hawaii and described "local Japanese" setting fires to guide Japanese bombers in the Philippines. This issue of Japanese American loyalty has continued as a contested subtheme in Pearl Harbor representations, creating sensitivity over the question of who was imagined to constitute "the nation" and "the enemy" in such a nationalistic time of war.

For most Japanese Americans, hearing the news of Pearl Harbor marks a vivid memory in the re-telling of this difficult time and represents a sharp divide. Although the attack certainly did not mark the beginning of anti-Japanese racism in America, which goes back to late-nineteenth- and early-twentieth-century restrictions on immigration, citizenship, and landholding, it did present a sudden rupture in "normal" life. Accounts by Japanese Americans often recalled a phone call, a radio announcement, or, if they lived in Hawaii, the sounds of bombs. After that day, any retention of Japanese customs, even "looking Japanese," could be taken as evidence of disloyalty. The reference to Pearl Harbor thus opened up memories about years marked by suspicion, fear, internment, and dislocation. Because these remembrances inevitably also anchored assumptions about group and individual identity, Pearl Harbor became the touchstone for larger stories about race and nation.

Tension has emerged among Japanese Americans over how to remember the rupture marked by the attack. Two narrative structures that some writers have labeled "compliance" (or "model minority") and "resistance" provide patterns that weave their way into countless Japanese American memoirs, books, academic writings, and commemorations. Though seldom expressed in any pure or simplified form, these labels can help focus contesting narratives. Lisa Lowe writes that the conflict and overlap of "stereotypes that construct Asians as the threatening 'yellow peril,' or alternatively, that pose Asians as the domesticated "model minority,' " are driven both by "complicated (national) anxieties regarding external and internal threats to the mutable coherence of the national body" and by the struggle to create a similar sense of "mutable coherence" within Japanese-Americans' definitions of identity.[5]

Compliance

During and immediately after the war, although disagreements raged in some internment camps over how Japanese Americans should respond to calls for loyalty and military service, the dominant representations focused less on any anger toward internment than on patriotism and a desire for reintegration into American life. This "compliance" or "model minority" narrative stressed pride—and success—in being American. The term "American" was often loaded with assumptions about opportunities to get a high level of education, to secure a well-paying job, to start a business, and to see children succeed and prosper. It also emphasized patriotism and support for the war effort in its many forms—from being peacefully relocated in camps to volunteering to fight in one of the two segregated battalions for Japanese Americans. The compliance narrative, shaped in dialogue with the wartime xenophobia, helped structure a hope that internment might be reconsidered if Japanese Americans could escape the designation as enemy. It held out the aspiration for reintegration into mainstream American life at the end of the war.

The Japanese American Citizens League (JACL) helped shape this compliance narrative. The league had been formed in 1929 to fight for the civil rights primarily of Japanese Americans, but also for Chinese Americans and others. Mike Masaoka, the head of the league during the war, favored a policy that would allow Japanese Americans to volunteer for army service and even suggested that Japanese Americans might be assigned particularly high-risk missions. He was one of the first Nisei (second-generation Japanese

Americans) to volunteer for the legendary 442d Regimental Combat Team and became one of the most famous Japanese Americans of his time.[6]

Many contemporary articles and letters written by internees and published in popular periodicals voiced the same aspiration for assimilation. In a letter written from resettlement "Camp Harmony" to the *New Republic* in June of 1942, Ted Nakashima listed the jobs and the undergraduate and graduate degrees held by his children and his nieces and nephews. He prefaced this information with an introduction to his Issei (first-generation) parents, "who brought up their children in the best American way of life. . . . My father, an editor, has spoken and written Americanism for forty years." Nakashima concluded by saying "what really hurts most is the constant reference to us evacuees as "Japs." " 'Japs' are the guys we are fighting. We're on this side and we want to help. Why won't America let us?" He followed all this with a stark and often sarcastic description of life in the "concentration camp."[7]

In 1943 the U.S. government did ask Japanese American males to choose between their "Japaneseness" and their "Americanness." At first, Japanese Americans were not allowed to serve in the U.S Army, but on February 1, 1943, the War Department created two segregated units in which Nisei men could serve. Two days later, the army issued the "Application for Leave Clearance Questionnaire," which every man in the camps over the age of seventeen had to complete. With only "yes" and "no" as permitted answers, question number 27 asked: "Are you willing to serve in the armed forces of the United States on combat duty, wherever ordered?" Number 28 asked: "Will you swear unqualified allegiance to the United States of America and faithfully defend the United States from any or all attacks by foreign or domestic forces, and foreswear any form of allegiance to the Japanese emperor, or any other foreign government, power, or organization?" Men who responded "Yes" to both questions were referred to within the Japanese American community as "Yes-Yes Boys" or as men who were "in." Those who answered "No" were referred to as "No-No Boys" or men who were "out." The Yes-Yes Boys were drafted and sent with the 442d Regimental Combat Team or with the 100th Battalion from Hawaii. The No-No Boys—over three hundred of them—were convicted of draft evasion and incarcerated.

The questions forced a stark choice. "Yes-yes" pledged allegiance to a government that had cast aside Japanese American rights as individual citizens; "no-no" constituted a brand of disloyalty subject to severe punishment. When they returned from prison, the No-No Boys often faced ostracism from Japanese American communities. John Okada's now well-known novel, *No-No Boy,* which deals sympathetically with the alienation of these men, written in 1957, went virtually unacknowledged until 1976, a forgetting that demonstrated the dominance of the compliance narrative, as many Japanese Americans sought to remember their community's loyalty and service to the United States.[8]

Photographs taken for the Wartime Relocation Authority (WRA), which was created to oversee the internment camps, exemplify another site of the early compliance narrative. Photographer Hikaru Iwasaki's captions emphasize the successful assimilation of his subjects into American culture. A typical one reads as follows: "Mr. Sashihara operated two drug stores and a 5 and 10 variety store. Mr. Shashihara is a graduate of the University of Southern California. . . . Mrs. Sashihara majored in Education at the University of California, Los Angeles, where she obtained her degree. Mr. and Mrs. Sashihara are a highly Americanized Issei (first generation) couple."[9] Mr. Iwasaki's captions, portraying a "model minority," seemed crafted to speed the end of internment and facilitate acceptance. Other photographers also generally portrayed a model community that was willing to be relocated as part of the war effort and was becoming more assimilated every day in the camps. To bolster this image, many pictures showed children in the camps singing the national anthem with flags in hand. The photographers were under orders *not* to photograph the armed guards, barbed wire, or guard towers around the camp. Internees were often depicted happily at work, going to school, and growing vegetables and flowers.[10]

Some of the photographers tried to highlight the injustice of the camps, but their images also suggested a clear assimilationist message. The photos of Dorothea Lange and of Ansel Adams, whose collection *Born Free and Equal* was published in 1944, emphasized injustice and implicitly advocated equal rights for Japanese Americans and the end of internment. *Life* magazine in 1944 ran a photo spread on Tule Lake Camp, similarly emphasizing a liberal critique of a democracy that would intern its citizens. Although it mentioned the issue of potential disloyalty (Tule Lake held the most No-No Boys), the article framed the regrettable injustice of internment as a call to end racism in American life and to nourish a tolerance that would set the United States apart from the ideologies of Axis nations.[11] American anthropologists, whom the government sent into the camps to study Japanese character and culture, also generally used their reports to critique ethnocentricity and to argue for assimilation.[12]

The 1951 war film *Go For Broke* epitomized the compliance/pluralistic emphasis. In this movie, the heroism of the soldiers of the 442d Regimental Combat Team shatters the racial prejudice against them and, in the end, unites all soldiers as "Americans." Takashi Fujitani, in a fine analysis of this film, points out how it provides an allegory that neatly fits with the cold war "script" of the security treaty between the United States and Japan signed in the same year. Japanese Americans portrayed as a "model minority" became analogous to Japan as a model ally in the cold war. Just as Japanese Americans, in this rendering, achieved equal citizenship through soldiering, so Japan regained sovereignty through forming a military alliance with the United States. In this film, as in other representations from the early 1950s, "the locations of Japan in the world and Japanese Americans in U.S. society were both homological and mutually reinforcing."[13] Masaoka served as a special consultant on the script. In two of the few other postwar Hollywood treatments of Japanese-American issues, John Sturges's *Bad Day at Black Rock* (1954) and Phil Karlson's *Hell to Eternity* (1960), the racial injustice toward Japanese Americans likewise became a cinemagraphic vehicle for critiquing American racism and endorsing a pluralistic, assimilationist nation.[14]

The most widely circulated Japanese American memoirs from the 1950s, while recounting the shock of Pearl Harbor and the disorientation of the camps, ended with a reassurance about the future. Mine Okubo's *Citizen 13660* (1946), which presented drawings and sparse text about internment, closed on a note of hope: "I relived momentarily the sorrows and the joys of my whole evacuation experience, until the barracks faded away into the distance. . . . My thoughts shifted from the past to the future."[15] Monica Sone's *Nisei Daughter* (1953) also concluded with the common assimilationist sentiment: "I was going back into [America's] mainstream, still with my Oriental eyes, but with an entirely different outlook, for now I felt more like a whole person instead of a sadly split personality. The Japanese and the American parts of me were now blended into one."[16]

During and after the war, then, the dominant representations by Japanese American leaders and postwar liberals structured a compliance narrative that focused on assimilation into a pluralistic America. These representations emphasized the ability of Japanese Americans to return to life as usual, to embrace dominant values, and to be successful. It fostered the forgetting—by both Japanese Americans and the rest of the country—of past racism and internment in order to accentuate a brighter future. In her 1973 memoir, *Farewell to Manzanar,* Jeanne Wakatsuki Houston recalls that "as I sought for ways to live agreeably in Anglo-American society, my memories of Manzanar, for many years, lived far below the surface. . . . I half-suspected that the place did not exist. So few people I met in those years had even heard of it. . . . Sometimes I imagined I had made the whole thing up, dreamed it."[17]

Resistance

When John Okada died in 1970, his *No-No Boy,* as well as his message of resistance in face of the binary choice between "Japanese" and "American," had gained little audience. *No-No Boy,* which opened with a remembering of Pearl Harbor's aftermath, had structured a darker story than the compliance narrative:

> December the seventh of the year 1941 was the day when the Japanese bombs fell on Pearl Harbor. As of that moment, the Japanese in the United States became, by virtue of their ineradi-

cable brownness and the slant eyes which, upon close inspection, will seldom appear slanty, animals of a different breed. The moment the impact of the words solemnly being transmitted over the several million radios of the nation struck home, everything Japanese and everyone Japanese became despicable.[18]

Okada's novel went on to present a picture of Japanese Americans who, because they were made to feel non-American, actively resisted the internment and the military drafting in the camps. Although Okada himself served in the U.S. army, he used this fictional account to interrupt the dominant postwar narrative, which stressed the jubilation of victory and the embrace of upward mobility and pluralism.

Stories of resistance, building upon dissenters during and after the war and forming a counternarrative to the compliance/model minority rendering, remained largely invisible in American culture until the 1970s. After the Immigration and Nationality Act of 1965 abolished national-origin quotas and exclusions, large numbers of immigrants from all over Asia arrived in the United States, giving support to movements to forge an ethnic identity called "Asian American." Many Asian immigrants could identify, painfully, with the Japanese experience. For example, the protagonist of Monique Thuy-Dung Truong's short story, "Kelly," speaks of her elementary school teacher: "You have to know that all the while she was teaching us history . . . she was telling all the boys in our class that I was Pearl and my last name was Harbor."[19] Moreover, civil rights movements and the Vietnam War had built a culture in which resistance could be a badge of pride. Resistance movements provided space and vocabulary to reflect about pasts that had remained silent and unremembered. Universities, reflecting the boom in social history and interdisciplinary studies, created ethnic studies programs or specific departments of Asian American studies. An interview with Peter Ota in Studs Terkel's "*The Good War*" summed up the new mood. Ota explained that beginning in the 1960s, Nisei and Sansei (third-generation Japanese Americans) were coming of age and had the distance, time, and English-language skills to reflect on internment and on the reactions of their parents and grandparents. While the Issei had reacted stoically and told the younger generations to do the same, it was the Sansei who became angry and resistant to the compliant history that they saw written and remembered. If war and internment were to happen today, Ota predicted, most Japanese Americans would now resist.[20]

As the resistance narrative gained cultural currency, Okada's work became a standard reference point in academic and popular writing about Japanese American identity and the World War II experience. Since its rediscovery in the 1970s *No-No Boy* has been "canonized as a Japanese American classic." It both shattered the image of the docile model minority and provided encouragement for new, ethnically grounded critiques of mainstream American life.[21]

The new status accorded to *No-No Boy* was part of a larger memory campaign to recover, reprint, and remember resistance after Pearl Harbor. New books and projects, often from sources with little visibility in their own time, elaborated and documented the theme. The diary of Japanese American social worker Charles Kikuchi, who worked with Japanese Americans in the years after internment, for example, received substantial attention when published in 1973 because it brought to light forgotten forms of resistance. Paul Spikard, in reviewing Kikuchi's work, suggested that it portrayed a "Nisei underclass" whose resistance to racial oppression was neither organized nor self-conscious and was targeted less against whites than against the behavioral expectations and social norms of other Japanese Americans. Resistance, writes Spikard, manifested itself in a variety of forms, from the No-No Boys and incarcerated draft resisters to the "Zoot-Suiters, good-time girls and others . . . [who] so embarrassed other Nisei that they appear nowhere in published accounts."[22] Other histories also highlighted protests and resistance.

The resistance narrative gained visibility along with the political action of groups (including the JACL) who fought to obtain redress for internment. Passage of the Japanese American Evacuation Claims Act in 1948 had assigned $38 million in reparations to internees, but these payments were miniscule compared to the amounts lost when people had been forced to abandon their homes and businesses in 1942.[23] With a cultural emphasis stressing compliance rather than victimization, demands for additional redress had gained few adherents. The generation who had lived in the camps generally maintained a silence. From the 1970s on, however, a new generation of Japanese American activists began organizing a national movement that ended the silence and, gradually, built broad support for redress. In 1983 the Commission on the Wartime Relocation and Internment of Civilians published *Personal Justice Denied,* recommending an official apology and compensation for all living victims of internment. On August 10, 1988, President Reagan signed the Civil Liberties Act, issuing the recommended apology and according $20,000 to each survivor of the internment camps. By this time, public discourse stressing "rights" and lauding resistance to radical injustice legitimated such legislation (although payments were over two years in actually coming).[24] Long delayed apologies and payment may be seen as both a cause and an effect of new narratives that stressed resistance against injustices based on race.

The year of the fiftieth anniversary of the bombing of Pearl Harbor further highlighted reconsiderations of the history of Japanese Americans, and internment took its place in America's rising memory boom. A few weeks before the anniversary day, a Japanese American writer in *Newsweek* questioned "what we are trying to remember" in the commemoration of the attack on Pearl Harbor and expressed fear that remembrance of that day might become "an orgy of American self-righteousness and a renewed demonization of Japanese and other perceived adversaries."[25] Apparently in response to similar concerns, President George H. W. Bush on December 7 again publicly apologized for internment. Three months later, the camp at Manzanar, California, became a National Historic Site. The Japanese American National Museum, located in Los Angeles, moved a barracks from Heart Mountain, Wyoming, into its exhibit hall and began to collect stories from internees.

Gradually, the internment gained more and more cultural visibility. The Smithsonian Institution put together an exhibit on internment that prominently featured the dilemma between choosing "no-no" or "yes-yes." New scholarship highlighted bleaker photographs from the camps by WRA Japanese American photographer Toyo Miyatake, contrasting the "alienation" projected by these photos with the assimilationist representations produced by others. Tomi Knaefler's *Our House Divided* (1991) was only one of the many new memoirs and histories that linked the history/memory of the war years directly to personal identities shaped by distrust coupled with vulnerability. A 1991 video by Rea Tajiri, *History and Memory,* tried to recreate images that had never been photographed, hitherto absent traces of what her family had experienced and witnessed during internment. Tajiri aimed to join these images with other visual icons from World War II to fill in the silences left by the preceding generation. Speaking for the Sansai, she remembers "living within a family full of ghosts. There was this place that they knew about. I had never been there, yet I had a memory of it. . . . We had lived with a lot of pain."[26] If the fiftieth anniversary touched off a flood of secondary memories of the "good war" and the "greatest generation" within some Americans, it triggered anxiety and protest about past wrongs for many Japanese Americans.

In this milieu, the JACL came under scrutiny for having been too compliant in the face of racism. In June 1989, for example, the JACL commissioned Deborah Lim, an attorney and instructor of Asian Studies at San Francisco State University, to study the JACL's wartime activities. Her report detailed the JACL's cooperation with military and camp authorities and buttressed the case for a previously proposed apology: "The JACL recognizes that a number of our community citizens were injured by persons acting individually and in the name of the JACL and that the JACL apologizes for their injuries, pain and injustice." The JACL's leadership shelved Lim's report and issued a substitute one and a far milder resolution, stating that draft resisters who nevertheless declared their loyalty to America "deserve a place of honor and respect" in the history of Japanese Americans. Later, the JACL would be pressured into apologizing more fully for working with, rather than resisting, internment.[27]

With time, the resistance narrative drew criticism as being too simplistic. Another formulation of history/memory called for resistance to the very idea of an essentialized dichotomy between compliance and resistance. Lisa Lowe's *Immigrant Acts,* for example, adopted a postmodern sensibility toward meaning, an understanding of the mutability of narrative, and a sensitivity to "the contradictions of immigrant marginality."[28] Caroline Chung Simpson's *An Absent Presence* also pointed out that scholars who, from the 1970s on, embraced resistant and ethnic-based novels such as *No-No Boy* often assumed that these books represented a local "counter-memory" to dominant, state-inspired views. But there were *many* local memories, she points out, and "official" compliance stories versus resistant "countermemories" is far too simplistic a framework. Both narratives simultaneously circulated in both large and localized history/memory, and they often blurred together.[29] The promise of American life both eluded and beckoned to Okubo's Citizen 13660. And not even Okada's No-No Boy, who felt a stirring of an "elusive insinuation of promise" (the closing line of the novel) could escape the doubleness of both asserting and reacting against the hyphenate identities that were, inevitably, both "in" and "out" at the same time.

*The Japanese American memorial
to patriotism during World War II*

The building of a monument to Japanese American patriotism during World War II, which was dedicated on November 9, 2000, in Washington, D.C., touched off a small-scale history war over what, and whom, to honor. Costing $11 million, privately funded, the monument was to memorialize the 33,000 Japanese Americans who had fought in the war and also to commemorate those who had suffered internment. While it was under construction, however, a protest movement grew around one of the quotations that was to be engraved on the monument. The quote, by Mike Masaoka, read, "I am proud that I am an American of Japanese ancestry. I believe in this nation's institutions, ideals and traditions; I glory in her heritage; I boast of her history; I trust in her future.—Mike M. Masaoka, Civil Rights Advocate, Staff Sergeant, 442d Regimental Combat Team."

Divisions over how to represent Masaoka—as a leader or a betrayer—filled Japanese American newspapers and wracked the community at the turn of the twenty-first century. The Committee for a Fair and Accurate Japanese American Memorial, which wanted Masaoka's quote removed, gathered hundreds of signatures on a protest petition to send to Interior Secretary Bruce Babbitt and the National Park Service.[30]

The website JaVoice.com became a center for protest and for a petition drive. The site requested a "Japanese American Memorial for All" and charged that the planned memorial did not adequately represent the Japanese American community. The website included the entirety of Masaoka's speech from which the quote was taken and argued that "in the face of severe discrimination and oppression, Masaoka and the JACL advocated full and complete cooperation with the U.S. Government." The site objected to the authority given to Masaoka as a representative of Japanese Americans and to the authority he claimed for himself. Masaoka, the website stated, claimed that "Japanese Americans would not protest exclusion and incarceration, and that they would go willingly when called upon to make this 'sacrifice.' " In this view, Masaoka was no "civil rights advocate" because he advocated only cooperation with the government rather than civil rights for Japanese Americans. Among many who endorsed the removal of Masaoka's name, Gary Okihiro of Columbia University wrote, "This is revisionist history at best (and I use the term 'history' politely here). . . . The body of scholarship contradicts [Park Service head Robert] Stanton's notion. Masaoka didn't even speak for Japanese Americans, and his words and deeds favored fascism and not democracy. Add my outrage to this latest of outrages."[31]

While clearly objecting to Masaoka and the JACL (the strongest disseminators of the compliance narrative during the war), JaVoice.com still wanted to honor both the compliers who joined the war (except for Masaoka) and the resistant No-Nos, who had stood up for their rights. The site declared that "the content of a people's patriotism must be more than their glorification of and loyalty to the government at any cost. Rather, patriotism is the unwavering commitment to the ideals of a nation and thus must recognize the necessity to uphold conscience and justice no matter what the obstacles."[32]

During this controversy, the Public Broadcasting Service aired Frank Abe's documentary film *Conscience and the Constitution,* which also represented Masaoka and the JACL as a compromised leadership.[33] Abe's film emphasized an alternative group of leaders whose "fair play committees" staged protests in the internment camps; actively opposed the incarceration of dissenters; published obstreperous newspapers, such as the *Rocky Shimpo;* and fought legal battles for the right to print dissenting views. The film centered around eighty-five Nisei who refused to be drafted from Heart Mountain Camp before having their constitutional rights restored. It also featured newspapermen like James Omura, editor of the *Rocky Shimpo,* who started newspapers within the camps, even using the Japanese language. When censored, Omura and others protested, successfully sued on the grounds of freedom of speech and press, and won the right to keep printing. Masaoka, by contrast, supported many of the internment policies against which these resisters fought.

Despite protests, the memorial board, chaired by retired rear admiral Melvin Chiogioji and backed by the Park Service, refused to alter the inscriptions. Many board members cited Masaoka's postwar lobbying to allow Issei to become naturalized citizens and his work on behalf of the 1964 Civil Rights Act.[34] The memorial now stands as a testament to the struggles within the history/memory of diverse Japanese Americans.

Among Japanese Americans, different groups vied over how to remember and over what to forget in the histories of the domestic aftermath of the Pearl Harbor attack. Marita Sturken, writing on the years of internment, notes that memory tells more than anything "about the stakes held by individuals and institutions in what the past means."[35] Not surprisingly, perhaps, disputes over whom and what a new monument should commemorate, sixty years after Pearl Harbor, refracted and brought new visibility to the clashing narratives of compliance, resistance, and mixes of the two.

9 Spectacular History

The cultural politics surrounding Pearl Harbor took shape within the country's media-rich mass market. The dramatic surprise, the tragedy and triumph, the mysteries of blame—all seemed especially well suited to the audience-grabbing formats of tabloid-style journalism and to spectacular formulas of Hollywood film. A hot item in memory boom culture, the representations of Pearl Harbor illustrated the blurred boundaries of history/memory/media in turn-of-the-century American life.

"The Shocking Truth Revealed"

"The Shocking Truth Revealed!" "The Explosive Truth!" Mass-marketed history often thrives on slogans, promises of revelations, and claims of final and definitive "truth." Such tabloid-style influences convey a particular agenda for the practice of historical inquiry. Whereas academic historical inquiry stresses context and complication, the tabloid aesthetic pushes histories that exaggerate claims, simplify and erase interpretive complexity, and sling around the word "truth" on the apparent assumption that no one would buy or read anything that did not claim it. I had considered entitling this book "The Shocking Truth Revealed" in parody of this genre. And such a title might, ironically, have been quite apt.

The "shocking truth" here advanced about history (though it is not so shocking to most historians) is that, like memory, history is inevitably selective, mediated, and structured. It arises situationally from particular times, places, and interpretive communities. Empirical evidence is essential to history, but its selection and interpretation remain so contingent, so dependent upon questions asked and upon diverse narrative and metaphorical frames, that any final "shocking truth" about a complex situation is unlikely to be "proved" to the satisfaction of all.

The dust jacket claims and literary techniques of many books that have tried to attract the general public's fascination with Pearl Harbor may be boiled down to a formula of three tabloid-style packaging attributes: revelatory promises, the assumption that "documents" provide unmediated access to "truth," and seemingly "authentic" personal stories. Shaped within the form of spectacular exposé, these three attributes flourished in the publishing climate of the memory boom. Three books, all from different interpretive perspectives, illustrated aspects of the tabloid-style spectacularity that so often accompanied the Pearl Harbor genre: Clausen and Lee's *Pearl Harbor*, Costello's *Days of Infamy*, and Stinnett's *Day of Deceit*.

Clausen and Lee's book rested behind a cover in which rays emanated from a circle labeled "The Explosive Truth." Its thesis—that a lack of intelligence coordination and the local commanders' deficiencies were to blame for the attack on Pearl Harbor—mirrored the conclusions of the congressional inquiry to which Clausen had submitted his report in 1946. Even so, the 1992 book recirculated these old conclusions as the "explosive truth," while the dust jacket's breathless prose exclaimed that "Henry Clausen is the last major living *witness*, the one person who can *reveal*, fifty years afterward, the *real truth* about Pearl Harbor" (italics mine). His inquiry, conducted in 1944 and 1945 and presented to Secretary of War Stimson in an eight-hundred-page report, as the book jacket puts it, "revealed a massive, inconceivable failure to exploit the priceless intelligence obtained by the United States in the months prior to Pearl Harbor." The fact that Clausen had advanced this conclusion (using less purple prose) in the mid-1940s and had been promulgating this "truth" for nearly fifty years presumably made it no less "explosive."

The promotional packaging for Clausen and Lee's book buttressed the claims of revelatory truth by invoking the authority of primary "documents." The book highlighted Clausen's personal and special access to documents and reprinted some facsimiles; the back cover consisted of a copy of a War Department document stamped "Secret." It was a memo from Henry Stimson to "Army Personnel" explaining that Major Henry C. Clausen was authorized to conduct the investigation supplementary to the Army Pearl Harbor Board and should be given "access to all records, documents, and information in your possession." This featured document authorized access to other documents! Of course, any historian understands that documents are always *interpreted* and that interpretation often depends upon many things—the context of the document, the context of the time within which it is interpreted, and the person doing the interpreting. Any critical reader should likewise grasp that access to documents granted in the 1940s could not likely produce much "explosive" news half a century later. But the Pearl Harbor formula for sales suppresses the idea of interpretation or contextuality and invites readers to enjoy access to documents as access to truth. The implicit assumption seems to be that documents speak for themselves and reflect "truth" in some unmediated way.

The cover of Costello's *Days of Infamy,* in similar fashion, announced fresh revelations. Costello's book was a well-reasoned and even rather modest account masked in promotional hyperbole about the "shocking, long-hidden truth" and "official cover-up." His thesis, drawing on his reading of recently declassified documents, blamed Roosevelt and Churchill's "strategic miscalculations" for the debacle and defended Kimmel and Short. The "miscalculations" turned out to be a secret agreement committing the United States to defend the British Empire in the Far East—a flawed strategy, according to Costello, that invited a preemptive strike by Japan. Another "intelligence miscalculation" failed to put sufficient priority on breaking the intercepted but encrypted Japanese naval communications that would have revealed the upcoming attack. These points contributed valuable detail and a thoughtful hindsighted *interpretation* of the complicated strategic decisions involved in the great-power maneuvering of 1941, but they hardly "shock" or establish some "hidden truth," as Costello himself acknowledged in the text of his book. More shocking, perhaps, were Costello's charges about General MacArthur's unpunished "dereliction" and a payoff to him by the Philippine president, but the cover copy blurred this separate case by bannering "MacArthur, Roosevelt, Churchill—How Their Secret Deals and Strategic Blunders Caused Disasters at Pearl Harbor and the Philippines." Between the covers of the book, Costello told a complicated story, but to the browser or casual reader, the book promised the kind of hyperbole and revelatory framework that had long appealed to those who accused Roosevelt of secret malfeasance and backdoor conspiracy. Costello wrote that "assigning accountability is at best an exercise of imperfect historical deduction . . . more subjective than objective," but his publisher's banner promised "The Shocking Truth Revealed."[1] Who would buy a book with a banner reading "An Exercise of Imperfect Historical Deduction!"?

Stinnett's *Day of Deceit* illustrated the formula of revelations, documents accessing "truth," and personal stories in exaggerated fashion. Unlike Costello, Stinnett advanced no nuance, either inside or out. Stinnett revived the old backdoor claims and slightly revised them in light of "new evidence." "The truth is clear: FDR knew," Stinnett wrote.[2] He claimed, moreover, that FDR actually provoked the attack and mounted a vast cover-up of his misdeeds.

Stinnett's first piece of evidence for his assertions was a vignette that opened the book. Although he conceded that its status as proof was "speculative," it is still worth examining his opening story in some detail. He recounted a twenty-two-minute meeting on the evening of December 7 among Edward R. Murrow, Colonel William Donovan, and FDR. Donovan, he stated, reported that the conversation dealt with public reactions to the attack and that Roosevelt seemed unsurprised by and actually welcomed the attack. Donovan's claim that FDR was not surprised, however, does not mesh with a direct quote, allegedly from FDR, that Donovan supposedly remembered: "They caught our ships like lame ducks! Lame ducks, Bill. We told them, at Pearl Harbor and everywhere else, to have the lookouts manned. But they still took us by surprise."[3] Apparently Stinnett thought that this no-surprise vignette buttressed his thesis that "FDR knew."

How did Stinnett "know" of this meeting? Stinnett reported

that Donovan had "disclosed the details" in 1953 to his executive assistant, William J. vanden Heuvel, who "summarized the recollections in his diary" (which remains solely in vanden Heuvel's possession), but the summary was verbally "confirmed" by vanden Heuval to Stinnett in 1998. Such "evidence" forces a hard consideration about individual oral testimony and the processes that mediate recollection.

Let's review. Stinnett opened with a vignette derived from a recollection by "Wild Bill" Donovan told a dozen years after a twenty-two-minute meeting and then rerendered into an aide's private diary that was, in turn, interpreted to Stinnett fifty-seven years after the twenty-two minutes had occurred. Out of this "evidence" Stinnett produced a direct quote from FDR (and one that arguably does not support his thesis anyway)! Since it is unlikely that Donovan actually remembered FDR's *exact* words, said twelve years earlier, with whom did the exact quote originate? With Donovan? With vanden Heuvel? With Stinnett? This vignette seems preposterous as "evidence" that "FDR knew." Its claim is illogical, and it would not stand even the flimsiest test of reliability as source material.

Perhaps the claim should just be ignored. Stinnett himself acknowledged that the vignette was "speculative." Instead, however, a different question should be posed. Why would anyone *open* a book with such weak and ill-argued hearsay? The question is almost rhetorical. Such a form is so familiar that any bookstore browser recognizes it. This opening vignette is part of a publisher's formula: open by telling a story about "real" people, not abstractions or forces. The story positions the author as an insider—one who has, in effect, eavesdropped and has a special access to "history." The quote, however specious or even illogical to someone reading endnotes or trying to fathom the argumentation, lends an aura of you-are-there authenticity to the more casual reader. Being "in" on this brief December 7 meeting, with heretofore unpublic "quotes" from FDR himself, beckons the reader into the author's all-knowing gaze.

Stinnett's book also featured a facsimile of a document: an eight-point plan set forth by a junior naval intelligence officer suggesting that the United States should sharply challenge Japan's expansionism in the Pacific. This document, in Stinnett's view, proves that the Roosevelt administration embarked on a deliberate policy of provocation in order to push Japan into attacking first. Numerous critics of the book pointed out that there is no evidence that FDR endorsed this particular plan. Cautious historians usually understand that files are filled with memos outlining various courses of action, and they exercise great caution in assuming that every lower-level memo represents policy. The Roosevelt administration did order some of the actions mentioned in the intelligence officer's memo (others it did not), but the existence of this memo in itself hardly sustains the claim that Roosevelt plotted the war. Still, by featuring an official document, the book again promotes itself as an insider perspective. And, further layering misleading claims, the promotional blurb even refers to Stinnett's book itself as a "document." In what seemed the perfect publisher's blurb for this Pearl Harbor genre, Tom Roeser of the *Chicago Sun-Times* wrote that Stinnett's book was "Perhaps the most revelatory document of our time." This blurb was prominently placed on the front cover of the second edition.

Such vignettes, the use of the word "document," and the cover exaggerations about these books say far less about FDR and Pearl Harbor than they do about how the tabloid-style influences present history/memory to the public. These books are filled with accounts of official memos and intricate points about intelligence procedures. How might such books sell? They must have bells and whistles grafted on: they must establish credibility by personal, insider stories; promise scandalous revelations; and lead with dramatic blurbs. Above all, they must assert their history as truth rather than interpretation. The Pearl Harbor story, tapping into the "greatest generation" memory boom and promising drama and intrigue, seemed a perfect commodity for revival within a tabloid culture that constructed history as spectacle.

E-history

Stinnett's "revelatory document" prompted immediate challenge and discussion, interchanges that illustrate the workings of a new venue for Pearl Harbor history/memory: the Internet.

In its most sensational claim, *Day of Deceit* argued that U.S. code breakers had read Japan's naval communications and thus knew the details of the attack. Previous accounts had claimed that the United States had not cracked Japan's *military* codes but only its *diplomatic* codes (Magic). According to Stinnett, the decoded naval messages, together with warnings from a Peruvian ambassador with insider information and from communications sent from Japan's own spies in Honolulu, proved that FDR had to know an attack was coming in retaliation for the embargoes and other provocations outlined in the eight-point plan.

Academic reviewers mostly dismissed these claims as insubstantial or long refuted. Most argued that it was implausible that the eight-point plan set forth Roosevelt's policy. The issues of the Peruvian ambassador and the Japanese spies had long been argued out by scholars on all sides of the blame controversy and hardly represented new material. Regarding the new, and most significant, issue of Japanese naval codes, two studies published at nearly the same time and also based on newly available naval records reached conclusions that differed from Stinnett's. One of these was Stephen Budiansky's *Battle of Wits*, a history of World War II code breaking. It dismissed Stinnett's key claim in a sentence: "Not a single AN [Japanese Navy] message transmitted at any time during 1941 was read by December 7."[4] Budiansky's conclusion, based on his detailed knowledge of code breaking, could not have been more directly in opposition to Stinnett's claim that "FDR knew."

Years ago, such debates would have ensued over the *longue durée*. Book reviews in scholarly journals might have appeared within nine months to two years; academic articles and books taking up aspects of the controversy might have come out within a couple of years. But the digital revolution—ironically growing out of the advances in computer technology made by the World War II code breakers themselves—has revolutionized historical discussions. The controversy over the naval codes and their decryption burst forth immediately and took place in almost-real time. Scholarly discussion that might have taken years in the "old," pre-Internet era before the 1990s now played out daily— and probably with wider distribution to interested parties.

The code debates became a dynamic discussion that illustrates a new, hybrid form of historical memory: e-discussions that can make accounts written in books seem too fixed. On the historical discussion site called History-Net (or H-Net), with its subgroups such as History-Diplomatic (H-Diplo) and History-Japan (H-Japan), Stinnett's claims sparked considerable comment. Budiansky, for example, explained on discussion boards the process and timetable of decoding; old decoders responded with their personal remembrances; other researchers contributed their thoughts. Elsewhere on the Internet, Stinnett held to his claims that U.S. summaries of intercepted Japanese radio messages "were current—contrary to the assertions of some [for example, Budiansky] who claim that the messages were not decoded and translated until later."[5] Comments on Stinnett's book on amazon.com and barnesandnoble.com, online booksellers that publish reviews and reactions from readers, fell predictably into the backdoor versus the Prange camps. One person, who claimed to be "a WWII history professor," wrote that Stinnett's "great" book "finally reveals the true diabolical, and opportunistic character of FDR." Another wrote that Stinnett's book "should not be in the history section it should be in the fantasy section" and recommended Gordon Prange instead.[6]

Internet sites and discussion boards circulate and contest the past in new ways, bringing into sharp relief the fluid and fragmented nature of history/memory. Debates about the past can instantly flower on the Internet and create new hybrid forms of history. Books, for example, almost immediately become augmented by diverse electronic amplifications and conversations (on History-Net, on publishers' websites, on amazon.com, and on many other discussion boards) that collectively render the books themselves entirely too static—indeed, almost quaint. Even more important, diverse communities of interest can come together around collections of information or recollections on specific topics. The Internet, as a purveyor of the memory boom, has sprouted thousands of different kinds of sites related to World War II, creating a remembered world so disparate (in both style and quality) that two historians in 2002 brought out a 225-page guide, called *World War II on the Web,* attempting to rate and annotate the top one hundred sites.[7] If not "spectacular" in its large-scale modes of attraction, the Internet's immediacy and broad access, providing a forum for memory activists, buffs, and collectors of all kinds, represent a different kind of spectacularity.

"The Movie and the Moment"

It was not the new "shocking truth" books or the Internet, however, that gave the Pearl Harbor attack high visibility at the turn of the twenty-first century. Crafting a spectacle that would completely ignore the various controversies over commanders' guilt, bungling bureaucracies, and decrypted codes, Hollywood began to hype what promoters hoped might be its biggest blockbuster ever: a $135 million film called, simply, *Pearl Harbor*. The film, posed to appeal to the "greatest generation" mania, presented opportunities to all involved. For the Walt Disney Company, it might boost profits; for Michael Bay, the director best known for *The Rock* (1996) and *Armageddon* (1998), it might demonstrate greater depth and substance as a filmmaker; for producer Jerry Bruckheimer, the potential for spectacular effects topped even that of his earlier hits, *Top Gun* and *Armageddon*. Randall Wallace (of *Braveheart*) added the idea of ending not with defeat but with Lieutenant Colonel Jimmy Doolittle's Tokyo raid, which could provide a flag-waving finale. The Pentagon supported the production to tout the bravery of World War II veterans and boost recruitment campaigns.[8]

Still, the road to the final screen was not easy. Disney executives tried to hold the line on the extravagant projected costs; Bay quit the project four times; both Bay and Bruckheimer deferred their fees from Disney to ante up more money to finance the film; there was concern about the film's box office appeal in Japan, America's largest international film market. Cooperation with the navy, however, helped. The navy permitted Bay and Bruckheimer to explode old, inactive warships that had been mothballed at Pearl Harbor and were slated to be sunk as part of a program to create artificial reefs. The incredible opportunity to blow up ten full-sized ships helped create the epic quality of the attack scene.

The navy also allowed the use of an aircraft carrier in the lead-up to the Doolittle raid.[9]

Pearl Harbor took its place within a tradition of films set against the dramatic event of the Japanese attack. Each earlier Pearl Harbor film had offered a chance to re-remember the coming of World War II and, in so doing, to fix a particular vision of American culture. Many of the individuals and groups who were acquainted with Pearl Harbor controversies waited apprehensively for the new film. Japanese commentators worried about Japan bashing. The JACL, which organized protests, feared possible hints about disloyalty and a subsequent backlash against Asians.[10] Pro-Chinese activists warned about soft-pedaling Japanese imperialism. Pro-Kimmel groups wondered whether their cause would be advanced or undercut. American veterans, whom the film's director had interviewed and sought to honor, probably hoped for some echo of their own remembered experiences. The history/memory of Pearl Harbor, after all, had multiple stakeholders.

Not to worry. The film managed to convey little sense of any context that might raise controversy. It sidestepped interpretations of the reasons for the appalling surprise, of the military or diplomatic miscalculations, of the clash between isolationists and interventionists, or of the racial politics of the 1940s and its current sensitivities. The U.S.-Japanese clash happened without national blame; Japanese American representations were mostly avoided (one scene that suggested a civilian Japanese dentist was a spy had to be reshot after protests); the African American mess attendant, Doris "Dorie" Miller (Cuba Gooding Jr.), heroically manned a machine gun he had never before fired; Kimmel looked handsome and worthy; the president and other officials in Washington appeared both forthright and stalwart (with Jon Voight's crippled FDR even preposterously rising to stand on his legs during a cabinet meeting in which he urged a strong response to the attack). Each character, it seemed, was cast as a member of the "greatest generation."[11] Transcending all of the diverse controversies, the film did what Hollywood does best: it choreographed what Geoff King has termed a "spectacular narrative," in which the real substance of the film was its special effects.

A Hollywood movie, of course, is not a history book, with its conventions of logic and argumentation. Cinema draws upon the traditions of oral and visual cultures to mix together nonlinear and often fractured combinations of images and sounds.[12] Because it is the business of filmmakers carefully to structure diverse sensory elements to maximize dramatic impact (and therefore to maximize audiences and profits), the so-called "high-concept" spectacle has assumed growing importance in Hollywood.

Emphasizing spectacle had become central to Hollywood's late-twentieth-century strategy to parry the threat of television, the small screen that could entice audiences to remain home and stay out of theaters. Fast-moving action sequences of enormous size and with multichannel sound also lured overseas markets by being able to leap cultural or language barriers. Whereas some media scholars have argued that the growing reliance on spectacle has undermined narrative in Hollywood films, Geoff King has argued that narrative and spectacle work together. Big-screen attractions encourage viewers to pause and stare, while narrative engages them in the mystery of the ending, in the desire to "find out" by moving along to the next and the next frame. Blockbusters that emphasize spectacle, according to King, still have the "oppositions and reconciliations" associated with narrative.[13]

The narrative of *Pearl Harbor* revolves around a love triangle. It opens with two friends, a very young Rafe and Danny, who love airplanes. Skipping ahead a few years, Rafe (Ben Affleck) meets a volunteer nurse, Evelyn (Kate Beckinsale); they fall in love; and he volunteers to fly for the Royal Air Force (RAF) because, he says, he wants his life "to matter." Evelyn and Danny (Josh Hartnett), both now stationed at peaceful Pearl Harbor, hear that Rafe has died in aerial combat, and Danny tries to console the woman whom his best friend had loved. Predictably Danny also falls in love with Kate, and she, reluctantly bowing to the fact of Rafe's death, reciprocates. Rafe returns and is furious at both; Kate learns that she is pregnant with Danny's child; the Pearl Harbor attack happens, providing the welcome action for which the audience has been waiting ninety minutes; and both Rafe and Danny then fly off with the Doolittle raid. Before Danny dies (in China after the raid), he tells Rafe about the forthcoming child; Rafe returns to marry Kate, settle down on the old farm after the war, and become a good father to the son, who—like his two fathers—heads toward a crop-dusting plane, fascinated with the spectacle of flight. The film ends with a reconciliation of diverse tensions through sacrifice (Danny's death), with masculine and feminine roles reinforced and passed on to the next generation, and with successful closure to the challenges that have faced citizens and nation. The plot is historically implausible (no actual person joined the RAF, survived the Pearl Harbor attack, and then flew with the Doolittle raid), simplistically sentimental (with little of the inner tension or character development of *From Here to Eternity*), and stitched together by painfully trite dialogue. In his moments of greatest affection for Kate, Rafe utters, "You are so beautiful it hurts." To underscore that the film had a very important point to make, it ends with a narration that clumsily cobbles together historical references from Thomas Paine and Martin Luther King: "The times tried our souls, and through the trials we overcame."[14]

The plot, however, did deliver a medium for explosions and special effects that recreated the bombing, death, and destruction—the kind of large-scale disaster spectacle for which Jerry Bruckheimer had become famous. If viewers often reported that the love story of the first ninety minutes was painfully boring, the subsequent battle scenes delivered what most expected. Bay aimed to make "the most advanced flying movie ever," and a squadron of planes, painted to match the period, carried cameras providing unusual vantage points. In addition, commented Bay, "we did a six-ship explosion, which was probably one of the biggest explosions ever done." Precisely timed with the oncoming planes, 350 bombs exploded in seven seconds. Computers created some of the invasion scene: digital planes and water were added with meticulous attention. The huge water tank at Rosarito Beach, Mexico, which had been used by the makers of *Titanic*, staged the USS *Oklahoma* as it rolled to its side and sank, with stuntmen dropping off into the water. Computer animators added in more sailors, fireballs, and smoke. The director of photography created a gorgeously colored film that, as the chaos of battle ensued, turned almost black and white by the use of hundreds of feet of black smoke and people covered in black oil. The seamless and carefully controlled combination of scale modeling, computer animation, and recreation produced the illusion of mayhem and disorder. The noise of bombardment and response further embellished the visually remarkable scene.[15]

Employing "spectacular narrative," *Pearl Harbor* drew from several Hollywood trends. First, it updated the Western. Because the infamy-and-triumph narrative of Pearl Harbor had drawn upon standard elements of frontier legend, it is not surprising that the film *Pearl Harbor* also articulated familiar frontier formulas: redemption through violence, application of superior technology, loyalty to friends and country, and assertive masculinity (including emphasis on personal honor), joined with traditional family values. The male heroes who exemplify all of these virtues are ordinary people, rural folks who grew up close to the land and ultimately return to it, yet are fascinated by the technology of flight. (The film is so uninterested in its female lead that her family, region, and interests remain unknown.) The values that *Pearl Harbor* exalts marked previous blockbusters that film critics have generally seen as "disguised Westerns," including Jerry Bruckheimer's *Independence Day, Twister* (1996), and *Armageddon*.[16]

Second, *Pearl Harbor* fed upon the accelerating World War II memory boom and "greatest generation" phenomenon. It became part of Hollywood's rediscovery of World War II. Although the film industry had promoted various Vietnam films (both pro- and antiwar) during the 1980s, the long neglect of World War II did not end until the 1990s. Steven Spielberg's *Schindler's List* and *Saving Private Ryan*, as well as *The Thin Red Line* (1999) and *U-571* (2000), brought audiences back to the heroic values and human dilemmas that the postwar cycle of combat films had explored. Like *Saving Private Ryan*, *Pearl Harbor* showcased its battle scene "authenticity," the quality that had also propelled Brokaw's oral histories of the "greatest generation" to the top of the best-seller lists. A $125 million, ten-hour television miniseries by Spielberg and Tom Hanks, *Band of Brothers* (2001), followed up on *Pearl Harbor*'s popularity by commemorating the fifty-seventh anniversary of the Normandy landings.

Third, the film mimicked the mix of love story, special effects, and music that had made *Titanic* (1997) one of the biggest blockbusters of the era. The huge popularity (and profitability) of *Ti-tanic* had recently reinforced Hollywood's long fascination for epic historical dramas in which personal love stories played out against disaster and destruction. *Titanic* had successfully combined the big-budget action spectacle, which held special appeal to young male viewers, with the kind of love story that would attract young women. The attack on Pearl Harbor seemed a superb opportunity to do the same. The film mixed historical appeal (shown in other recent films such as *Braveheart* and *The Patriot*) plus disaster spectacle (Bruckheimer's specialty) plus a love story that accentuated manliness, loyalty, and patriotism (following *From Here to Eternity*'s appeal to an earlier generation).

Finally, *Pearl Harbor* raised marketing hype to new levels. Unlike Hollywood films that were designed for niche markets, "blockbusters" were fashioned to appeal to all categories of filmgoers and even to those who did not regularly attend. The blockbuster aimed to become such a central cultural experience that people who did not see it would feel deficient and left out of the "everybody" who went and then talked about the film.[17] In the case of *Pearl Harbor,* the promotional apparatus went over the top. The entertainment giant Walt Disney Company worked carefully on timing and publicity. It opened its publicity campaign a year before release, showing previews accompanying the Revolutionary War epic, *The Patriot*. It developed a state-of-the-art website and licensed two film-related products, a Hamilton Pilot watch and Ray-Ban sunglasses.[18] For a signature song, Bruckheimer and Bay turned to songwriter Diane Warren, whose many previous hits and five Academy Award nominations included tearjerkers for *Armageddon* and other Bruckheimer spectacles, and to singer Faith Hill, who had topped the charts with sentimental hits from the country genre. The resulting "There You'll Be" is heard over the closing credits of the film.

Premiering on Memorial Day, 2001, the film attracted special press coverage because of its calculated timing. It helped that Disney spent more than $5 million providing journalists and others with transportation to and lodging in Hawaii. There, a lavish party—complete with an eighty-person Hawaiian choir and a navy band—entertained two thousand guests aboard the nuclear aircraft carrier *John C. Stennis*. Military officials, who had read an early draft of the script and redlined dialogue they felt might convey an antimilitary tone, joined the celebration. "My thanks to Disney for honoring our World War II veterans, recognizing those who currently serve, and building a bridge to our future," Admiral Thomas Fargo proclaimed. Throughout the filming, everyone associated with the project repeatedly stated that it would honor veterans; by its opening, it would have seemed almost unpatriotic *not* to have covered the film as a news story. A database search of headlines in the three months leading up to the release showed that the film had gained far more mention than had previous high-concept films such as *Titanic, Jurassic Park,* and *Star Wars.* Many theaters held special promotions for veterans and facilitated postfilm exchanges between veterans and members of the audience. *Pearl Harbor* became news rather than simply entertainment. "It was a total marketing blitz, and I can't imagine anyone who didn't know 'Pearl Harbor' was opening on Memorial Day," said Paul Dergarabedian, president of a firm that tracks box office returns.[19]

Pearl Harbor's debut as a celebration of the "greatest generation" triggered a barrage of other Pearl Harbor–related products. Starting over a month before the premier, bookstores debuted a glossy, large-format hardback (a coffee table book?) called *The Movie and the Moment.* This book epitomized the blurring of Hollywood and history, interspersing pictures from the film with photos from 1941 and telling stories about the making of the film next to accounts of the attack itself. Later came the novelized version of the story, written by Randall Wallace, the author of *Braveheart.*[20] The Internet spawned many websites related to Pearl Harbor themes. Among them, the National Geographic Society offered maps, photographs, eyewitness accounts, timelines, and a section to post memories or queries.[21] Bookstores featured tables of new and reissued books on Pearl Harbor. Prange's books continued to be featured classics, while Stinnett's well-timed offering replayed backdoor themes. Often displayed side by side, Prange and Stinnett's volumes continued to represent the bipolarity of Pearl Harbor interpretations, the two basic discursive traditions related to blame that had shaped most Pearl Harbor narratives since 1941. *Life* released a book called *Pearl Harbor: America's Call to Arms.* This special "collector's edition" featured photos from the era and cited "debts" to Gordon Prange and Walter Lord for its textual portions. Virtually every magazine and newspaper ran Pearl Harbor stories during May; there was 30 percent more news coverage of Pearl Harbor before May 2001 than at the time of even the fiftieth anniversary in 1991. The week of the film's opening, for example, *Newsweek* offered a fourteen-page spread on the film and the event and used a cover photo with a scene of Affleck and Beckinsale embracing.[22] *People* magazine, in typical "greatest generation" style, did a seven-page illustrated presentation of stories from individual veterans.[23]

Pearl Harbor sparked a craze for World War II nostalgia products in the summer of 2001. Spinoffs officially associated with the film, as well as freelanced tie-ins, popped up everywhere. Hasbro released a new line of Pearl Harbor–themed GI Joe figures, trying to revive its once popular but now lagging brand. The February previews of fall women's fashions offered new lines inspired by the 1940s. "If Pearl Harbor connects with people, the emotional ties to the movie will fuel the fashion trends," said the entertainment editor at *Women's Wear Daily.*[24]

Television documentaries about Pearl Harbor promised to merge the appeal of the memory boom with that of the new "reality" shows, such as *Survivor,* which were currently sweeping the ratings. Television moguls apparently believed that audiences, primed by the hype over both the Bruckheimer film and reality programs, would tune into past stories of "real" challenges. At least six special broadcasts on Pearl Harbor spread out over four nights and eleven hours just before Memorial Day. ABC rebroadcast *Pearl Harbor: Two Hours That Changed the World* with David Brinkley, a documentary made ten years earlier for the fiftieth anniversary. MSNBC offered *Pearl Harbor: Attack on America,* hosted by Persian Gulf War general Norman Schwarzkopf, who stressed the lesson of readiness. The Travel Channel presented *Secrets of Pearl Harbor,* concentrating on the USS *Greeneville*'s February 2001 sinking of the Japanese fishing boat and featuring an interview with its commander. And the History Channel contributed a four-segment program: "Unsung Heroes," which provided tales of courage; "The Real Story of Pearl Harbor," giving historical context; "One Hour over Tokyo," on the Doolittle raid; and "History vs. Hollywood: Pearl Harbor," a panel discussion by experts. Public relations specialists pointed out the calculated (and free) snowball effect that this massive television coverage had on the film's promotion.[25]

Of all the programs that splashed onto the small screen, perhaps the oddest was the highly promoted *Pearl Harbor: Legacy of Attack,* shown on the National Geographic Channel and NBC. Narrated by Tom Brokaw and featuring appearances by Stephen Ambrose, it intermixed interviews with now elderly survivors and accounts of the attack itself with the current story of underwater explorer Robert Ballard (who found the *Titanic*), trying unsuccessfully to locate and salvage one of the sunken Japanese midget submarines that had infiltrated Pearl Harbor on the morning of December 7. The two-hour program, with its disjointed juxtapositions between the 1941 attack and the 2001 salvage story, ended with a promoter's dream: underwater interior shots of the *Arizona* itself. In 1987 the National Park Service had planned to videotape some of the underwater site for educational purposes, but it had been forced to cancel the attempt when many survivors opposed such visual invasion of the sacred tomb.[26] This time, however, Brokaw's impeccable credentials as a sanctifier of the "greatest generation" apparently smoothed the camera's way.

In Brokaw's presentation, as in most of the Pearl Harbor–related documentaries, the "lessons" of Pearl Harbor seemed most frequently carried by the voices of veterans who recounted their memories. Their messages echoed some of the themes of "sentimental militarism" found in the war films of the late 1940s and 1950s, without the battle-weary harshness. They recalled a comradeship that was unlike anything in civilian life and honored qualities of individual heroism. Their memories, upon which the complexities of international politics hardly intruded, intermingled their own coming of age with metaphors of the country's imagined loss of innocence. The Brokaw documentary closed by structuring the meanings of Pearl Harbor through parallels between the national and the personal. Visual images of the nation's military rebuilding after the attack, for example, mixed with comments from veterans such as "I learned to be a man." Maturity, manliness, and military strength blurred together in spoken and visual images.[27]

Many newly packaged DVDs and videocassettes also flooded the market. Fox brought out a refurbished version of *Tora! Tora! Tora!*, accompanied by a documentary about the making of the movie. Questar issued a two-disk set called *Remember Pearl Harbor,* containing the John Ford film *December 7,* along with several documentaries and other features. The uncut version of John Ford's film and Frank Capra's *Know Your Enemy: Japan,* with additional newsreels and interviews, came out from Kit Parker Films under the title *John Ford's December 7th: The Pearl Harbor Story.* The History Channel issued a two-disk set, *Pearl Harbor: The Definitive Documentary of the Day That Will Forever Live in Infamy,* packaging relevant programs that had aired on its channel, and *World War II: The War in the Pacific.* Other wartime and postwar entertainment films and newsreels had new prominence on video shelves and cable television's "classic" channels.

With all the hoopla, the timing, and the visibility provided by associated products, the opening of *Pearl Harbor* was bound to be profitable. The $75.2 million taken in over the Memorial Day weekend was the second highest in Hollywood's history up to that time (next to *The Lost World: Jurassic Park 2*). The film, however, fell short of the overblown expectations. Unenthusiastic viewers and negative reviews created a reverse snowball effect: the second weekend's attendance fell 50 percent, the third dropped another 50 percent, and the fourth sank 36 percent. Though hardly a failure, especially in some international markets (including Japan, where advertising emphasized the love story rather than the attack and where some dialogue was altered), *Pearl Harbor* disappointed both investors and critics. After so much promotion, its mediocrity sparked widespread ridicule: "Snora! Snora! Snora!" The *New York Times,* in one of the kinder reviews, called the movie "extravagantly average," concluding that although May 25 (the film's premier) would not "live in infamy," it could appropriately suggest a line adapted from Churchill: "Never have so many spent so much on so little."[28] A historian for the Pearl Harbor Association dubbed the film "overdone overkill."[29]

Before the widespread publicity for *Pearl Harbor,* market research had shown that young adults aged 19–24 generally could not identify Pearl Harbor.[30] The hype for the film during the spring and summer of 2001, however, riveted attention onto December 7, 1941, and re-affirmed Pearl Harbor's status as one of the most widely circulated icons of American history.

Pearl Harbor's visibility as an icon had, in fact, been building throughout the 1990s. On both a professional and a popular level, people reengaged the old, highly political debates over blame and context. Publishers dressed up histories with tabloid formulas, promising revelations of "shocking truths" coming from "documents." More than anything else, however, Pearl Harbor became a convenient site for fascination with spectacle, disaster, and survival that was so characteristic of mass-mediated, late-twentieth-century American culture. *Pearl Harbor,* the movie, with its associated public appearances by veterans and promotional offshoots, sketched the attack in memory and secondary memory as a place where spectators could embrace moral certitude and suspend the complexities of international affairs. Viewers were beckoned into the memory boom's imagined World War II—a land of daring men and loyal women who enthusiastically took up the work of war, finished the job, and then went home to create families and raise more sons and daughters who would, in their turn, do the same.

Pearl Harbor memories had become so prominent and ubiquitous in American culture by the summer of 2001 that a stranger to the planet might have imagined that the bombs had just been dropped. Less than four months after *Pearl Harbor*'s premiere, these freshened memories would leap back into virtually every headline in the country.

10 Day of Infamy

September 11, 2001

"INFAMY!" headlined news stories across the country on September 11 and 12, 2001. Live on television and through repetitive images, Americans had witnessed planes slamming into the World Trade Center and smoke rising from the Pentagon. The surprise bombing of Pearl Harbor became the first frame of reference for the attack. No one needed to command the widespread use of Pearl Harbor imagery. Commentators around the country spontaneously invoked it, and many Americans seemed actually to "experience" the attacks through the memories that the Pearl Harbor–hyped summer of 2001 had helped forge. In the first cabinet-level discussions after the attack, officials repetitiously alluded to Pearl Harbor. President George W. Bush noted in his daily diary, "The Pearl Harbor of the 21st century took place today."[1]

Although diverse narratives about Pearl Harbor had circulated among Americans since 1941, by the summer of 2001, memory-boom culture had become saturated as never before with books, videos, films, and recollections of the 1941 attack. "Infamy" provided a sign that was culturally legible to almost everyone. It invoked a familiar narrative about a sleeping nation, a treacherous attack, homeland casualties, the need to pull together to victory, and eventual triumph. It evoked the ethos of the "greatest generation."

Why do people turn to the past for frameworks to understand their present? How do stories that circulate in a nation's memories interact with current experiences to reshape narratives of both? David Lowenthal has suggested that people turn to the past for "reaffirmation of belief and action; the guidance of example; and the awareness of personal and communal identity."[2] Amid the completely unexpected, it may seem reassuring to discern some familiar pattern, to domesticate the strangeness of the present by invoking the familiarity of a past shared and reconstituted in memory. The Pearl Harbor story itself had taken shape within the conventions of earlier frontier legends of challenge and triumph. Now, Pearl Harbor could be to 9/11 what the Last Stand and the Alamo had been to Pearl Harbor: a widely recognized iconic tale of threat and harm that worked to rally patriotism, marshal manly virtues, and promise eventual and righteous triumph to a nervous nation. The Pearl Harbor story, however, could also raise more complicated issues of fixing blame for intelligence failures and of the nation's relationship with immigrant communities.

"The evil ones have roused a mighty nation"

Political and media commentary after the attacks of September 11, 2001, elaborated Pearl Harbor allusions. "This is the second Pearl Harbor. I don't think that I overstate it," said Republican Senator Charles Hagel from Nebraska, one of dozens of members of Congress who made similar remarks. The head of New York City's Port Authority declared, "This is significantly worse than Pearl Harbor," and Eliot A. Cohen, a professor of strategic studies, wrote in the *New Republic*, "This is our generation's Pearl Harbor." The *New Yorker's* "Talk of the Town" reprinted its column from December 20, 1941, drawing parallels in the "mood" in New York City after both attacks.[3]

Analysts found it difficult to resist the rhetorical traditions associated with Pearl Harbor. The Senate's Republican Policy

Committee, in a statement called "Americans Who Died On American Soil," wrote that the "murderous and diabolical attack would awaken a slumbering giant."[4] An editorial writer at TravelGolf.com reprinted Yamamoto's "sleeping" quote and somberly wrote that "while America slept, it condemned itself to repeat the errors of *appeasement*."[5] ABC's Peter Jennings compiled a story on how September 11 had further stimulated Americans' newfound interest in Pearl Harbor. And sixty years after the American Folklife Center at the Library of Congress had called on folklorists to audiotape the responses of average citizens to the Pearl Harbor tragedy, its director again appealed to Americans to document their thoughts and feelings about 9/11 on tape. "Telling our own stories in times of crisis helps us to manage our feelings," she said.[6] Counterposing and comparing these 1941 and 2001 interviews then formed the core of a documentary for American Radio Works.[7]

Not surprisingly (especially for a Texan), President George W. Bush built upon the Western rhetorical styles that had structured the Pearl Harbor story during World War II. Perpetrators, he assured Americans, would be hunted down and smoked out. He recalled the "wanted dead or alive" posters of the Old West, rhetorically painted Osama bin Laden's name on them, and offered reward money to current-day bounty hunters. In the months that followed, he avoided any complex discussion of international affairs, explaining the attack and America's global response within the simple framework of good versus evil. "Evil," "evil ones," and "evildoers" were the president's recurring words. Delving into the bag of Pearl Harbor rhetorical traditions, Bush proclaimed at a prayer breakfast on the attack's second-month anniversary, "The evil ones have roused a mighty nation." Like FDR, Bush created new propaganda bureaus to project this message, and presidential adviser Karl Rove hurried to Hollywood to request studio cooperation in establishing helpful movie themes. Jerry Bruckheimer, whose *Black Hawk Down* (2001) was playing in the theaters, worked with the Defense Department and the Pentagon on the idea of a reality television series based on the war in Afghanistan.[8]

When President Bush presented his first speech after the attack, Tom Brokaw presided over NBC's before-and-after analysis. Brokaw invited fellow "greatest generation" popularizer Stephen Ambrose as a guest commentator. Just before the president reached the podium, Brokaw set the stage for an explicit World War II comparison, asking Ambrose if he could remember a more dramatic appearance by a president. "All of us over fifty years of age can remember Franklin Delano Roosevelt on December 8th, 1941," replied Ambrose (displaying questionable math skills). After the speech, Brokaw again turned to Ambrose, referring to him as "America's folk hero," and asked whether Bush's speech was as unifying and memorable as FDR's. Ambrose spoke approvingly of the president's turn of phrase, suggesting that there were lines "we could all be drawn in by" and that would resonate with Americans far into the future. His nominees for remembrance were "Freedom and fear are at war" and "This will not be an age of terror; it will be an age of freedom."[9]

Ambrose proved incorrect about the staying power of these presidential phrases, but such media frames—developed over and over in television, radio, newspapers, and magazines—suggested that knowledge of Pearl Harbor and World War II, above all, somehow had prime relevance to understanding current international threats and responses. The president, who had already installed a bust of World War II commander and later president Dwight David Eisenhower in the Oval Office, advanced a formula that was memorable (and also highly troublesome to America's allies). He declared in his 2002 State of the Union Address that Americans were fighting an "axis of evil." By uniting the World War II term "axis" (which had designated the alliance among Germany, Italy, and Japan) with Reagan's anti-Soviet term "evil" (empire), Bush recalled both of America's monumental twentieth-century struggles in a single phrase.

In fact, the Pearl Harbor analogy became so widely used in the immediate aftermath of 9/11 that its appropriateness also became a matter of debate and discussion. A few commentators began to point out divergences: The loosely organized Al Qaeda network was not a nation-state, and its battle tactics had little relevance to the huge men-and-machines campaigns of World War II. Pearl Harbor was a U.S. military base; the World Trade Center was an international, and civilian, financial entrepot—a veritable United Nations of global capitalism. In World War II, FDR embraced an international coalition and vilified the impulses of isolationism and unilateralism; Bush's call for international support, phrased as "either you are with us, or you are with the terrorists," fell squarely within the anti-internationalist rhetoric of American exceptionalism.[10]

Journalist David Brooks, in the conservative *Weekly Standard,* compared the American media responses to the two attacks, arguing that American culture had changed between 1941 and 2001.[11] After Pearl Harbor, he suggested, Americans seemed less anxious, more optimistic, and less prone to self-criticism; most seemed eager, even relieved, finally to shoulder their responsibilities in a world that had already been at war for years. "None of today's self-doubting gloominess troubled America as it entered World War II."[12] The subtext of this comparison seemed to be that America had been a better, more balanced, and more patriotic place sixty years ago than it was in the supposedly divided, overwrought, and self-centered present. Ironically, this overgeneralized and dubious comparison of the two aftermaths itself seemed to represent the very gloomy and self-flagellistic journalistic commentary that Brooks pretended to criticize. The Pearl Harbor comparison provided a vehicle for his already well-known conservative critique of contemporary culture.

Whether endorsing, critiquing, or moralizing over the 1941/2001 comparisons, however, commentators seemed unable to escape writing about the September attacks in the shadow of Pearl Harbor memories. As ever, the icon of Pearl Harbor provided rich rhetorical resources for experiencing and interpreting the present.

Pearl Harbor parallels continued to creep into discussions about the aftermath of 9/11 in diverse ways. When New York Mayor Rudolph W. Giuliani called for the establishment of a memorial on the former World Trade Center's ground, controversies immediately arose over appropriate plans and designs for the sacred site upon which people had died. As at the *Arizona* Memorial in Hawaii, the marking of sacred space was proving contentious. Commentators who worried over the antiterrorist campaign's abridgement of domestic civil liberties consistently raised the negative specter of the race-based fear that had swept the country after Pearl Harbor and had justified the internment of Japanese Americans. In San Francisco Japanese Americans folded two thousand paper cranes to symbolize solidarity with Muslim Americans who might experience persecution; in Washington the JACL and forty other organizations rallied at the National Japanese American Memorial to Patriotism to call for unity and tolerance for difference. By contrast, those who advocated a stronger policy in dealing with possible internal threats approvingly advanced legal precedents from the post–Pearl Harbor period. In addition, as after 1941, questions arose about America's intelligence-gathering capabilities. Senator Richard Shelby of Alabama, among others, suggested that the attack was "a failure of great dimensions on the part of U.S. intelligence."[13] This last issue, about an intelligence failure, landed in especially complicated political terrain.

Warnings of new Pearl Harbors

Though muted by calls for unity and patriotism, critical voices pointed out that a major attack on America had hardly come unheralded. For a decade, many security analysts had warned of growing vulnerabilities such as cyberwarfare, chemical and biological terrorism, and other unconventional attacks. In the aftermath of the cold war, went the argument, the United States faced threats of a new nature and was not revamping its security systems to meet them. Often, to punctuate their warnings, analysts had invoked the Pearl Harbor metaphor.

For example, during the 1990s, pumped by the widespread fear that massive computer failure might hit at the turn of the millennium (the so-called Y2K, or "year 2000 phenomenon"), a veritable cottage industry of experts, think tanks, and lobbyists touted the possibility of an "electronic Pearl Harbor."[14] With the Internet revolution and the growing reliance on computers in every business and bureaucracy, these experts on cybersecurity claimed, the nation urgently needed new spending priorities.

Security analysts also regularly invoked Pearl Harbor narratives to argue for a space-based antimissile shield and improved intelligence gathering. In 2001, after President George W. Bush took office, the new secretary of defense, Donald Rumsfeld, warned that the United States faced a "space Pearl Harbor" unless Congress supported an expensive new program to bring space under the umbrella of U.S. military power. Rumsfeld championed the technological and bureaucratic restructuring of U.S. military and intelligence establishments. Repeatedly alluding to the dangers of a surprise attack, the defense secretary stated that America's intelligence problem was what kept him awake at night. He often recommended reading Wohlstetter's book to make his case.[15] The president himself, while on the campaign trail in 2000, had used Pearl Harbor allusions to argue for vast increases in the defense budget as well.[16] And the U.S. Commission on National Security/21st Century, a task force headed by retired air force general Charles G. Boyd, reported to Congress a few months before September 11 that it would take a major disaster such as Pearl Harbor to awaken the country to its perilous security environment.[17]

September 11 seemed the obvious fulfillment of these predictions of security "Pearl Harbors" over the past decade. Why had Americans been allowed to "sleep" through these clear warnings? Osama bin Laden, after all, had issued unambiguous threats. Why were intelligence agencies and others ill prepared?

A few analysts and politicians, drawing on the precedent of the post–Pearl Harbor investigations, immediately requested an inquiry into the lapses and the lessons associated with the 9/11 attacks. On October 11, 2001, for example, Republican senator John McCain of Arizona on NBC's *Meet the Press* proposed a special commission "not in order to hang somebody at the yardarm or to disgrace anyone, but so that we will not make the mistakes again that we made before and can reorganize our intelligence services." Democratic senator Joseph Lieberman drew explicitly on the Pearl Harbor precedent to advocate a similar step. The White House remained reluctant, however, warning that an inquiry might divert the ongoing fight against terrorism and aggravate partisan or bureaucratic infighting.[18] Political responsibility for the surprise attack and the strategic changes that might be required for improvement were issues that would likely far into the future intertwine with perspectives about Pearl Harbor in-

quiries and controversies—except that partisan political position-
ing was reversed. Democratic leaders studiously avoided implying any backdoor-to-war conspiracies such as the Republican
arch-isolationists had leveled after 1941, but the visibility of Pearl
Harbor analogies implicitly raised questions that loaded calls for
postattack investigations with partisan implications.

"Sept. 11 will help us remember Dec. 7"

The relevance of Pearl Harbor to 9/11, and vice versa, became the
guiding motif behind the Pearl Harbor sixtieth anniversary ceremonies, which took place on December 7, 2001, at World War II
memorials in Hawaii.[19] With more than three thousand people
attending, two commemorations took place in Oahu, one at the
Arizona Memorial and another at the Punchbowl National Memorial Cemetery of the Pacific. The ceremonies began at 7:55 A.M.,
the same time that the first Japanese bombs had fallen. Most of the
Pearl Harbor veterans who gathered at the *Arizona* Memorial, including twenty-one USS *Arizona* survivors, were in their eighties,
and doubts that they would ever gather again prompted strong
emotions.

Repeatedly, December 7 and September 11 were symbolically
connected, a kind of passing of the baton to a new, potentially
great generation. The state of Hawaii and local businesses had
helped bring some 600 New York City police officers, firefight-
ers, and families as guests. About 350 family members of those
who had perished in the World Trade Center also attended. These
New Yorkers tossed flowers into the water to float amid the rain-
bows of oil still leaking from the USS *Arizona*.[20]

In Washington, President Bush marked the anniversary by de-
claring December 7 National Pearl Harbor Remembrance Day,
and he called on federal offices to fly their flags at half-staff on this
and every December 7 in the future in order to honor the "greatest of generations." His proclamation explicitly assigned meanings to "our collective national memory" of Pearl Harbor: "a symbol of American military valor and American resolve, but also a
reminder of the presence of evil in the world and the need to

remain ever vigilant against it." Then he flew to Norfolk, Virginia, to gather with twenty-five witnesses to the Pearl Harbor attack and speak from the deck of the USS *Enterprise,* the first aircraft carrier to launch strikes against the Taliban in Afghanistan. "What happened at Pearl Harbor was the start of a long and terrible war for America," he said. "Yet out of that surprise attack grew a steadfast resolve that made America freedom's defender." His language explicitly linked his actions to the causes of World War II. "We've seen their kind before," he said. "The terrorists are the heirs to fascism. They have the same will to power, the same disdain for the individual, the same mad global ambitions. And they will be dealt with in just the same way. Like all fascists, the terrorists cannot be appeased; they must be defeated."[21] Frank Capra, director of World War II's *Why We Fight* series, could have written the lines.

Addressing the anxiety that Japanese listeners might feel over the Pearl Harbor analogies, the president directly mentioned the current Japanese alliance. Noting that Japan had passed from enemy to ally, he remarked that "Today our two navies are working side by side in the fight against terror. The bitterness of 60 years ago has passed away. The struggles of our war in the Pacific now belong to history."[22]

Other ceremonies took place around the country. At Ground Zero in New York City, the recovery workers paused in their rubble removal long enough to light a thirty-foot Christmas tree, adorned with an American flag, atop the ruins of the Twin Towers. Mayor Giuliani recalled Pearl Harbor, pledging that this generation would fight as willingly as the one that had rallied in 1941. Former president George H. Bush presided over two ceremonies, one outside the National Museum of the Pacific War in Fredericksburg, Texas (where a room was dedicated in his name) and one to open a new wing at the National D-Day Museum in New Orleans in honor of those who had fought in the Pacific War. The parallels between 1941 and 1991 structured both speeches, and the former president proudly compared his son's leadership to that of Franklin Roosevelt.[23]

If Pearl Harbor analogies presented President Bush as a war leader assuming the challenge of leading a new "greatest generation," however, they also continued to raise the issue of intelligence failures and a board of inquiry. In May 2002, sensational revelations hit the media matrix: well before September 11, FBI offices in Phoenix and Minneapolis had asked headquarters to step up investigations of suspicious people enrolled in flight-training schools, and the president himself had reportedly been briefed about intelligence that pointed to some kind of (unspecified) imminent attack. In large red letters, *Time* magazine fronted its cover with a special report called "Why America Slept." Below were the teasers: "What Bush Knew before 9/11. Why So Little Was Done. How the System Is Still Broken."[24] Pearl Harbor metaphors kept coming. Conservative columnist Cal Thomas, for example, wrote that the incompetence of the FBI and CIA could be overcome only by a "morale boost like Lt. Col. Jimmy Doolittle's air raid on Japan, which restored America's confidence."[25] John Prados, a historian of intelligence gathering before Pearl Harbor, headlined an article "Our Pearl Harbor: The Latest NSA Revelations Suggest the 9/11 Plot Could Have Been Foiled."[26] While many people called for some kind of independent, blue-ribbon inquiry, the White House continued to oppose the idea, arguing that such a move would hamper ongoing intelligence efforts. Instead, the House Permanent Select Intelligence Committee and the Senate Select Committee on Intelligence, which had established a Joint Inquiry Committee into 9/11, began holding classified and public hearings in June 2002.[27]

The Bush administration used the new "Pearl Harbor" to support an overhaul of strategic direction and of intelligence and security procedures. A group called the Project for the New American Century (PNAC) had been lobbying for dramatic changes in American military posture and policy since its formation in 1997. The PNAC advanced a new strategic doctrine of preemptive attack, advocated new space-based systems, and argued that the United States needed to remove from power Iraqi president Saddam Hussein and establish a strong U.S. military presence in the oil-rich Persian Gulf. Such technological and strategic changes might have to come slowly, PNAC acknowledged, unless there were a "catastrophic and catalyzing event—like a new Pearl Harbor."[28] Under Bush, members of PNAC, such as Elliott Abrams, Paul

Wolfowitz, Richard Perle, and Richard Armitage, now occupy top posts in the government, and they moved to deploy anxieties about terrorism on behalf of a new National Security Strategy, issued in September 2002, and a vigorous plan for "regime change" in Iraq. The Bush administration also put together a proposal for a new department of homeland security, designed to improve coordination among various intelligence and security bureaucracies by providing a more unified command. It would be, according to the new National Security Strategy, the "largest government reorganization since the Truman Administration created the National Security Council," a 1947 creation that had, of course, taken place against the backdrop of Pearl Harbor inquiries.[29]

However, was 9/11 being investigated? In the fall of 2002, the public congressional hearings on intelligence failures, which highlighted stories of the prior warnings and deficiencies in America's security apparatus, created pressure for a larger, independent inquiry.[30] After months of resisting pressure from Congress and families of victims, President Bush reluctantly agreed to such a step, but appointees and procedures became contentious issues.[31] Such an inquiry, of course, would have some power to frame issues of blame and the lessons that should flow from them. After Republican victories in congressional elections in November, the president and Congress agreed to establish a ten-member panel with a chair to be chosen by the president and with a very limited power to issue subpoenas. Henry Kissinger, the former secretary of state in the highly secretive administration of Richard Nixon, was named chair but resigned less than three weeks later, amid controversy. Kissinger announced that he was unwilling to meet congressional expectations that he divulge the client list of his consulting firm, a stipulation designed to avoid any appearance of conflict of interest. Former Republican governor of New Jersey Thomas H. Kean was then appointed to replace Kissinger, and Lee H. Hamilton became the Democratic appointee for vice chairman. The panel began its work but remained largely out of the public's eye.[32]

Although the president's mainstream political opponents avoided overt backdoor interpretations of 9/11 when calling for an independent inquiry, others did raise the charge. Gore Vidal, no stranger to controversial writing, had long propounded the backdoor interpretation of Pearl Harbor. Vidal had endorsed Stinnett's *Day of Deceit* by writing that Stinnett's "smoking guns" showed that "the famous surprise attack was no surprise to our war-minded rulers, and . . . a small price to pay for the 'global empire' over which we now so ineptly preside." Along with Stinnett's book and the backdoor revival of the late 1990s, Vidal himself had published a novel, *The Golden Age* (2000), set in policymaking circles on the eve of the Pearl Harbor attack. Mixing completely fictional people together with fictional people with the names of "real" people, Vidal constructed a presumably insider perspective on the lead-up to Pearl Harbor. In Vidal's fictional words, for example, isolationist Democratic senator Albert Gore Sr. of Tennessee commented on Franklin Roosevelt in 1941: "He's like a magician. He keeps us occupied with England and the Atlantic and Lend-Lease and then while he's doing tricks with his European hand, the other is provoking Japan into attacking us so he can live up to his campaign promise that, if elected, no sons of yours will ever fight in a foreign war—unless, of course, we are attacked." Vidal claimed to base his writing in historical research and insisted that despite its categorization as "fiction," the book advanced historical understandings. In an afterword, he justified his backdoor novel by saying that "it was well known" in 1941 that Roosevelt had provoked Japan to attack, but Vidal left moot the question of whether or not the president had understood the attack would come at Pearl Harbor.[33]

Having so immersed himself in 1941, Vidal turned to 2001 and found a similar pattern. Both Democrats and Republicans had long pursued a policy of U.S. dominance over Central Asia's oil-rich lands, he argued. When the Taliban in Afghanistan would not cooperate with U.S. oil companies, the "oil and gas Bush-Cheney junta" deliberately chose to ignore clear warnings about Al-Qaeda's plans in order to panic the American public into supporting a war to bring Afghanistan under U.S. domination. Osama bin Laden and the Taliban, he claimed, had received U.S. threats against them two months before 9/11, raising the possibility that they had been provoked to attack. "A replay of the 'day of infamy' in the Pacific sixty-two years earlier?" asked Vidal.[34] Both Pearl Harbor and 9/11 justified an expanding American empire, he declared, but with one difference. "The truth about Pearl Harbour is obscured to this day. But it has been much studied. 11 September, it is plain, is never going to be investigated if Bush has anything to say about it."[35] Metaphors of Pearl Harbor, emerging at first to suggest "infamy," could bend in diverse directions.

The increased circulation of memories of Pearl Harbor in American media and politics after 1991 emerged along with diverse cultural and political phenomena. Some of these were the fiftieth-year commemorations of Pearl Harbor; an emphasis in international politics on identity and restitution for victims' claims; the broad memory boom in American culture; the conservative "Republican revival" after the mid-1990s; the determined effort to exonerate commanders Kimmel and Short; the mobilization of military lobbying groups associated with disputes in the "history wars"; the post–cold war security concerns about new "Pearl Harbors" in the making; the increased circulation of popular history on television, the Internet, and film; and the *"Titanic* effect," which propelled historical spectacle to the movie screen. By 2000, the icon of Pearl Harbor had become so prominent in American culture that the attack no longer seemed a distant event. To a new generation that had never experienced anything of World War II, Pearl Harbor became a familiar secondary memory—which then, suddenly, became even more vividly alive on September 11, 2001.

The ubiquity of the Pearl Harbor frame on September 11 shaped memories of both events. The Pearl Harbor attack, over the past sixty years, had become a symbolic part of many different historical narratives. Hardly a stable signifier, Pearl Harbor had held a prime place in both histories that stressed the president's leadership and those that emphasized his incompetence and perfidy. It structured lessons about the necessity of preparedness and war and also about the postatomic imperative of pursuing negotiation and conflict avoidance. Pearl Harbor provided the beginning for stories that both vilified Japan as an enemy and rehabilitated it as an ally. It sparked Japanese American memories of both compliance and resistance. The publicity campaign associated with the movie *Pearl Harbor,* capped by the attacks of September 11, however, elevated a "greatest generation" narrative far above all others. In most invocations, immediately after September 11, Pearl Harbor provided a relatively uncomplicated call for national unity and personal commitment to a war to the end against "evil." This was the Pearl Harbor narrative that had emerged so strongly in the last decade's memory boom and in the previous summer's obsessive interest in *Pearl Harbor,* the movie. The relative stabilization of this symbol, of course, also reflected the near-consensus with which the country backed the new war against terrorism in its early days.

At the same time that the shock of September 11 reshaped Pearl Harbor into a relatively uncomplicated and uncontested symbol (at least at first), the remembrance of Pearl Harbor worked to "forget" other possibly relevant pasts. In every American conflict of the past quarter century, for example, the specter of the Vietnam War had cast at least as durable a shadow as World War II. Indeed, the "bad war" and the "good war" had often vied with each other, as partisans used the symbolic languages of each to construct different foreign policy positions. In the Persian Gulf War of 1991, the first George Bush had gone to great lengths to portray Iraqi president Saddam Hussein as a new Hitler, against whose aggression there could be no appeasement. Others, however, feared "quagmire" and warned against pursuing a war without an exit strategy. (The limited goals pursued in the Persian Gulf War, in one sense, represented a compromise between the supposed lessons of these two historical frames.) The widespread popular invocation of Pearl Harbor after 9/11, however, promoted the World War II analogies so thoroughly that the Vietnam words of "quagmire" or "backlash" initially disappeared as if by magic. Pearl Harbor and the "greatest generation's" World War II became the reigning popular metaphor for foreign policy action.

Scholars of memory emphasize the constant interaction between past and present in shaping the meanings of both. Pearl Harbor had, over the years, signified many different messages for many different groups, and after the 1990s it had become one of the most recognizable icons of American history. In September 2001, however, the memories and meanings suddenly had a fresh, tragic context. Pearl Harbor became a "date which will live" intertextually with the interpretations of September 11.

Pearl Harbor as "history of the second degree"

Whatever the diverse meanings that cluster around the icon of Pearl Harbor, there is yet another sense in which Pearl Harbor's prominence in history/memory has been important. In nearly every representation of Pearl Harbor, the attack constitutes a dramatic "turning point," with personalized heroes and villains. No matter how disparate and inconsistent with each other, narratives centering on Pearl Harbor project an event-centered history. They present a defining event for internationalism versus isolationism; for enhancing big government; for "awakening" the country to the need for preparedness; for forging a "great generation"; for losing innocence and assuming manhood; for conflict (or reconciliation) among Pacific powers; and for the insider/outsider dilemmas relating to race and nation. In American culture, in short, Pearl Harbor serves as a dramatic fulcrum upon which a wide variety of themes in history/memory turn. Collectively, these narratives all reinforce the idea of event-driven history.

Such turning point stories, however, can be problematic in many ways. First, Pearl Harbor stories tend to be nation-centric. The attack on Pearl Harbor, after all, is hardly a major iconic event for other countries—even for Japan. To the extent that Pearl Harbor assumes a unique historical importance, American vulnerability is remembered even as vulnerabilities, grievances, and political chronologies of other nations may be pushed to the sidelines. The very emphasis on Pearl Harbor (even reinforced by this book) builds upon a tradition of national history in which World War II makes its appearance on December 7, 1941.

Moreover, turning point narratives of Pearl Harbor suggest emplotments of the past that are centered on the detail of conspicuous events, linked together in frequently overblown or all-too-clear cause and effect relationships. A focus on Pearl Harbor in its detail as an event will often downplay the *longue durée* that Fernand Braudel and other historians have sought to illuminate.

Economic trends, geopolitical movements, cultural changes that slowly over time condition and set contexts for "events" may find their way into Pearl Harbor history/memory, but accounts of the attack itself often telescope or even eclipse context and divert attention to small-scale detail and the influence of particular personalities.

Finally, in emphasizing history as a didactic guide to the future or promising revelation of a final "truth," Pearl Harbor stories often work against broad intellectual currents in every field of physical and social knowledge, most of which stress relational, positional, and unstable meanings.[36] Indeed, assumptions of stabilized history/memory run counter to the very concepts of history or memory. Pierre Nora, in his monumental work *Realms of Memory,* tried to redefine history as being "less interested in events themselves than in the construction of events over time." Nora was "less interested in 'what actually happened' than in its perpetual reuse." Nora, in short, sought to embed history in history.

This book, focused on an icon that has been enmeshed and continually recirculated in America's media culture, has attempted to work against the revelatory and event-centered tradition that generally seeks to uncover the "reality" of the past and to stabilize historical meaning. By examining Pearl Harbor's various meanings in diverse media over six decades, it has implicitly built upon Nora's call for "a history that is interested in memory not as remembrance but as the overall [and ever-changing] structure of the past within the present: history of the second degree."[37]

Notes

Introduction

1 The term "rhetorical resources" is borrowed, with thanks, from conversations with Norman Rosenberg. By this term, I mean those evocative rhetorical conventions that come to stand, as a kind of shorthand, for larger stories and meanings.

2 A useful definition of "collective memory"—sometimes also called "social memory," "popular memory," "public memory," or "historical memory"—is presented by Zelizer, "Reading the Past against the Grain": "Collective memory comprises recollections of the past that are determined and shaped by the group. By definition, collective memory thereby presumes activities of sharing, discussion, negotiation, and, often, contestation. Remembering becomes implicated in a range of other activities having as much to do with identity formation, power and authority, cultural norms, and social interactions as with the simple act of recall. Its full understanding thus requires an appropriation of memory as social, cultural, and political action at its broadest level. . . . From the perspective of memory studies, the most promising discussions in the academy have granted a fluidity to the distinction between history and memory" (pp. 214–216).

3 There are a number of different, sometimes interrelated, traditions in writings on historical memory. For my project the seminal work by Halbwachs, *On Collective Memory*, has proved most useful. Halbwachs was the first sociologist to theorize memory as a social activity—that is, how different memories persist in individuals who identify themselves with different groups, depending on their particular pres-

ent situations. Halbwachs (whose most important contributions appeared in French during the 1940s and 1950s and were translated into English in 1975) stressed the multiplicity and social situatedness of collective memories, emphasizing that memories persist when they are useful to, and therefore reinforced by, a particular group. "Every collective memory requires the support of a group delimited in space and time" (p. 22). Collective memory, according to Halbwachs, may become "historical memory" for future generations, who were not directly involved, through social institutions such as books, commemorations, festivals, and other means by which interpretations of the past are stored. Thus, an important work that builds on Halbwachs is Connerton, *How Societies Remember*, which expands upon Halbwachs's idea of socially constructed memory to examine the role of habit and ritual performance in solidifying memories of various social groups.

Seminal works by French scholars on historical memory include Nora's influential *Realms of Memory*, which examines French "memory sites"; see also Nora's collaborator, Le Goff, *History and Memory*, and Foucault, *Language, Counter-Memory, Practice*. Foucault wrote about "popular memory" and developed the idea of "counter-memory"—residual or resistant popular memories that withstand official constructions of the past (pp. 113–196). Building on these works, a special issue on memory and countermemory appeared in *Representations* 26 (spring 1989).

Many other examinations of memory sites illuminate the ways in which they both express the messages and aims of established elites and challenge official meanings. See, for example, Mosse, *Fallen Soldiers*; Winter, *Sites of Memory, Sites of Mourning*; Bodnar, *Remaking America*; Gillis, ed., *Commemorations*; Piehler, *Remembering War*; Savage, *Standing Soldiers, Kneeling Slaves*; Reardon, *Pickett's Charge*; Blight, *Race and Reunion*; West, *Domesticating History*; Seelye, *Memory's Nation*; Hein and Seldon, eds., *Censoring History*; and Levinson, *Written in Stone*.

Holocaust scholars have tended to see historical memory as the expression of the popular memory of specific communities and individuals. See, among many others, Friedländer, *Memory*; Langer, *Holocaust Testimonies*; Young, *The Texture of Memory*; LaCapra, *History and Memory after Auschwitz*; Linenthal, *Preserving Memory*; and articles in the journal *History and Memory*. James Young advances the useful terms "texture of memory" and "collected memory" to suggest the multiplicity that the term "collective memory" may tend to suppress.

American scholars such as Kammen, *Mystic Chords of Memory*, often associate collective memory with nonelite popular culture. See also many of the essays in Thelen, ed., *Memory and American History;* Lipsitz, *Time Passages;* and West, Levine, and Hiltz, eds., *America's Wars in Asia.*

   A sampling of other books that emphasize the dispersion and multiplicity of collective memories include Samuel, *Theaters of Memory;* Bal, Crewe, and Spitzer, eds., *Acts of Memory;* Tai, ed., *The Country of Memory;* Yoneyama, *Hiroshima Traces;* Igarashi, *Bodies of Memory;* and Fujitani, White, and Yoneyama, eds., *Perilous Memories.* Confino, "Collective Memory and Cultural History," 1388–1389, and Tai, "Remembered Realms," present useful theoretical analyses.

4   Carlyle, "On History Again" [1833]; quoted in Assmann, "Texts, Traces, Trash," 131.

5   Kundera, *Testaments Betrayed,* 128.

6   Kirshenblatt-Gimblett, *Destination Culture,* 187. On silences, see especially Trouillot, *Silencing the Past,* 26.

7   The idea of media "re-membering" comes from Baty, *American Monroe;* see also Young, *The Texture of Memory,* ix. The centrality of media is also stressed in Huyssen, "Present Pasts."

8   Maier, "A Surfeit of Memory?," warns that a kind of static memorialization and enervating melancholy about the past may crowd out more dynamic and historicized understandings. Lowenthal (*The Past Is a Foreign Country,* 187, 205–207, and *Possessed by the Past*) similarly warns that the preoccupation with "heritage" operates against history. Both Lowenthal and Kammen, *Mystic Chords of Memory,* explore the idea that "heritage" and "history" have different, often irreconcilable, goals.

9   Winter, "Film and the Matrix of Memory," elaborates the important role of "memory activists," taking the phrase from work by Carol Gluck.

1. *Infamy: Reinvigorating American Unity and Power*

1   Documents from National Archives, reprinted in *America's Entry into World War Two.*

2   Slotkin, *The Fatal Environment,* 435–476, 477 (quote), 498; Rosenberg, *Custer.*

3   In addition to Slotkin, see Kasson, *Buffalo Bill's Wild West,* 244–249, on Buffalo Bill Cody's presentation of the Custer story.

4   Slotkin, *The Fatal Environment,* 498.

5   Brear, *Inherit the Alamo;* Roberts and Olson, *A Line in the Sand.*

6   Kammen, *Mystic Chords of Memory,* 487; Dower, *War without Mercy,* 12.

7   "Pictures of the Nation's Worst Naval Disaster Show Pearl Harbor

Hell," *Life*, February 1942, 30–35; "Pearl Harbor Damage Revealed," *Life*, December 1942, 31–37.

8 Koshiro, "Japan's World," 425–426. On memory and nation in the Pacific War, see also the introduction in Fujitani, White, and Yoneyama, eds., *Perilous Memories*, 1–29.

9 Don Reid and Sammy Kaye, "Let's Remember Pearl Harbor" (Republic Music, 1941).

10 Poster in author's private collection.

11 Quoted in Prange, with Dillon and Goldstein, *Pearl Harbor,* 15.

12 Quoted in ibid., 13–14.

13 Quoted in ibid., 18.

14 Roeder, *The Censored War,* and M. Adams, *The Best War Ever,* examine how the censored "visual experience" established the media traces that have come to delineate "experience" itself. On memory and film, see also Rosenstone, ed., *Revisioning History;* and Chambers and Culbert, eds., *World War II, Film, and History.* On film propaganda and the war, see especially Koppes and Black, *Hollywood Goes to War;* Doherty, *Projections of War;* and Dower, *War without Mercy.*

15 Toshiya, "The Other and the Machine," 71.

16 On *December 7* see especially Skinner, "December 7," and G. White and Yi, "*December 7.*"

17 For analysis of this wartime diversity theme, see Alpers, "This Is the Army."

18 Dower, *War without Mercy,* 3–180.

19 Richard W. Steele, " 'The Greatest Gangster Movie Ever Filmed,' " 225, 233. See also A. Winkler, *The Politics of Propaganda,* and Koppes and Black, "What to Show the World."

20 Basinger, *The World War II Combat Film;* Schatz, "World War II and the Hollywood 'War Film' "; Donald, "Awakening a Sleeping Giant."

21 Appy, " 'We'll Follow the Old Man.' "

22 On gender ideology, foreign policy, and the cold war, see E. Rosenberg, " 'Foreign Affairs' after World War II"; Dean, *Imperial Brotherhood;* several of the essays in Appy, ed., *Cold War Constructions;* and books by Cynthia Enloe, especially *Bananas, Beaches and Bases; The Morning After;* and *Maneuvers.* On gender ideology in wartime Japanese films, see especially Freiberg, " '*China Nights*' (Japan, 1940)."

23 Reeves, *The Power of Film Propaganda,* 239–240.

24 Jeffreys-Jones: *Cloak and Dollar,* 115–130, and "Why Was the CIA Established in 1947?"

25 Quoted in Jeffreys-Jones, "Why Was the CIA Established in 1947?," 26.

26 Jeffreys-Jones, *Cloak and Dollar,* 115–130.

27 Kahn, "The Intelligence Failure of Pearl Harbor," 52.

28 Sherry, *Preparing for the Next War,* 47 (quote), 54.

29 Quoted in ibid., 131.

30 United States Strategic Bombing Survey: Summary Report (Pacific War), July 1, 1946, 32; at http://www.trumanlibrary.org/whistlestop/ study_collections/bomb/large/strategic_bombing.htm (October 20, 2002).

31 Gaddis, *We Now Know,* 35–36.

32 *Victory at Sea,* NBC, 1952–1953; directed by M. Clay Adams and produced by Henry Salomon; Rollins, " 'Victory at Sea' "; Bartone, " 'Victory at Sea.' " On television in the 1950s, see Tichi, *Electronic Hearth.* An example of the endurance of the *Victory at Sea* structure is *Battlefield: Pearl Harbor* (Cromwell Productions, 2000), which aired on the History Channel in 2001.

33 Divine, *The Sputnik Challenge,* 23; Snead, *The Gaither Committee,* 60; Sasaki, "Cold War Diplomacy," 11–15.

34 Sherry, *Preparing for the Next War,* 238. On the rise of the national security state, see especially Leffler, *A Preponderance of Power;* Hogan, *A Cross of Iron;* and Sherry, *In the Shadow of War.*

35 Walter Lippmann, *Washington Post,* May 15, 1958.

36 Frank Gaffney Jr., "Do We Really Want 'Denuclearization'?" *Washington Times,* December 14, 1993.

37 On nationalism, see Hobsbawm and Ranger, eds., *The Invention of Tradition;* Anderson, *Imagined Communities.*

38 Lord, *Day of Infamy,* 218.

2. Backdoor Deceit: Contesting the New Deal

1 Reardon, *Pickett's Charge,* and Keegan, *The Battle for History,* provide discussions of two other contested histories of military events.

2 Quoted in D. Winkler and Lloyd, eds., *Pearl Harbor and the Kimmel Controversy,* 65.

3 Melosi, *The Shadow of Pearl Harbor,* 14–16; Doenecke, *Storm on the Horizon,* 320–322 points out that most anti-interventionists endorsed the war, after Pearl Harbor, but remained critical of Roosevelt's prewar policy toward Japan.

4 Ibid., 35; D. Winkler and Lloyd, eds., *Pearl Harbor and the Kimmel Controversy,* 66. Admiral William H. Standley, a member of the investigation, did not believe that Kimmel was fairly treated by the report and disassociated himself from its conclusions.

5 Melosi, *The Shadow of Pearl Harbor,* 42–57.

6 Ibid., 67–73.

7   Ibid., 89–110; D. Winkler and Lloyd, eds., *Pearl Harbor and the Kim mel Controversy*, 66–67. Admiral Ernest J. King and Secretary Knox refused to endorse the navy's inquiry, arguing that naval officers needed to accept a share of the blame.

8   Melosi, *The Shadow of Pearl Harbor*, 113–127; D. Winkler and Lloyd, eds., *Pearl Harbor and the Kimmel Controversy*, 68.

9   U.S. Congress, Joint Committee on the Investigation of the Pearl Harbor Attack, *Investigation of the Pearl Harbor Attack*. S. Smith, ed., *Investigations of the Attack on Pearl Harbor*, is useful. Two opposing views of the committee's work are Clausen and Lee, *Pearl Harbor*, versus Toland, *Infamy*, 187–255, and Stinnett, *Day of Deceit*, 257. See also Melosi, *The Shadow of Pearl Harbor*, 144–148.

10 U.S. Congress, Joint Committee on the Investigation of the Pearl Harbor Attack, *Investigation of the Pearl Harbor Attack*, "Minority Report," 505.

11 Ibid., 506, 571.

12 Ibid., 501, 500.

13 Flynn: *The Final Secret, The Road Ahead*, and *The Roosevelt Myth*.

14 Morgenstern, *Pearl Harbor*.

15 Essays in Barnes, ed., *Perpetual War for Perpetual Peace*.

16 Beard, *President Roosevelt and the Coming of the War*. Craig, "The Not-So-Strange Career of Charles Beard," makes this point. Interestingly, the popular textbook by Charles and Mary Beard, *A Basic History of the United States*, 469, avoided placing responsibility for Pearl Harbor.

17 Tansill, *Back Door to War*; Barnes, ed., *Perpetual War for Perpetual Peace*.

18 Seth W. Richardson, "Why Were We Caught Napping at Pearl Harbor?" *Saturday Evening Post*, May 24, 1947, 20–21, 76–80 (quote, 80). This thesis about underestimation of the enemy has reappeared in many subsequent books and articles, such as Clarke, *Pearl Harbor Ghosts*.

19 Cabell Phillips, "Ten Years Ago This Friday," *New York Times Magazine*, December 2, 1951, 9–12; various "letters," *New York Times Magazine*, December 16, 1951, 4–6.

20 Theobald, *The Final Secret*, v–xiii, ix.

21 Kimmel, *Admiral Kimmel's Story*. Then see, for example, "Admiral Kimmel's Own Story of Pearl Harbor: Excerpts from Admiral Kimmel's Story," *U.S. News*, December 10, 1954, 66–77; J. F. Sonnett, "Reply," *U.S. News*, January 28, 1955, 116–117; "Review: Admiral Kimmel's Story," *Time*, January 17, 1955, 94; "Did F. D. R. Needle Japs to Bomb Pearl Harbor?" and "Discussion," *Saturday Evening Post*, May 15, 1954, 10, and June 19, 1954, 4.

22 Morison, "The Lessons of Pearl Harbor," *Saturday Evening Post*, Octo-

ber 28, 1961, 24, 27; "Review," with reply and rejoinder, of Theobald's *Final Secret* in *Saturday Review*, May 29, 1954, 13, and July 3, 1954, 23. For his larger work, see Morison, *History of United States Naval Operations in World War II.*

23   Wohlstetter, *Pearl Harbor.*

24   Current, Williams, and Freidel, *American History,* 805.

25   William F. Rickenbacker, "Dissent from an Anti-Revisionist," *National Review,* January 19, 1967, 34.

26   Prange, with Dillon and Goldstein: *At Dawn We Slept,* and *Pearl Harbor,* xi, 549 (quotes).

27   Prange, with Dillon and Goldstein, *Pearl Harbor,* 43–44, 39 (quote).

28   Morison, "The Lessons of Pearl Harbor," 27; Prange, with Dillon and Goldstein, *Pearl Harbor.* An excellent recent summary of this general perspective is presented by Norman L. Polmar's symposium presentation in D. Winkler and Lloyd, eds., *Pearl Harbor and the Kimmel Controversy,* 46–49.

29   Layton, with Pineau and Costello, *"And I Was There"*; Richardson and Dyer, *On the Treadmill to Pearl Harbor;* Toland, *Infamy,* 336.

30   Rusbridger and Nave, *Betrayal at Pearl Harbor.*

31   Prange, with Dillon and Goldstein, *Pearl Harbor,* viii.

32   Clarke, *Pearl Harbor Ghosts,* 70.

33   Hayden White writes that "while events may occur in time . . . their functions as elements of a story are imposed upon them by discursive techniques" that are tropological (*Figural Realism,* 9). For more on narrative construction and history writing, see especially his "Literary Theory and Historical Writing," and "Historical Emplotment and the Problem of Truth in Historical Representation" in this volume, 1–42.

34   Dean, "Theorizing Conspiracy Theory."

35   Melley, *Empire of Conspiracy,* 159.

36   Wills, *A Necessary Evil.*

3. Representations of Race and Japanese-American Relations

1   Quoted in Koppes and Black, *Hollywood Goes to War,* 253.

2   Robinson, *By Order of the President.*

3   *Collier's,* December 8, 1942.

4   Quoted in Wyden, *Day One,* 294.

5   On animalization, see Dower, *War without Mercy,* 77–93; 182–187; and Renov, "Warring Images."

6   "How to Tell Japs from the Chinese," *Life,* December 22, 1941, 81–82. See also M. K. Johnson, " 'No Certain Way.' "

7 "Explaining Jones-san," *Newsweek*, September 3, 1945, 23; Compton Pakenham, "With His Trick Mind, the Japanese Fools Himself," *Newsweek*, July 2, 1945, 48.

8 F. S. Wickware, "Japanese Language: Perfect for Hiding Facts or Saying What You Don't Mean," *Life*, September 7, 1942, 58.

9 Koppes and Black, *Hollywood Goes to War*, 250.

10 Dower, *War without Mercy*, 147–164; Donald, "Awakening a Sleeping Giant," 42.

11 Koppes and Black, *Hollywood Goes to War*, 251–252.

12 The starting point for postwar U.S.-Japan relations is Dower, *Embracing Defeat*. Koshiro, *Trans-Pacific Racisms*, 15–48, discusses how the culture of the cold war accommodation muted and complicated earlier racisms on both sides.

13 See, for example, the 1892 poem "East and West," by the noted Japan expert Ernest Francisco Fenollosa, in his *East and West*, v–vi, 3–55; Henning, *Outposts of Civilization*, 98, on the turn of the century; Igarashi, *Bodies of Memory*; and Simpson, *An Absent Presence*, on the cold war era.

14 Dwight Martin, "Don't Hug Me Too Tight," *Time*, December 10, 1951, 38.

15 Toshio Hashimoto as told to William Welsh, "I Bombed Pearl Harbor," *Flying*, August 1951, 16–18.

16 Kennan, *American Diplomacy*, 50.

17 Edwin O. Reischauer, "The Real Meaning of Pearl Harbor," *American Heritage*, December 5, 1981, 104–105. For his broader perspective see his *The United States and Japan*.

18 W. Williams, *The Tragedy of American Diplomacy*, 198–199.

19 Paul Boyer, *By the Bomb's Early Light*, 196–210.

20 The self-defense argument, which had been rejected by the Tokyo War Crimes Trial but advanced by some historians, is laid out in Minear, *Victors' Justice*, 149–159.

21 On the various cultural rememberings and forgettings of the atomic bomb in the United States and in Japan, see Hein and Selden, eds., *Living with the Bomb*.

22 Igarashi, *Bodies of Memory*, 13, 19–46; Koshiro, "Japan's World"; Dower, *Embracing Defeat*, 290–296. An influential recent challenge to the benign emperor view is Bix, *Hirohito*.

23 Orr, *The Victim as Hero*.

24 Marchetti, *Romance and the "Yellow Peril*," 178–179. See also S. Johnson, *The Japanese through American Eyes*.

25 Lord, *Day of Infamy*.

26 "The Pacific Boils Over," *Victory at Sea*, NBC, 1952–1953.

27 Iriye, "*Tora! Tora! Tora!*"

28 Basinger, *The World War II Combat Film*, 193.

29 *None but the Brave* (1965), although not about Pearl Harbor itself, perhaps went the farthest in portraying Japanese foot soldiers favorably, even finding a way to imagine a kind of U.S.-Japanese alliance forming in the midst of World War II itself!

30 Quoted in John S. Lang, "Samurai Spirit Lives on in Japan's Economic Drive," *U.S. News and World Report*, November 19, 1984, 48.

31 For summaries of the journalism and popular writing related to this theme, see Moeller, "Pictures of the Enemy," 35–38; Dower, "Graphic Japanese, Graphic Americans," and Wampler, "Reversals of Fortune?," both in Iriye and Wampler, eds., *Partnership*; and Ishii, "Through the Lens of Pearl Harbor."

32 Vogel, *Japan as Number One*. See also Prestowitz, *Trading Places*, and C. Johnson, *MITI and the Japanese Miracle*. Vogel reflects on the popularity of his book in Vogel, *Is Japan Still Number One?* 1–67.

33 Bergsten, Ito, and Noland, *No More Bashing*, 2–6; Moeller, "Pictures of the Enemy," 37.

34 Vincent Canby, "Japan Unfolds through Many Images," *New York Times*, June 14, 1992.

35 Other books (both sensational and more scholarly) included Choate, *Agents of Influence*; Holstein, *The Japanese Power Game*; Dietrich, *In the Shadow of the Rising Sun*; Wolferen, *The Enigma of Japanese Power*; and Fallows, *Looking at the Sun*.

36 Spokesman quoted in Barry Hillenbrand and James Walsh, "Fleeing the Past?" *Time*, December 2, 1991; Clarke, *Pearl Harbor Ghosts*, 227.

37 For details on Japan's Yankee bashing, see Ishii, "Through the Lens of Pearl Harbor."

38 See Barry Hillenbrand and James Walsh, "Fleeing the Past?" *Time*, December 2, 1991.

39 Friedman and Lebard, *The Coming War with Japan*.

40 Robert B. Reich, "The Pearl Harbor Metaphor," *Harper's*, January 1992, 20–21.

41 In addition to Halbwachs, *On Collective Memory*, see especially Lowenthal, *The Past Is a Foreign Country*, 210–217.

4. Commemoration of Sacrifice

1 Chidester and Linenthal, eds., *American Sacred Space*, ix–x.

2 Quoted in Otto Friedrich, "Day of Infamy," *Time*, December 2, 1991, 32–33.

3 Slackman, *Remembering Pearl Harbor*; Linenthal, *Sacred Ground*, 178–187.

4 Wisniewski, *Pearl Harbor and the USS* Arizona *Memorial*, 55–56.

5 Ibid., 57 (quote).

6 Delgado, "Memorials, Myths and Symbols."

7 Nora, *Realms of Memory*, 1:6; Neal, *National Trauma and Collective Memory;* Eber and Neal, eds., *Memory and Representation.*

8 Connerton, *How Societies Remember,* writes "commemorative ceremonies prove to be commemorative only in so far as they are performative" (5).

9 On World War I memorialization, see especially Winter, *Sites of Memory, Sites of Mourning;* Sherman, *The Construction of Memory in Interwar France;* King, *Memorials of the Great War in Britain;* Lloyd, *Battlefield Tourism.* See also Mosse, *Fallen Soldiers;* Winter and Sivan, eds., *War and Remembrance;* Evans and Lunn, *War and Memory;* Gillis, ed., *Commemorations;* Piehler, *Remembering War.*

10 A reverential tone and first-person accounts also structure Jasper, Delgado, and Adams, *The USS* Arizona.

11 Chidester and Linenthal, *American Sacred Space,* ix–x, 16.

12 Kirshenblatt-Gimblett, *Destination Culture,* 159.

13 The quote in the heading above is from Levinson, *Written in Stone,* 7.

14 Linenthal, *Sacred Ground,* 182.

15 Quoted in ibid., 185–186.

16 Quoted in Zinsser, "At Pearl Harbor There are New Ways to Remember," 74.

17 Quoted in ibid., 74.

18 Chidester and Linenthal, *American Sacred Space,* 4. Both Clarke, *Pearl Harbor Ghosts,* and Linenthal, *Sacred Ground,* detail the many controversies showing the cultural volatility of the site.

19 Linenthal, *Sacred Ground,* 198–199; Clarke, *Pearl Harbor Ghosts,* 114.

20 Quoted in Chidester and Linenthal, *American Sacred Space,* 5; Linenthal, *Sacred Ground,* 199.

21 White, "Moving History."

22 As discussed in Linenthal, *Sacred Ground,* 192–193.

23 Zinsser, "At Pearl Harbor There Are New Ways to Remember," 80; Ferguson and Turnbull, *Oh, Say, Can You See?,* interpret the memorial as a militarized space in which citizenship became defined as "hierarchical, authoritarian, bellicose" (xvii).

24 On the Vietnam memorial, see Scruggs and Swerdlow, *To Heal a Nation;* Hass, *Carried to the Wall;* Johnston, "Political Not Patriotic"; McMahon, "Contested Memory."

25 Linenthal, *Sacred Ground,* 199.

26 See citations in introduction, note 3.

27 Foucault, *Power/Knowledge,* 107–133.

28 A small article on each event appeared in the *New York Times:* "Navy Invites Survivors to Pearl Harbor Rites," April 6, 1962, 5, and R. V. Denenberg, "The New Visitor Center at Pearl Harbor," December 7,

1980, magazine, 1, 19, but the *Reader's Guide* lists no major articles on either event.

5. Bilateral Relations: Pearl Harbor's Half-Century Anniversary and the Apology Controversies

1   Quoted in Watanabe, "1991," 269; James Fallows, "Remember Pearl Harbor How?" *The Atlantic,* December 1991, 22–26.
2   Dingman, "Reflections on Pearl Harbor Anniversaries Past," 288–290.
3   This point is well developed in Hein and Selden, eds., *Living with the Bomb.*
4   Quoted in Linenthal, *Sacred Ground,* 204.
5   Quoted in Otto Friedrich, "Pearl Harbor: Day of Infamy," *Time,* December 2, 1991, 33; Watanabe, "1991," 273–275.
6   Dingman, "Reflections on Pearl Harbor Anniversaries Past," 290–291.
7   Watanabe, "1991," 269–275; Linenthal, *Sacred Ground,* 233–244, 249; Joe Treen, "Bloody Sunday," *People,* December 9, 1991, 40–45; Clarke, *Pearl Harbor Ghosts,* 122.
8   Barry Hillenbrand and James Walsh, "Fleeing the Past," *Time,* December 2, 1991, 70–71; McGeorge Bundy, "Pearl Harbor Brought Peace," *Newsweek,* December 16, 1991, 8; Ralph Kinney Bennet, "Legacy of Pearl Harbor," *Reader's Digest,* December 1991, 65–66; Alexander Cockburn, "Anniversaries: Pearl Harbor, Vietnam," *The Nation,* December 23, 1991, 802–803. R. Alton Lee, "Remembering Pearl Harbor," *USA* 120 (November 1991): 80–85, draws upon the standard view advanced by Roberta Wohlstetter and Gordon Prange.
9   Watanabe, "1991," 269–278.
10 Quoted in Thomas Mallon, "The Golden Pearl: Infamy Commemorated," *American Spectator,* March 1992, 36–42.
11 The quote in the heading above is from an interactive computer display in the *Arizona* Memorial Visitors' Center.
12 G. White, "Moving History," 726.
13 Ibid., 733.
14 Linenthal, *Sacred Ground,* 191.
15 Quoted in Zinsser, "At Pearl Harbor There Are New Ways to Remember," 82; G. White, "Moving History," 718.
16 G. White, "Moving History," 734.
17 Ibid., 710.
18 G. White, "Moving History"; Ferguson and Turnbull, *Oh, Say, Can You See?* 146, 224.
19 Delgado, "Memorials, Myths and Symbols," 320.

20 Jack McClenahan, "USS *Arizona* Monument to Expand Museum and Visitor Center," *Naval Affairs*, May 2000.

21 Watanabe, "1991," 275–276; Thorsten, "Treading the Tiger's Tail."

22 Thorsten, "Treading the Tiger's Tail," 328.

23 Ibid.

24 For example, Lifton and Mitchell, *Hiroshima in America;* Perlman, *Imaginal Memory;* Yoneyama, *Hiroshima Traces;* Maclear, *Beclouded Visions;* Davis, *Deracination.*

25 Various perspectives on the issue of Nanjing are discussed in Yang, "The Malleable and the Contested." Major studies of Japanese abuses include P. Williams and Wallace, *Unit 731,* and Yoshiaki and O'Brien, *Comfort Women.*

26 Cumings, *Parallax Visions,* 46–61, for example, argues that Pearl Harbor was a "garden-variety aggression" (at least against the United States) that cannot be justly compared to the mass killing of innocent civilians by the atomic bomb.

27 Dan Rather, *CBS Evening News,* March 2, 2001. See also Richard Cohen, "How Often Must We Say I'm Sorry," *Union Tribune* (San Diego), March 1, 2001; Tony Perry, "Once Again, Pearl Harbor Is Center of American-Japanese Conflict," *Los Angeles Times,* March 18, 2001, A-14; John Gregory Dunne, "The American Raj," *New Yorker,* May 7, 2001, 46–54.

28 On individual claims for reparations against Japan, see Hein, "Claiming Humanity and Legal Standing."

29 For context, see essays in Hein and Selden, eds., *Living with the Bomb* and *Censoring History;* K. Connie Kang, "Protestors Decry Japan's New History Textbooks," *Los Angeles Times,* April 18, 2001, B-1, 7; Mark Magnier, "School Districts in Japan Reject Controversial History Textbook," *Los Angeles Times,* February 3, 2001, points out that few districts adopted the controversial text.

30 Quoted in "U.S. and Japan Renew Partnership: Ex-Foes Mark Peace Treaty's 50th Anniversary at Ceremony in San Francisco," *Washington Post,* September 9, 2001.

31 Shin'ya Fujiwara, "In Japan, Waiting for the Captain to Appear," *New York Times,* February 17, 2001, A-17.

6. The Memory Boom and the "Greatest Generation"

1 Terkel, "*The Good War,*" 1.

2 For example, Scott, "Experience."

3   Hunt, "Remembering World War II." On Pearl Harbor specifically, see, for example, La Forte and Marcello, eds., *Remembering Pearl Harbor*, and Berry, *"This Is No Drill!"*

4   Pearl Harbor Survivor's Medal, establishing legislation, http://www .foxfall.com/fmc-phs.htm (November 16, 2002).

5   See especially Winter, "The Generation of Memory"; Lowenthal, *The Past Is a Foreign Country*, xv–xix, 40–44; and Kammen, *Mystic Chords of Memory*, 537–570.

6   Kammen, *Mystic Chords of Memory*, 535–537.

7   Lowenthal, *The Past Is a Foreign Country*, 40–44.

8   Huyssen: *Twilight Memories* and "Present Pasts."

9   Iyer, *The Global Soul*; Appadurai, *Modernity at Large*; Appadurai, ed., *Globalization*.

10 Winter, "The Generation of Memory," 90 (quote).

11 Rosenzweig and Thelan, *The Presence of the Past*.

12 Brokaw, *The Greatest Generation*, xix.

13 Ibid., xviii–xx.

14 Ibid., ix.

15 See also Rick Marin, "Raising a Flag for Generation W.W. II," *New York Times*, April 22, 2001.

16 Introductory promotional material preceding *Tora! Tora! Tora!*, "The Pearl Harbor Collection," Fox Video.

17 Donna Petrozzello, "Dan Davids Makes History," *Broadcasting and Cable*, August 31, 1998.

18 Joint Resolution No. 10, August 16, 1999, at http://www.njleg.state .ng.us/9899/Bills/p199 (November 16, 2000).

19 Congressman Jack Quinn, "Press Release", at http://www.house.gov (November 6, 2000).

20 Ibid. Examples of opposition, even from those who favored veterans' causes, can be found, for example, on a public forum and discussion sponsored by the conservative website Free Republic at http://www .freerepublic.com (November 6, 2000).

21 *Philadelphia Inquirer*, December 8, 2002; Clarke, *Pearl Harbor Ghosts*, xiv–xv.

22 Art Chapman, "New National Museum Gallery Explores Pacific War," *Star-Telegram* (Fort Worth), June 28, 1999; Linenthal, *Sacred Ground*, 188.

23 Lourdes Medrano Leslie, "A Pearl Harbor Buff Keeps Stories Alive," *Star Tribune* (Minneapolis), July 4, 2001.

24 Blight, *Race and Reunion*, 339–380; O'Leary, *To Die For*, 129–171.

25 "High kitsch" quote in Michael Kimmelman, "Turning Memory into Travesty," *New York Times*, March 4, 2001; cartoon in *Los Angeles*

Times, October 16, 2000. Other critical reviews are collected at http://www.savethemall.org while favorable commentary is at http://www.wwiimemorial.com.

26 Spencer S. Hsu and Linda Wheeler, "WWII Memorial on Mall Gets Final Approval," *Washington Post,* May 23, 2001, B-1.

27 See the website and press announcement of the Veterans' Oral History Project, American Folklife Center, Library of Congress, at http://www.loc.gov (November 19, 2000).

28 A selection of the Pearl Harbor Day interviews may be heard at Veterans' Oral History Project, at http://www.loc.gov/folklife/pearl harbor/pearl-about.html (December 6, 2001).

29 Quoted in Rick Marin, "Raising a Flag for Generation W. W. II," *New York Times,* April 22, 2001.

7. The Kimmel Crusade, the History Wars, and the Republican Revival

1 Lacy McCrary, "Fighting to Restore a Father's Rank," *Philadelphia Inquirer,* December 7, 1998.

2 Spector's own book covering Pearl Harbor is *Eagle against the Sun.*

3 Clausen and Lee, *Pearl Harbor,* 3.

4 Ibid., 2–4.

5 Historians of signals intelligence have convincingly refuted Rusbridger and Nave's main argument by pointing out that Japanese naval codes (JN-25) had indeed been broken but that a different and superior code system had been introduced during 1941 that was not cracked until the following year. See especially Aldrich: "Conspiracy or Confusion?" and *Intelligence.*

6 Costello, *Days of Infamy.*

7 Gannon, "Reopen the Kimmel Case." Gannon extended his arguments on behalf of Kimmel in *Pearl Harbor Betrayed.* Gannon argued that Kimmel had been treated unjustly and blamed officials in Washington but charged ineptitude and failure rather than a backdoor conspiracy.

8 Beach, *Scapegoats.*

9 Quoted in Cripps, "So Their Eyes Won't Glaze Over," 77.

10 Yoneyama, "For Transformative Knowledge," and Linenthal, "Anatomy of a Controversy." Other essays in Linenthal and Engelhardt, eds., *History Wars,* also examine the *Enola Gay* controversy. See also Harwit, *An Exhibit Denied;* Hogan, ed., *Hiroshima;* and Nobile, ed., *Judgment at the Smithsonian.*

11 Karal Ann Marling and John Wetenhall, "Patriotic Fervor and the Truth about Iwo Jima," *Chronicle of Higher Education*, September 26, 1993.

12 Levinson, *Written in Stone*, 29–75. See also M. Wallace, *Mickey-Mouse History*.

13 Nash, Crabtree, and Dunn, *History on Trial*, 188–193.

14 Clausen and Lee, *Pearl Harbor*, 2.

15 Ibid., 289.

16 For the evidence Clausen gathered for the 1946 report, see U.S. Congress, Joint Committee on the Investigation of the Pearl Harbor Attack, part 35 of the *Investigation of the Pearl Harbor Attack* hearings before the Joint Committee.

17 Clausen and Lee, *Pearl Harbor*, 297–298; Kaiser, "Conspiracy or Cock-up?"

18 Quoted in Schultz, "Resurrecting the Kimmel Case," 44.

19 All quotes are from Schultz, "Resurrecting the Kimmel Case," 45–46. For the text of the hearings, "Remarks at the Meeting of the Office of the Secretary of Defense and Members of the Kimmel Family Dealing with the Posthumous Restoration of the Rank of Admiral for Rear Admiral Husband E. Kimmel, United States Navy, April 27, 1995, Washington, D.C.," see http://users.erols.com/nbeach/kimmel.html (November 20, 2000).

20 Kevin Baker, "The Guilt Dogging the Greatest Generation," *New York Times*, November 12, 2000. See the Dorn report at http://www.ibiblio.org/pha/pha/dorn/ (October 2002).

21 See especially the website "Admiral Husband Edward Kimmel," maintained by his family, at http://www2.fwi.com/~tkimmel/Husband.htm (October 20, 2001).

22 Lacy McCrary, "Fighting to Restore a Father's Rank," *Philadelphia Inquirer*, December 7, 1998.

23 Quoted in Kevin Baker, "The Guilt Dogging the Greatest Generation," *New York Times*, November 12, 2000.

24 Winkler and Lloyd, eds., *Pearl Harbor and the Kimmel Controversy*.

25 Quoted in ibid., 26, 29, 61.

26 Quoted in Charles J. Lewis and Eric Rosenberg, "Congress Poised to Clear Officers Disgraced over Pearl Harbor Raid," *Post-Intelligencer* (Seattle), September 29, 2000. See also David Greenberg, "Who Lost Pearl Harbor?" *Slate*, December 7, 2000, at http://slate.msn.com (December 10, 2000).

27 Quoted in Charles J. Lewis and Eric Rosenberg, "Congress Poised to Clear Officers Disgraced over Pearl Harbor Raid," *Post-Intelligencer* (Seattle), September 29, 2000.

28 Quoted in Kevin Baker, "The Guilt Dogging the Greatest Generation," *New York Times*, November 12, 2000.

29   Stinnett, *Day of Deceit.*

30   Dunn, in welcoming remarks to the Naval Historical Foundation symposium; in Winkler and Lloyd, eds., *Pearl Harbor and the Kimmel Controversy.*

31   Quoted in Ollie Reed Jr., "A Family's Battle for Honor," *Albuquerque Tribune,* December 7, 2001, A-1. A restatement of his position and efforts to keep the cause alive is detailed in "Edward R. Kimmel's Remarks," May 26, 2002, at http://www2.fwi.com/~tkimmel/ERKO8 .htm (October 15, 2002).

8. Japanese Americans:
Identity and Memory Culture

1   This chapter is co-authored with Katy Forsyth.

2   Quoted in *Maui News,* April 25, 2000.

3   Felicity Barringer, "Remembering Pearl Harbor Has Its Risks," *New York Times,* June 4, 2001, C-11.

4   Robinson, *By Order of the President,* provides details.

5   Lowe, *Immigrant Acts,* 38–39. See also Spickard, *Japanese Americans,* 93–132.

6   On Masaoka, see Fujitani, "*Go for Broke,* the Movie"; Masaoka with Hosokawa, *They Call Me Moses Masaoka.* For an official history of the JACL, see "About JACL," at http://www.jacl.org/about .html (May 30, 2002). For more on the JACL and compliance, see especially Takahashi, *Nisei/Sansei,* 85–96.

7   Ted Nakashima, "Concentration Camp: U.S. Style," *New Republic,* June 15, 1942, 822–823.

8   Yogi, " 'You Had to Be One or the Other.' "

9   "War Relocation Authority Photographs of Japanese-American Evacuation and Resettlement, 1942–1945," Bancroft Library, at http://www .oac.cdlib.org:80/dynaweb/ead/calher/jvac/@Generic_BookView;cs = default;ts = default?DwebQuery = war + relocation + authority&D web SearchAll =1 (July 10, 2001) (caption quote at vol. 78, sec. I, WRA no. 91).

10   Ibid.; Patterson, "Resistance to Images of the Internment."

11   *Life,* March 29, 1944.

12   Starn, "Engineering Internment"; Simpson, *An Absent Presence,* 43–75; Dower, *War without Mercy,* 120–122.

13   Sturken, "Absent Images of Memory," 41–42.

14   Fujitani, "*Go for Broke,* the Movie," 253 (quote), 255.

15   Okubo, *Citizen 13660,* 209.

16 Sone, *Nisei Daughter,* 238.

17 Houston and Houston, *Farewell to Manzanar,* 162.

18 Okada, *No-No Boy,* vii.

19 Truong, "Kelly," 42.

20 Terkel, *"The Good War,"* 28.

21 Amoko, "Resilient Imaginations," 35–54; Yogi, " 'You Had to Be One or the Other.' "

22 Kikuchi and Modell, *The Kikuchi Diary;* Spikard, "Not Just the Quiet People." Among many histories emphasizing resistance, see Spickard, *Japanese Americans,* 93–132; Irons, *Justice at War;* and Daniels, *Prisoners without Trial.*

23 The Japanese American Historical Museum claims this amount represented "less than ten cents for every dollar lost." "Japanese American Incarceration Facts," at http://www.janm.org/nrc/internfs.html (May 30, 2002).

24 Takezawa, *Breaking the Silence;* Hatamiya, *Righting a Wrong.*

25 Gene Oishi, "Our Neighbors Called Us 'Japs,' " *Newsweek,* November 25, 1991.

26 Davidov, " 'The Color of My Skin'," 239; Knaefler, *Our House Divided;* Rea Tajiri, producer and director, *History and Memory,* distributed by Electronic Arts Intermix (New York, 1991), as analyzed in Sturken, "Absent Images of Memory," 42, 46, and Renov, "Warring Images," 112–115.

27 For the text of the Lim report and other resolutions, see "Japanese American Voice," at http://www.javoice.com (May 30, 2002).

28 Lowe, *Immigrant Acts,* 38–39.

29 Simpson, *An Absent Presence,* 15–16.

30 Annie Nakao, "Furor over Memorial to Japanese Americans," *San Francisco Examiner,* July 7, 2000.

31 Quoted in "Japanese American Voice," at http://www.javoice.com (May 30, 2002), which contains dozens of similar quotes and links to articles related to the controversy. For a history of the controversy sympathetic to the protesters, see Francis Y. Sogi and Yeiichi (Kelly) Kuwayama, "Japanese Americans Disunited," at http://www.javoice.com/pamphlet1.html (May 30, 2002).

32 "Home," http://www.javoice.com (June 20, 2001).

33 *Conscience and the Constitution,* at http://www.itvs.org/conscience/ (May 20, 2002).

34 Annie Nakao, "Furor over Memorial to Japanese Americans," *San Francisco Examiner,* July 7, 2000.

35 Sturken, "Absent Images of Memory," 34.

9. *Spectacular History*

1   Costello, *Days of Infamy,* 332.

2   Stinnett, *Day of Deceit,* 3.

3   Quoted in ibid.

4   Budiansky, *Battle of Wits,* 8. See also Prados, *Combined Fleet Decoded;* and Alvarez, *Secret Messages.* For a fairly typical academic dismissal of Stinnett's book, see the review by Philip Zelikow in *Foreign Affairs* 79 (March/April 2000): 153–155. A summary of refutations of Stinnett is Judith Greer, "Did FDR Know?" at http://www.salon.com/books/ feature/2001/06/14/fdr/print.html (June 13, 2001), and a detailed critique is a review by Philip H. Jacobsen in *Cryptologia* 24 (April 2000): 110–118.

5   Robert B. Stinnett, "Pentagon Still Scapegoats Pearl Harbor Fall Guys," at http://www.independent.org/tii/news/011203Stinnett.html (June 3, 2002).

6   H-Net commentaries can be accessed by going to http://www2.h-net.msu.edu/and running the search engine on "Cryptography and Pearl Harbor" and "Budiansky"; reviewer quotes are from the *Day of Deceit* page at http://barnesandnoble.com (June 3, 2002). A catalog of relevant books and reviews is "The Literature of Intelligence: A Bibliography of Materials, with Essays, Reviews, and Comments," at http://intellit.muskingum.edu/intellsite/wwiipearl_folder/wwiipearltoc.html (May 30, 2002).

7   Smith and Jensen, *World War II on the Web.*

8   Lawrence Suid, "Pearl Harbor: Bombed Again," *Naval History,* August 2001.

9   *Newsweek,* May 14, 2001, 44–58.

10 Sarah Tippit, "Japanese Americans Protest New 'Pearl Harbor' Film," May 21, 2001; at http://dailynews.yahoo.com/h/nm/20010521/en/ film-pearlharbor_4.html (May 23, 2001).

11 For a spoof of the effort to avoid offense, see Bruce McCall, "Blitzkrieg! the Movie," *New Yorker,* July 2, 2001, 35.

12 Rosenstone, *Visions of the Past,* 12–16.

13 G. King, *Spectacular Narratives,* 4–5, 32–40.

14 An extended critique of *Pearl Harbor* as "history" is Lawrence Suid, "Pearl Harbor: Bombed Again," *Naval History,* August 2001.

15 Various articles in *Newsweek,* May 14, 2001, 44–58; Probst, "One Nation, under Siege"; Magid, "Earning Their Wings."

16 G. King, *Spectacular Narratives,* 22–33, 39–49.

17 Ibid., 9.

18 Lola Smallwood, "Enough with the Hype Machine for Explosive 'Pearl Harbor,'" *St. Paul Pioneer Press*, June 11, 2001, 7F.

19 Ibid.; quote in Tony Perry, "The Pentagon's Little 'Pearler,'" June 4, 2001, at http://www.theage.com.au/entertainment/2001/06/04/ FFX0IA3PHNC.html (September 23, 2002).

20 Sunshine and Felix, eds., *The Movie and the Moment*; R. Wallace, *Pearl Harbor*.

21 "Remembering Pearl Harbor," http://www.nationalgeographic.com/ pearlharbor (November 2, 2002).

22 *Newsweek*, May 14, 2001, 44–58.

23 "Moment of Truth," *People Magazine*, May 28, 2001, 51–58.

24 Julian E. Barnes, "Joe's Back, and Looking for a Ride," *New York Times*, May 25, 2001; quote in Samantha Critchell, "'Pearl Harbor' Helps Inspire Revival of 1940s Style," *Star Tribune* (Minneapolis), May 26, 2001, E5. On the emergence of Hollywood spinoffs, see G. King, *Spectacular Narratives*, 175–190.

25 Smallwood, "Enough with the Hype Machine for Explosive 'Pearl Harbor'"; Claudia Rosett, "Revisiting Pearl Harbor," May 21, 2001, at http://interactive.wsj.com/articles;SB990040225358637245.htm (May 21, 2001).

26 Linenthal, *Sacred Ground*, 191.

27 *Pearl Harbor: Legacy of Attack*, ABC, May 27, 2001; on "sentimental militarism," see Appy, "'We'll Follow the Old Man,'" 74–105.

28 A. O. Scott, "War Is Hell, but Very Pretty," *New York Times*, May 25, 2001, "Weekend," 1, 20.

29 Robert Sullivan, "What Really Happened," *Time*, June 4, 2001, 70.

30 Jess Cagle, "Cinema," *Time*, June 4, 2001, 69.

10. Day of Infamy: September 11, 2001

1 Woodward, *Bush at War*, 37.

2 Lowenthal, *The Past Is a Foreign Country*, xx.

3 First two quotes from Charles Babington, "Bush to Address Nation," *Washington Post*, September 11, 2001; Eliot A. Cohen, "Make War, Not Justice," at http://www.thenewrepublic.com/092401/cohen092401 .html (September 25, 2001); "The Talk of the Town," at http://www .newyorker.com/FROM_THE_ARCHIVE/ARCHIVES/?010917fr_ar chive08 (September 15, 2001).

4 U.S. Senate Republican Policy Committee, "Americans Who Died on American Soil," September 21, 2001, at http://www.senate.gov/ ~rpc/releases/1999/fr092101.htm (November 7, 2001).

5 Guy E. Torrey IV, "On A Nation Shocked from Slumber," Septem-

ber 13, 2001, at http://www.travelgolf.com/d...ments/editorials/torrey-wtc-disaster.htm (November 7, 2001).

6   Library of Congress, "The Day after the Day Which Will Live in Infamy, Continuing the Tradition," at http://www.loc.gov/folklife/pearlharbor/pearl-about.html (December 6, 2001).

7   John Biewen and Elana Hadler Perl, "Days of Infamy: December 7 and 9/11," American Radio Works, September 2002, at http://www.americanradioworks.org/features/daysofinfamy/index.html (September 9, 2002).

8   "President Holds Prime Time News Conference," October 11, 2001, at http://whitehouse.gov/news/releases/2001/10/print/20011011-7.html (October 30, 2001); CNN Newsreport, November 11, 2001 (including quote); Xan Brooks, "That's Militainment," *The Guardian*, May 22, 2002.

9   *NBC Nightly News* live coverage of the "Declaration of War on Terrorism," September 20, 2001. I would like to thank Matt Diediker for his help providing the documentation on this point.

10 Some examples of the resistance to the Pearl Harbor analogy include Stanley Hoffmann, "On the War," *New York Review of Books*, November 1, 2001; David M. Kennedy, "Fighting an Elusive Enemy," *New York Times*, September 16, 2001; Eugene Leach, "World Trade Center Attack—No Pearl Harbor," *Hartford Courant*, September 14, 2001. See also Robert W. Martin, "The 9-11 Tragedy and the Attack on Pearl Harbor: Can We Compare?" at http://militaryhistory.about.com/library/weekly/aa091301a.htm (November 7, 2001).

11 David Brooks, "After Pearl Harbor," *Weekly Standard*, December 10, 2001, 25–29.

12 Ibid., 25.

13 Quoted in Martin, "The 9-11 Tragedy and the Attack on Pearl Harbor: Can We Compare?" On monument-building, see Michael Kimmelman, "Out of Minimalism, Monuments to Memory," *New York Times*, January 13, 2002, sec. 2: 1. On civil liberties, see Kenji G. Taguma, "Japanese Americans Urge Calm before Stereotyping Suspects," September 12, 2001, at "New California Media," http://www.ncmonline.com/content/ncm/2001/sep/0912calm.html (November 7, 2001); "Press Release," September 19, 2001, Japanese American Citizens League, at http://www.jacl.org/current_prs/01091900.htm (May 30, 2002); "60 Years Later, 'It's Our Turn,'" December 8, 2001, at http://dallasnews.com/attack_on_america/spirit/stories/STORY.eaa48dca9b.bo.af.0.a4.c73c2.html (December 12, 2001); Stephen Schwartz, "The Right Way to Lock Up Aliens," *Weekly Standard*, December 10, 2001, 12–13.

14 "Electronic Pearl Harbor," at http://www.soci.niu.edu/~crypt/other/

harbor.htm (May 23, 2001), provides a large collection tracing the origins and the popularization of the term "electronic Pearl Harbor."

15 Woodward, *Bush at War*, 22–23; Otto Kreisher, "Rumsfeld Is Coy on Weapons in Space," *Union Tribune* (San Diego), May 9, 2001, A-1.

16 For Bush's campaign speech, at the Citadel military academy, see Center for Defense Information, "Presidential Transition, 2001," at http://www.cdi.org/hotspots/Election2000/ (September 5, 2001).

17 The United States Commission on National Security/21st Century, "Road Map for National Security: Imperative for Change," at http://www.nssg.gov/PhaseIIIFR.pdf (March 8, 2003).

18 Austin Bay, "The World Trade Center Attack: 21st Century Pearl Harbor," at http://www.strategypage.com/onpoint/articles/2001091l.asp (November 7, 2001); "Inquiry of Pre-Attack Intelligence Sought," *New York Times*, October 22, 2001. Among the many other calls for an inquiry based on the Pearl Harbor model is Nikolas K. Gvosdev, "An Investigation—Now!" at http://historynewsnetwork.org/articles/article.huml?id=298 (September 26, 2001).

19 The quote in the heading is from an editorial, *Post-Intelligencer* (Seattle), December 7, 2001.

20 "60 Years Later, 'It's Our Turn.'"

21 "National Pearl Harbor Remembrance Day Proclamation," at http://www.whitehouse.gov/news/releases/2001/12/20011207-2.html (December 11, 2001); quotes from "Bush on Pearl Harbor Anniversary," December 7, 2001, at http://www.dallasnews.com/national/STORY.ea7f5ab75e.93.88.fa.7c23198c8d.html (December 12, 2001).

22 Quoted in "Bush Remembers Pearl Harbor aboard USS *Enterprise*," at http://www.cnn.com/2001/ALLPOLITICS/12/07/rec.bush.pearl/index.html (December 11, 2001).

23 "Elder Bush Praises Pearl Harbor Vets' Service," December 8, 2001, at http://www.dallasnews.com/texas_southwest/STORY.eaa49b83af.bo.af.o.a4.85fld.html (December 11, 2001).

24 *Time*, May 27, 2002.

25 Cal Thomas, "Go on the Offensive, Like a Doolittle Raid," *Des Moines Register*, June 6, 2002.

26 John Prados, "Our Pearl Harbor," June 21, 2002, at http://www.prospect.o...atures/2002/06/prados-j-06-21.html (June 24, 2002).

27 See three editorials in the *New York Times*, June 13, 2002: Warren Rudman and Gary Hart, "Restructuring for Security"; Bob Herbert, "A Closer Look"; and William Safire, "The 'Big Ear' Gone Deaf."

28 Project for the New American Century, "Rebuilding America's Defenses: Strategy, Forces and Resources for a New Century," September 2000, at http://www.newamericancentury.org (October 12, 2002).

29 "The National Security Strategy," September 20, 2002, at http://www.whitehouse.gov/nsc/nss.html (October 20, 2002).

30   For example, Michael Elliott, "Could 9/11 Have Been Prevented?" September 11, 2002, at http://www.time.com/time/nation/article/0,8599,333835,00.html (October 5, 2002); Patrick E. Tyler, "Feeling Secure, U.S. Failed to Grasp bin Laden Threat," *New York Times,* September 8, 2002, 1.

31   "Bush Accepts Independent but 'Focused' 9/11 Probe," September 20, 2002, at http://www.cnn.com/2002/ALLPOLITICS/09/20/independent .probe (October 15, 2002).

32   *Washington Post,* November 28, 2002, December 2, 2002, December 14, 2002, December 17, 2002.

33   Vidal, *The Golden Age,* 172, 466.

34   Vidal, *Dreaming War,* 15. Another book by Vidal, *Perpetual War for Perpetual Peace,* borrowed its title from Harry Elmer Barnes's back-door classic.

35   Sunder Katwala, "Gore Vidal Claims 'Bush Junta' Complicit in 9/11," *Guardian Unlimited,* October 27, 2002.

36   Berkhoffer, *Beyond the Great Story;* Suny, "Back and Beyond."

37   Nora, ed., *Realms of Memory,* 1: xxiv.

Bibliography

Note: For the many newspaper, popular periodical, film, and website sources, see the notes.

Adams, Ansel. *Born Free and Equal: Photographs of the Loyal Japanese-Americans at Manzanar Relocation Center, Inyo County, California*. New York: U.S. Camera, 1944.

Adams, Michael C. C. *The Best War Ever: America and World War II*. Baltimore, Md.: Johns Hopkins University Press, 1994.

Aldrich, Richard J. "Conspiracy or Confusion? Churchill, Roosevelt and Pearl Harbor." *Intelligence and National Security* 7, no. 3 (1992): 335–346.

——. *Intelligence and the War against Japan: Britain, America, and the Politics of Secret Service*. Cambridge: Cambridge University Press, 2000.

Alpers, Benjamin L. "This Is the Army: Imagining a Democratic Military in World War II." *Journal of American History* 85, no. 1 (June 1998): 129–163.

Alvarez, David J. *Secret Messages: Codebreaking and American Diplomacy, 1930–1945*. Lawrence, Kans.: University Press of Kansas, 2000.

Ambrose, Stephen E. *Citizen Soldiers: The U.S. Army from the Normandy Beaches to the Bulge to the Surrender of Germany, June 7, 1944–May 7, 1945*. New York: Simon and Schuster, 1997.

——. *D-Day, June 6, 1944: The Climactic Battle of World War II*. New York: Simon and Schuster, 1994.

America's Entry into World War Two. Fredericksburg, Tex.: Awani Press, 1995.

Amoko, Apollo. "Resilient ImagiNations: *No-No Boy, Obasan* and the Limits of Minority Discourse." *Mosaic* 33, no. 3 (September 2000): 35–54.

Anderson, Benedict R. *Imagined Communities: Reflections on the Origin and Spread of Nationalism.* London: Verso Editions/NLB, 1983.

Appadurai, Arjun. *Modernity at Large: Cultural Dimensions of Globalization.* Minneapolis: University of Minnesota Press, 1996.

——, ed. *Globalization.* Durham, N.C.: Duke University Press, 2001.

Appy, Christian G. " 'We'll Follow the Old Man': The Strains of Sentimental Militarism in Popular Films of the Fifties." In Kuznick and Gilbert, eds., *Rethinking Cold War Culture,* 74–105.

——, ed. *Cold War Constructions: The Political Culture of United States Imperialism, 1945–1966.* Amherst: University of Massachusetts Press, 2000.

Assmann, Aleida. "Texts, Traces, Trash: The Changing Media of Cultural Memory." *Representations,* no. 56 (1996): 123–134.

Bal, Mieke, Jonathan V. Crewe, and Leo Spitzer, eds. *Acts of Memory: Cultural Recall in the Present.* Hanover, N. H.: University Press of New England, 1999.

Barnes, Harry Elmer, ed., with the collaboration of William Henry Chamberlin. *Perpetual War for Perpetual Peace: A Critical Examination of the Foreign Policy of Franklin Delano Roosevelt and Its Aftermath.* New York: Greenwood Press, 1969; first printing, 1953.

Bartone, Richard C. " 'Victory at Sea': A Case Study in Official Telehistory." *Film and History* 11, no. 4 (December 1991): 115–129.

Basinger, Jeanine. *The World War II Combat Film: Anatomy of a Genre.* New York: Columbia University Press, 1986.

Baty, S. Paige. *American Monroe: The Making of a Body Politic.* Berkeley: University of California Press, 1995.

Beach, Edward Latimer. *Scapegoats: A Defense of Kimmel and Short at Pearl Harbor.* Annapolis, Md.: Naval Institute Press, 1995.

Beard, Charles A. *President Roosevelt and the Coming of the War, 1941: A Study in Appearances and Realities.* New Haven, Conn.: Yale University Press, 1948.

Beard, Charles A., and Mary R. Beard. *A Basic History of the United States.* New York: Doubleday, Doran, 1944.

Bergsten, C. Fred, Takatoshi Ito, and Marcus Noland. *No More Bashing: Building a New Japan–United States Economic Relationship.* Washington, D.C.: Institute for International Economics, 2001.

Bernardi, Daniel, ed. *Classic Hollywood, Classic Whiteness.* Minneapolis: University of Minnesota Press, 2001.

Berkhoffer, Robert F., Jr. *Beyond the Great Story: History as Text and Discourse.* Cambridge, Mass.: Harvard University Press, 1997.

Berry, Henry. *"This Is No Drill!" Living Memories of the Attack on Pearl Harbor.* New York: Berkley Books, 1992.

Bix, Herbert P. *Hirohito and the Making of Modern Japan.* New York: HarperCollins, 2000.

Blight, David W. *Race and Reunion: The Civil War in American Memory.* Cambridge, Mass.: Harvard University Press, 2001.

Bodnar, John E. *Remaking America: Public Memory, Commemoration, and Patriotism in the Twentieth Century.* Princeton, N.J.: Princeton University Press, 1992.

Borg, Dorothy, and Shumpei Okamoto. *Pearl Harbor as History: Japanese-American Relations, 1931–1941.* New York: Columbia University Press, 1973.

Boyer, Paul S. *By the Bomb's Early Light: American Thought and Culture at the Dawn of the Atomic Age.* New York: Pantheon, 1985.

Bradley, James, with Ron Powers. *Flags of Our Fathers: Heroes of Iwo Jima.* New York: Delacorte Press, 2001.

Brear, Holly Beachley. *Inherit the Alamo: Myth and Ritual at an American Shrine.* Austin: University of Texas Press, 1995.

Brokaw, Tom. *The Greatest Generation.* New York: Random House, 1998.

Browne, Nick, ed. *Refiguring American Film Genres: History and Theory.* Berkeley: University of California Press, 1998.

Budiansky, Stephen. *Battle of Wits: The Complete Story of Codebreaking in World War II.* New York: Free Press, 2000.

Burstein, Daniel. *Yen!: Japan's New Financial Empire and Its Threat to America.* New York: Simon and Schuster, 1988.

Butler, Judith P., and Joan Wallach Scott, eds. *Feminists Theorize the Political.* New York: Routledge, 1992.

Carnes, Mark C., ed. *Past Imperfect: History According to the Movies.* New York: Henry Holt, 1995.

Chambers, John Whiteclay, II, and David Culbert, eds. *World War II, Film, and History.* New York: Oxford University Press, 1996.

Chang, Iris. *The Rape of Nanking: The Forgotten Holocaust of World War II.* New York: Basic Books, 1997.

Chidester, David, and Edward Tabor Linenthal, eds. *American Sacred Space.* Bloomington: Indiana University Press, 1995.

Choate, Pat. *Agents of Influence.* New York: Knopf, 1990.

Clarke, Thurston. *Pearl Harbor Ghosts: The Legacy of December 7, 1941.* 2d ed. New York: Ballantine Books, 2001.

Clausen, Henry C., and Bruce Lee. *Pearl Harbor: Final Judgement.* New York: Da Capo Press, 2001. First published 1992.

Confino, Alon. "Collective Memory and Cultural History: Problems of Method." *American Historical Review* 102, no. 5 (December 1997): 1386–1403.

Connerton, Paul. *How Societies Remember.* New York: Cambridge University Press, 1989.

Costello, John. *Days of Infamy: Macarthur, Roosevelt, Churchill, the Shocking Truth Revealed: How Their Secret Deals and Strategic Blunders Caused Disasters at Pearl Harbor and the Philippines.* New York: Pocket Books, 1994.

——. *The Pacific War.* New York: Rawson Wade, 1981.

Craig, Campbell. "The Not-So-Strange Career of Charles Beard." *Diplomatic History* 25, no. 2 (spring 2001): 251–274.

Crichton, Michael. *Rising Sun.* New York: Ballantine Books, 1993.

Cripps, Thomas. "So Their Eyes Won't Glaze Over: How Television News Defined the Debate over the Smithsonian's *Enola Gay* Exhibit." *Wide Angle* 20, no. 2 (April 1998): 77–104.

Cumings, Bruce. *Parallax Visions: Making Sense of American–East Asian Relations.* Durham, N.C.: Duke University Press, 2002.

Current, Richard N., T. Harry Williams, and Frank Freidel. *American History: A Survey.* 2d ed. New York: Knopf, 1966.

Daniels, Roger. *Prisoners without Trial: Japanese Americans in World War II.* New York: Hill and Wang, 1993.

Davidov, Judith Fryer. "The Color of My Skin, the Shape of My Eyes: Photographs of the Japanese-American Internment by Dorothea Lange, Ansel Adams and Toyo Miyatake." *Yale Journal of Criticism* 9, no. 2 (fall 1996).

Davis, Walter A. *Deracination: Historicity, Hiroshima, and the Tragic Imperative.* Albany: State University of New York Press, 2001.

Dean, Jodi. "Theorizing Conspiracy Theory." *Theory and Event* 4, no. 3 (2000).

Dean, Robert D. *Imperial Brotherhood: Gender and the Making of Cold War Foreign Policy.* Amherst: University of Massachusetts Press, 2001.

Delgado, James P. "Memorials, Myths and Symbols: The Significance of the *Arizona* Memorial." *Valley Forge Journal* 5, no 4 (1991): 310–326.

Dietrich, William S. *In the Shadow of the Rising Sun: The Political Roots of American Economic Decline.* University Park: Pennsylvania State University Press, 1991.

Dingman, Roger. "Reflections on Pearl Harbor Anniversaries Past." *Journal of American–East Asian Relations* 3, no. 3 (fall 1994): 279–293.

Divine, Robert A. *The Sputnik Challenge.* New York: Oxford University Press, 1993.

Doenecke, Justus D. *Storm on the Horizon: The Challenge to American Intervention, 1930–1941.* Lanham, Md.: Rowman and Littlefield, 2000.

Doherty, Thomas Patrick. *Projections of War: Hollywood, American Culture, and World War II.* New York: Columbia University Press, 1999.

Donald, Ralpha R. "Awakening a Sleeping Giant: The Pearl Harbor Attack on Film." *Film and History* 27, no. 1 (summer 1997): 40–46.

Dower, John W. *Embracing Defeat: Japan in the Wake of World War II.* New York: W. W. Norton/New Press, 1999.

——. "Graphic Japanese, Graphic Americans: Coded Images in U.S.-Japanese Relations." In Iriye and Wampler, eds., *Partnership.*

——. *War without Mercy: Race and Power in the Pacific War.* New York: Pantheon Books, 1986.

Eber, Dena E., and Arthur G. Neal, eds. *Memory and Representation: Constructed Truths and Competing Realities.* Bowling Green, Ohio: Bowling Green State University Popular Press, 2001.

Edgerton, Gary R., and Peter C. Rollins. *Television Histories: Shaping Collective Memory in the Media Age.* Lexington: University Press of Kentucky, 2001.

Enloe, Cynthia H. *Bananas, Beaches & Bases: Making Feminist Sense of International Politics.* Berkeley: University of California Press, 1990.

——. *Maneuvers: The International Politics of Militarizing Women's Lives.* Berkeley: University of California Press, 2000.

——. *The Morning After: Sexual Politics at the End of the Cold War.* Berkeley: University of California Press, 1993.

Evans, Martin, and Kenneth Lunn. *War and Memory in the Twentieth Century.* New York: Berg, 1997.

Fallows, James M. *Looking at the Sun: The Rise of the New East Asian Economic and Political System.* New York: Pantheon Books, 1994.

Fenollosa, Ernest Francisco. *East and West: The Discovery of America and Other Poems.* New York: Thomas Y. Crowell, 1893.

Ferguson, Kathy E., and Phyllis Turnbull. *Oh, Say, Can You See? The Semiotics of the Military in Hawaii.* Minneapolis: University of Minnesota Press, 1999.

Flynn, John T. *The Final Secret of Pearl Harbor.* New York: J. T. Flynn, 1945.

——. *The Road Ahead: America's Creeping Revolution.* New York: Devin-Adair, 1949.

——. *The Roosevelt Myth.* New York: Devin-Adair, 1948.

Foucault, Michel. *Language, Counter-Memory, Practice: Selected Essays and Interviews.* Translated by Donald F. Bouchard and Sherry Simon. Ithaca, N.Y.: Cornell University Press, 1977.

——. *Power/Knowledge: Selected Interviews and Other Writings 1972–1977.* Translated by Colin Gordon et al. Edited by Colin Gordon. New York: Pantheon Books, 1980.

Freiberg, Freda. " '*China Nights*' (Japan 1940): The Sustaining Romance of Japan at War." In Chambers and Culbert, eds., *World War II, Film, and History,* 31–46.

Friedländer, Saul. *Memory, History, and the Extermination of the Jews of Europe.* Bloomington: Indiana University Press, 1993.

Friedman, George, and Meredith LeBard. *The Coming War with Japan.* New York: St. Martin's Press, 1991.

Fujitani, Takashi. "*Go for Broke,* the Movie: Japanese American Soldiers in U.S. National, Military, and Racial Discourses." In Fujitani, White, and Yoneyama, eds., *Perilous Memories,* 255–262.

Fujitani, Takashi, Geoffrey M. White, and Lisa Yoneyama, eds. *Perilous*

Memories: The Asia-Pacific War(s). Durham, N.C.: Duke University Press, 2001.

Gaddis, John Lewis. *We Now Know: Rethinking Cold War History.* New York: Oxford University Press, 1997.

Gannon, Michael V. *Pearl Harbor Betrayed: The True Story of a Man and a Nation under Attack.* New York: Holt, 2001.

——. "Reopen the Kimmel Case." *Proceedings of the United States Naval Institute* 12, no. 120 (December 1994): 51–56.

Gillis, John R., ed. *Commemorations: The Politics of National Identity.* Princeton, N.J.: Princeton University Press, 1994.

Gluck, Sherna Berger, ed. *Rosie the Riveter Revisited: Women, the War, and Social Change.* New York: Penguin, 1988.

Halbwachs, Maurice. *On Collective Memory.* Edited, translated, and with an introduction by Lewis A. Coser. Chicago: University of Chicago Press, 1992.

Harwit, Martin. *An Exhibit Denied: Lobbying the History of Enola Gay.* New York: Copernicus, 1996.

Hass, Kristin Ann. *Carried to the Wall: American Memory and the Vietnam Veterans Memorial.* Berkeley: University of California Press, 1998.

Hatamiya, Leslie T. *Righting a Wrong: Japanese Americans and the Passage of the Civil Liberties Act of 1988.* Stanford, Calif.: Stanford University Press, 1993.

Hein, Laura. "Claiming Humanity and Legal Standing: Contemporary Demands for Redress from Japan for Its World War II Policies." In Torpey, ed., *Politics and the Past.*

Hein, Laura, and Mark Selden, eds. *Censoring History: Citizenship and Memory in Japan, Germany, and the United States.* Armonk, N.Y.: M. E. Sharpe, 2000.

——. *Living with the Bomb: American and Japanese Cultural Conflicts in the Nuclear Age.* Armonk, N.Y.: M. E. Sharpe, 1997.

Heinrichs, Waldo. "The *Enola Gay* and Contested Public Memory." Paper presented at Workshop on Public Memory, Tokyo, June 22–24, 2002.

Henning, Joseph M. *Outposts of Civilization: Race, Religion, and the Formative Years of American-Japanese Relations.* New York: New York University Press, 2000.

Hobsbawm, Eric J., and Terence O. Ranger, eds. *The Invention of Tradition.* New York: Cambridge University Press, 1992.

Hogan, Michael J. *A Cross of Iron: Harry S. Truman and the Origins of the National Security State, 1945–1954.* New York: Cambridge University Press, 1998.

——, ed. *Hiroshima in History and Memory.* New York: Cambridge University Press, 1996.

Holmes, Linda Goetz. *Unjust Enrichment: How Japan's Companies Built Postwar Fortunes Using American POWs*. Mechanicsburg, Pa.: Stackpole Books, 2001.

Holstein, William J. *The Japanese Power Game: What It Means for America*. New York: Scribner, 1990.

Houston, Jeanne Wakatsuki, and James D. Houston. *Farewell to Manzanar: A True Story of Japanese American Experience during and after the World War II Internment*. Boston: Houghton Mifflin, 1973.

Hunt, Richard A. "Remembering World War II: The Role of Oral History." *Public Historian* 16, no. 2 (1994): 83–88.

Huyssen, Andreas. "Present Pasts: Media, Politics, Amnesia." In Appadurai, ed., *Globalization*, 57–77.

———. *Twilight Memories: Marking Time in a Culture of Amnesia*. New York: Routledge, 1995.

Igarashi, Yoshikuni. *Bodies of Memory: Narratives of War in Postwar Japanese Culture, 1945–1970*. Princeton, N.J.: Princeton University Press, 2000.

Iriye, Akira. *The Origins of the Second World War in Asia and the Pacific*. New York: Longman, 1987.

———. *Pearl Harbor and the Coming of the Pacific War: A Brief History with Documents and Essays*. Boston: Bedford/St. Martin's, 1999.

———. *Power and Culture: The Japanese-American War, 1941–1945*. Cambridge, Mass.: Harvard University Press, 1981.

———. *"Tora! Tora! Tora!"* In Carnes, ed., *Past Imperfect*, 228–231.

Iriye, Akira, and Robert A. Wampler, eds. *Partnership: The United States and Japan, 1951–2001*. New York: Kodansha International, 2001.

Irons, Peter H. *Justice at War: The Story of the Japanese American Internment Cases*. New York: Oxford University Press, 1983.

Ishihara, Shintaro. *The Japan That Can Say No: Why Japan Will Be First among Equals*. New York: Simon and Schuster, 1990.

Ishii, Osamu. "Through the Lens of Pearl Harbor: America's Economic, Social, and Cultural Frictions with Japan, and Memories of the Pacific War, 1982–1993." Paper presented at Workshop on Public Memory, Tokyo, June 22–24, 2002.

Iyer, Pico. *The Global Soul: Jet Lag, Shopping Malls, and the Search for Home*. New York: Knopf, 2000. Distributed by Random House.

Jasper, Joy Waldron, James P. Delgado, and Jim Adams. *The USS Arizona: The Ship, the Men, the Pearl Harbor Attack, and the Symbol That Aroused America*. New York: St. Martin's Press, 2001.

Jeffreys-Jones, Rhodri. *Cloak and Dollar: A History of American Secret Intelligence*. New Haven, Conn.: Yale University Press, 2002.

———. "Why Was the CIA Established in 1947?" *Intelligence and National Security* 12, no. 1 (January 1997): 21–40.

Johnson, Chalmers A. *MITI and the Japanese Miracle: The Growth of Industrial Policy, 1925–1975.* Stanford, Calif.: Stanford University Press, 1982.

Johnson, M. K. " 'No Certain Way to Tell Japanese from Chinese': Racist Statements and the Marking of Difference." *Explorations in Ethnic Studies* 18, no. 2 (July 1995): 159–176.

Johnson, Sheila K. *The Japanese through American Eyes.* Stanford, Calif.: Stanford University Press, 1988.

Johnston, Steven. "Political Not Patriotic: Democracy, Civil Space, and the American Memorial/Monument Complex." *Theory and Event* 5, no. 2 (2001).

Kahn, David. "The Intelligence Failure of Pearl Harbor." *Foreign Affairs* 70, no. 5 (winter 1991): 138–152.

Kaiser, David. "Conspiracy or Cock-Up? Pearl Harbor Revisited." *Intelligence and National Security* 9, no. 2 (April 1994): 354–372.

Kammen, Michael G. *Mystic Chords of Memory: The Transformation of Tradition in American Culture.* New York: Knopf, 1991.

Kasson, Joy S. *Buffalo Bill's Wild West: Celebrity, Memory, and Popular History.* New York: Hill and Wang, 2000.

Keegan, John. *The Battle for History: Re-Fighting World War II.* New York: Vintage Books, 1996.

Kennan, George Frost. *American Diplomacy, 1900–1950.* Chicago: University of Chicago Press, 1951.

Kikuchi, Charles, and John Modell. *The Kikuchi Diary: Chronicle from an American Concentration Camp.* Urbana: University of Illinois Press, 1973.

Kimmel, Husband E. *Admiral Kimmel's Story.* Chicago: H. Regnery, 1955.

King, Alex. *Memorials of the Great War in Britain: The Symbolism and Politics of Remembrance.* New York: Berg, 1998.

King, Geoff. *Spectacular Narratives: Hollywood in the Age of the Blockbuster.* New York: I. B. Tauris Publishers, 2000.

Kirshenblatt-Gimblett, Barbara. *Destination Culture: Tourism, Museums, and Heritage.* Berkeley: University of California Press, 1998.

Knaefler, Tomi. *Our House Divided: Seven Japanese American Families in World War II.* Honolulu: University of Hawaii Press, 1991.

Koppes, Clayton R., and Gregory D. Black. *Hollywood Goes to War: How Politics, Profits, and Propaganda Shaped World War II Movies.* New York: Free Press, 1987.

——. "What to Show the World: The Office of War Information and Hollywood, 1942–45." *Journal of American History* 64, no. 1 (June 1977): 87–105.

Koshiro, Yukiko. "Japan's World and World War II." *Diplomatic History* 25, no. 3 (summer 2001): 425–442.

——. *Trans-Pacific Racisms and the U.S. Occupation of Japan.* New York: Columbia University Press, 1999.

Kundera, Milan. *Testaments Betrayed: An Essay in Nine Parts.* New York: Harper Perennial, 1996.

Kuznick, Peter J., and James Burkhart Gilbert, eds. *Rethinking Cold War Culture.* Washington, D.C.: Smithsonian Institution Press, 2001.

LaCapra, Dominick, *History and Memory after Auschwitz.* Ithaca, N.Y.: Cornell University Press, 1998.

La Forte, Robert S., and Ronald E. Marcello, eds. *Remembering Pearl Harbor: Eyewitness Accounts by U.S. Military Men and Women.* Wilmington, Del.: Scholarly Resources, 1991.

Langer, Lawrence L. *Holocaust Testimonies: The Ruins of Memory.* New Haven, Conn.: Yale University Press, 1991.

Layton, Edwin T., and John Costello and Roger Pineau. *"And I Was There": Pearl Harbor and Midway—Breaking the Secrets.* New York: William Morrow, 1985.

Leffler, Melvyn P. *A Preponderance of Power: National Security, the Truman Administration, and the Cold War.* Stanford, Calif.: Stanford University Press, 1992.

Le Goff, Jacques. *History and Memory.* Translated by Steven Rendall and Elizabeth Clayman. New York: Columbia University Press, 1992.

Levinson, Sanford. *Written in Stone: Public Monuments in Changing Societies.* Durham, N.C.: Duke University Press, 1998.

Lifton, Robert Jay, and Greg Mitchell. *Hiroshima in America: Fifty Years of Denial.* New York: Putnam's Sons, 1995.

Linenthal, Edward Tabor. "Anatomy of a Controversy." In Linenthal and Engelhardt, eds., *History Wars,* 9–62.

——. *Preserving Memory: The Struggle to Create America's Holocaust Museum.* New York: Viking, 1995.

——. *Sacred Ground: Americans and Their Battlefields.* Urbana: University of Illinois Press, 1993.

Linenthal, Edward Tabor, and Tom Engelhardt, eds. *History Wars: The Enola Gay and Other Battles for the American Past.* New York: Metropolitan Books/Henry Holt, 1996.

Lipsitz, George. *Time Passages: Collective Memory and American Popular Culture.* Minneapolis: University of Minnesota Press, 1990.

Lloyd, David W. *Battlefield Tourism: Pilgrimage and the Commemoration of the Great War in Britain, Australia and Canada, 1919–1939.* New York: Berg, 1998.

Lord, Walter. *Day of Infamy.* New York: Holt, 1957.

Lowe, Lisa. *Immigrant Acts: On Asian American Cultural Politics.* Durham, N.C.: Duke University Press, 1996.

Lowenthal, David. *The Past Is a Foreign Country.* New York: Cambridge University Press, 1985.

——. *Possessed by the Past: The Heritage Crusade and the Spoils of History.* New York: Free Press, 1996.

Maclear, Kyo. *Beclouded Visions: Hiroshima-Nagasaki and the Art of Witness.* Albany: State University of New York Press, 1999.

Magid, Ron. "Earning Their Wings." *American Cinematographer* 82, no. 5 (May 2001): 50–57.

Maier, Charles. "A Surfeit of Memory? Reflection on History, Melancholy, and Denial." *History and Memory* 5, no. 4 (1993): 136–151.

Marchetti, Gina. *Romance and the "Yellow Peril": Race, Sex, and Discursive Strategies in Hollywood Fiction.* Berkeley: University of California Press, 1993.

Marling, Karal Ann and John Wetenhall. Iwo Jima: Monuments, Memories, and the American Hero. Cambridge Mass.: Harvard University Press, 1991.

Masaoka, Mike, with Bill Hosokawa. *They Call Me Moses Masaoka.* New York: William Morrow, 1987.

McMahon, Robert J. "Contested Memory: The Vietnam War and American Society, 1975–2001." *Diplomatic History* 26, no. 2 (spring 2002): 159–184.

Melley, Timothy. *Empire of Conspiracy: The Culture of Paranoia in Postwar America.* Ithaca, N.Y.: Cornell University Press, 2000.

Melosi, Martin V. *The Shadow of Pearl Harbor: Political Controversy over the Surprise Attack, 1941–1946.* College Station, Tex.: Texas A and M University Press, 1977.

Minear, Richard H. *Victors' Justice: The Tokyo War Crimes Trial.* Princeton, N.J.: Princeton University Press, 1971.

Moeller, Susan D. "Pictures of the Enemy: Fifty Years of Images of Japan in the American Press, 1941–1992." *Journal of American Culture* 19, no. 1 (spring 1996): 29–42.

Morgenstern, George. *Pearl Harbor: The Story of the Secret War.* New York: Devin-Adair, 1947.

Morison, Samuel Eliot. *History of United States Naval Operations in World War II.* 15 vols. Boston: Little, Brown, 1947–1962.

Mosse, George L. *Fallen Soldiers: Reshaping the Memory of the World Wars.* New York: Oxford University Press, 1990.

Nash, Gary B., Charlotte A. Crabtree, and Ross E. Dunn. *History on Trial: Culture Wars and the Teaching of the Past.* New York: Knopf, 1997. Distributed by Random House.

Neal, Arthur. *National Trauma and Collective Memory: Major Events in the American Century.* Armonk, N.Y.: M. E. Sharpe, 1998.

Nobile, Philip, ed. *Judgment at the Smithsonian.* New York: Marlowe, 1995.

Nora, Pierre, ed. *Realms of Memory: Rethinking the French Past.* 3 vols. English edition edited by Lawrence D. Kritzman. Translated by Arthur Goldhammer. New York: Columbia University Press, 1996–1998.

Nornes, Abé Mark, and Fukushima Yukio, eds. *The Japan/America Film*

Wars: World War II Propaganda and Its Cultural Contexts. Chur, Switzerland: Harwood Academic Publishers, 1994.

Okada, John. *No-No Boy.* Seattle: University of Washington Press, 1979; first printing, 1957.

Okubo, Miné. *Citizen 13660.* New York: Columbia University Press, 1946.

O'Leary, Cecilia Elizabeth. *To Die For: The Paradox of American Patriotism.* Princeton, N.J.: Princeton University Press, 1999.

Orr, James Joseph. *The Victim as Hero: Ideologies of Peace and National Identity in Postwar Japan.* Honolulu: University of Hawaii Press, 2001.

Patterson, Anita Haya. "Resistance to Images of the Internment: Mitsuye Yamada's 'Camp Notes.' " *MELUS* 23, no. 3 (fall 1998): 103–127.

Pearl Harbor: America's Call to Arms. Editors of *Life Magazine.* New York: Time, 2001.

Perlman, Michael. *Imaginal Memory and the Place of Hiroshima.* Albany: State University of New York Press, 1988.

Piehler, G. Kurt. *Remembering War the American Way.* Washington, D.C.: Smithsonian Institution Press, 1995.

Prados, John. *Combined Fleet Decoded: The Secret History of American Intelligence and the Japanese Navy in World War II.* New York: Random House, 1995.

Prange, Gordon William, with Donald M. Goldstein and Katherine V. Dillon. *At Dawn We Slept: The Untold Story of Pearl Harbor.* New York: McGraw-Hill, 1981.

——. *Pearl Harbor: The Verdict of History.* New York: McGraw-Hill, 1986.

Prestowitz, Clyde V. *Trading Places: How We Allowed Japan to Take the Lead.* New York: Basic Books, 1988.

Probst, Christopher. "One Nation, under Siege." *American Cinematographer* 82, no. 5 (May 2001): 36–49.

Reardon, Carol. *Pickett's Charge in History and Memory.* Chapel Hill: University of North Carolina Press, 1997.

Reeves, Nicholas. *The Power of Film Propaganda: Myth or Reality?* London: Cassell, 1999.

Reischauer, Edwin O. *The United States and Japan.* New York: Viking Press, 1962. First published 1950.

Renov, Michael. "Warring Images: Stereotype and American Representations of the Japanese." In Nornes and Yukio, eds., *The Japan/America Film Wars,* 95–118.

Richardson, James O., and George C. Dyer. *On the Treadmill to Pearl Harbor: The Memoirs of Admiral James O. Richardson as Told to Vice Admiral George C. Dyer.* Washington, D.C.: Naval History Division, Department of the Navy, 1973.

Roberts, Randy and James Stuart Olson. *A Line in the Sand: The Alamo in Blood and Memory.* New York: Free Press, 2001.

Robinson, Greg. *By Order of the President: FDR and the Internment of Japanese Americans.* Cambridge, Mass.: Harvard University Press, 2001.

Roeder, George H., Jr. *The Censored War: American Visual Experience during World War Two.* New Haven, Conn.: Yale University Press, 1993.

Rollins, Peter. " 'Victory at Sea': Cold War Epic." In Edgerton and Rollins, eds., *Television Histories.*

Rosenberg, Bruce A. *Custer and the Epic of Defeat.* University Park: Pennsylvania State University Press, 1974.

Rosenberg, Emily S. " 'Foreign Affairs' after World War II: Connecting Sexual and International Politics." *Diplomatic History* 18, no. 1 (winter 1994): 59–70.

Rosenstone, Robert A. *Visions of the Past: The Challenge of Film to Our Idea of History.* Cambridge, Mass.: Harvard University Press, 1995.

——, ed. *Revisioning History: Film and the Construction of a New Past.* Princeton, N.J.: Princeton University Press, 1995.

Rosenzweig, Roy, and David P. Thelen. *The Presence of the Past: Popular Uses of History in American Life.* New York: Columbia University Press, 1998.

Rusbridger, James, and Eric Nave. *Betrayal at Pearl Harbor: How Churchill Lured Roosevelt into World War II.* New York: Summit Books, 1991.

Samuel, Raphael. *Theatres of Memory.* New York: Verso, 1994.

Sasaki, Takuya. "The Cold War Diplomacy and Memories of the Pacific War: A Comparison of the American and Japanese Cases." Paper presented at Workshop on Public Memory, Tokyo, June 22–24, 2002.

Savage, Kirk. *Standing Soldiers, Kneeling Slaves: Race, War, and Monument in Nineteenth-Century America.* Princeton, N.J.: Princeton University Press, 1997.

Schatz, Thomas. "World War II and the Hollywood 'War Film.' " In Browne, ed., *Refiguring American Film Genres,* 89–128.

Schultz, Fred L. "Resurrecting the Kimmel Case." *Naval History* 9, no. 4 (July 1995): 43–46.

Scott, Joan W. "Experience." In Butler and Scott, eds., *Feminists Theorize the Political,* 22–40.

Scruggs, Jan C., and Joel L. Swerdlow. *To Heal a Nation: The Vietnam Veterans Memorial.* New York: Harper and Row, 1985.

Seelye, John. *Memory's Nation: The Place of Plymouth Rock.* Chapel Hill: University of North Carolina Press, 1998.

Sherman, Daniel J. *The Construction of Memory in Interwar France.* Chicago: University of Chicago Press, 1999.

Sherry, Michael S. *In the Shadow of War: The United States since the 1930s.* New Haven, Conn.: Yale University Press, 1995.

——. *Preparing for the Next War: American Plans for Postwar Defense, 1941–45.* New Haven, Conn.: Yale University Press, 1977.

Simpson, Caroline Chung. *An Absent Presence: Japanese Americans in Post-war American Culture, 1945–1960.* Durham, N.C.: Duke University Press, 2001.

Skinner, James M. "December 7: Filmic Myth Masquerading as Historical Fact." *Journal of Military History* 55, no. 4 (October 1991): 507–516.

Slackman, Michael. *Remembering Pearl Harbor: The Story of the USS Arizona Memorial.* Honolulu: Arizona Memorial Museum Association, 1993.

Sledge, E. B. *With the Old Breed at Peleliu and Okinawa.* New York: Oxford University Press, 1990. First published 1981.

Slotkin, Richard. *The Fatal Environment: The Myth of the Frontier in the Age of Industrialization, 1800–1890.* New York: Atheneum, 1985.

Smith, J. Douglas, and Richard Jensen. *World War II on the Web: A Guide to the Very Best Sites.* Wilmington, Del.: Scholarly Resources, 2002.

Smith, Stanley H., ed. *Investigations of the Attack on Pearl Harbor: Index to Government Hearings.* New York: Greenwood Press, 1990.

Snead, David L. *The Gaither Committee, Eisenhower, and the Cold War.* Columbus: Ohio State University Press, 1999.

Sone, Monica Itoi. *Nisei Daughter.* Boston: Little, Brown, 1953.

Spector, Ronald H. *Eagle against the Sun: The American War with Japan.* New York: Free Press, 1985.

Spickard, Paul R. *Japanese Americans: The Formation and Transformations of an Ethnic Group.* New York: Twayne, 1996.

———. "Not Just the Quiet People: The Nisei Underclass." *Pacific Historical Review* 68, no. 1 (1999): 78–94.

Starn, Orin. "Engineering Internment: Anthropologists and the War Relocation Authority." *American Ethnologist* 14, no. 4 (1986): 700–720.

Steele, Richard W. " 'The Greatest Gangster Movie Ever Filmed': *Prelude to War.*" *Prologue: The Journal of the National Archives* 4, no. 4 (winter 1979): 220–235.

Stinnett, Robert B. *Day of Deceit: The Truth about FDR and Pearl Harbor.* New York: Touchstone, 2000.

Sturken, Marita. "Absent Images of Memory: Remembering and Reenacting the Japanese Internment." In Fujitani, White, and Yoneyama, eds., *Perilous Memories.*

Sunshine, Linda, and Antonia Felix, eds., *The Movie and the Moment.* New York: Hyperion, 2001.

Suny, Ronald Grigor. "Back and Beyond: Reversing the Cultural Turn?" *American Historical Review* 107 (December 2002): 1476–1499.

Tai, Hue-Tam Ho. "Remembered Realms: Pierre Nora and French National Memory." *American Historical Review* 106, no. 3 (June 2001): 906–923.

———, ed. *The Country of Memory: Remaking the Past in Late Socialist Vietnam.* Berkeley: University of California Press, 2001.

Takahashi, Jere. *Nisei/Sansei: Shifting Japanese American Identities and Politics.* Philadelphia: Temple University Press, 1997.

Takezawa, Yasuko I. *Breaking the Silence: Redress and Japanese American Ethnicity.* Ithaca, N.Y.: Cornell University Press, 1995.

Tansill, Charles Callan. *Back Door to War: The Roosevelt Foreign Policy, 1933–1941.* Chicago: H. Regnery, 1952.

Terkel, Studs. *"The Good War": An Oral History of World War Two.* New York: Ballantine Books, 1985.

Terry, Wallace, ed. *Bloods: An Oral History of the Vietnam War.* New York: Random House, 1984.

Thelen, David, ed. *Memory and American History.* Indianapolis: Indiana University Press, 1989.

Theobald, Robert Alfred. *The Final Secret of Pearl Harbor: The Washington Contribution to the Japanese Attack.* New York: Devin-Adair, 1954.

Thorsten, Marie. "Treading the Tiger's Tail: American and Japanese Pearl Harbor Veterans' Reunions in Hawaii and Japan." *Cultural Values: Journal of Cultural Research* 6, no. 3 (2002): 317–340.

Tichi, Cecelia. *Electronic Hearth: Creating an American Television Culture.* New York: Oxford University Press, 1991.

Toland, John. *Infamy: Pearl Harbor and Its Aftermath.* Garden City, N.Y.: Doubleday, 1982.

Torpey, John, ed. *Politics and the Past: On Repairing Historical Injustices.* Lanham, Md.: Rowman and Littlefield, 2001.

Toshiya, Ueno. "The Other and the Machine." In Nornes and Yukio, eds., *The Japan/America Film Wars,* 71–95.

Trouillot, Michel-Rolph. *Silencing the Past: Power and the Production of History.* Boston: Beacon Press, 1995.

Truong, Monique Thuy-Dung. "Kelly." *Amerasia Journal* 17, no. 2 (fall/winter 1991): 41–48.

U.S. Congress. Joint Committee on the Investigation of the Pearl Harbor Attack. *Investigation of the Pearl Harbor Attack. Report of the Joint Committee on the Investigation of the Pearl Harbor Attack.* Seventy-ninth Congress, Second Session (November 15, 1945–May 31, 1946). Washington, D.C.: U.S. Government Printing Office, 1946. Microfilm edition, 40 parts.

Vidal, Gore. *Dreaming War: Blood for Oil and the Cheney-Bush Junta.* New York: Thunder's Mouth Press, 2002.

——. *The Golden Age.* New York: Doubleday, 2000.

——. *Perpetual War for Perpetual Peace: How We Got to be so Hated.* New York: Thunder's Mouth Press, 2002.

Vogel, Ezra F. *Japan as Number One: Lessons for America.* Cambridge, Mass.: Harvard University Press, 1979.

——. *Japan Still Number One?* Subang Jaya, Malaysia: Pelanduk Publications, 2000.

Wallace, Mike. *Mickey-Mouse History and Other Essays on American Memory.* Philadelphia: Temple University Press, 1996.

Wallace, Randall. *Pearl Harbor.* New York: Hyperion, 2001.

Wampler, Robert A. "Reversals of Fortune? Shifting U.S. Images of Japan as Number One, 1979–2000." In Iriye and Wampler, eds., *Partnership.*

Watanabe, Toru. "1991: American Perceptions of the Pearl Harbor Attack." *Journal of American–East Asian Relations* 3, no. 3 (fall 1994) 269–278.

West, Patricia. *Domesticating History: The Political Origins of America's House Museums.* Washington, D.C.: Smithsonian Institution Press, 1999.

West, Philip, Steven I. Levine, and Jackie Hiltz, eds. *America's Wars in Asia: A Cultural Approach to History and Memory.* Armonk, N.Y.: M. E. Sharpe, 1998.

White, Geoffrey M. "Moving History: The Pearl Harbor Film(s)." In Fujitani, White, and Yoneyama, eds., *Perilous Memories*, 267–295.

White, Geoffrey, and Jane Yi. "*December 7:* Race and Nation in Wartime Documentary." In Bernardi, ed., *Classic Hollywood.*

White, Hayden V., ed. *Figural Realism: Studies in the Mimesis Effect.* Baltimore, Md.: Johns Hopkins University Press, 1999.

Williams, Peter, and David Wallace. *Unit 731: Japan's Secret Biological Warfare in World War II.* New York: Free Press, 1989.

Williams, William Appleman. *The Tragedy of American Diplomacy.* New York: Dell, 1962. First published 1959.

Wills, Garry. *A Necessary Evil: A History of American Distrust of Government.* New York: Simon and Schuster, 1999.

Winkler, Allan M. *The Politics of Propaganda: The Office of War Information, 1942–1945.* New Haven, Conn.: Yale University Press, 1978.

Winkler, David F., and Jennifer M. Lloyd, eds. *Pearl Harbor and the Kimmel Controversy: The Views Today.* Washington, D.C.: Naval Historical Foundation, 2000.

Winter, Jay. "Film and the Matrix of Memory." *American Historical Review* 106, no. 3 (June 2001): 857–864.

——. "The Generation of Memory: Reflections on the 'Memory Boom' in Contemporary Historical Studies." *Bulletin of the German Historical Institute* 27, no. 3 (fall 2000): 69–92.

——. *Sites of Memory, Sites of Mourning: The Great War in European Cultural History.* New York: Cambridge University Press, 1995.

Winter, Jay, and Emmanuel Sivan, eds. *War and Remembrance in the Twentieth Century.* New York: Cambridge University Press, 1999.

Wisniewski, Richard A. *Pearl Harbor and the USS* Arizona *Memorial: A Pictorial History.* Rev. ed. Honolulu: Pacific Printing and Publishing, 1986.

Wohlstetter, Roberta. *Pearl Harbor: Warning and Decision.* Stanford, Calif.: Stanford University Press, 1962.

Wolferen, Karel Van. *The Enigma of Japanese Power: People and Politics in a Stateless Nation.* New York: Knopf, 1989.

Woodward, Bob. *Bush at War*. New York: Simon and Schuster, 2002.

Wyden, Peter. *Day One: Before Hiroshima and After*. New York: Simon and Schuster, 1984.

Yang, Daqing. "The Malleable and the Contested: The Nanjing Massacre in Postwar China and Japan." In Fujitani, White, and Yoneyama, eds., *Perilous Memories*.

Yogi, Stan. "You Had to Be One or the Other: Oppositions and Reconciliation in John Okada's *No-No Boy*." *MELUS* 21, no. 1 (1996): 63–77.

Yoneyama, Lisa. "For Transformative Knowledge and Postnational Public Spheres: The Smithsonian *Enola Gay* Controversy." In Fujitani, White, and Yoneyama, eds., *Perilous Memories*.

——. *Hiroshima Traces: Time, Space, and the Dialectics of Memory*. Berkeley: University of California Press, 1999.

Yoshiaki, Yoshimi, and Suzanne O'Brien. *Comfort Women: Sexual Slavery in the Japanese Military during World War II*. New York: Columbia University Press, 2000.

Young, James Edward. *The Texture of Memory: Holocaust Memorials and Meaning*. New Haven, Conn.: Yale University Press, 1993.

Zelizer, Barbie. "Reading the Past against the Grain: The Shape of Memory Studies." *Critical Studies in Mass Communication* 12, no. 2 (1995): 214–239.

Zinsser, William. "At Pearl Harbor There are New Ways to Remember." *Smithsonian* 22, no. 9 (1991): 72–83.

Index

EMILY ROSENBERG is the De Witt Wallace Professor of History at Macalester College. She is the author of *Financial Missionaries to the World: The Politics and Culture of Dollar Diplomacy, 1900–1930* (paperback edition, Duke, 2003); (with John Murrin, Paul Johnson, James McPherson, Gary Gerstle, and Norman Rosenberg) *Liberty, Equality, Power: A History of the American People* (revised edition, 2002); *World War I and the Growth of United States Predominance in Latin America* (1986); *Spreading the American Dream: American Economic and Cultural Expansion* (1982); and (with Norman Rosenberg) *In Our Times: America since 1945* (revised edition, 2003).

Library of Congress Cataloging-in-Publication Data

Rosenberg, Emily S.
A date which will live : Pearl Harbor in American memory /
Emily S. Rosenberg.
p. cm. — (American encounters/global interactions)
Includes bibliographical references and index.
ISBN 0-8223-3206-x (cloth : alk. paper)
1. Pearl Harbor (Hawaii), Attack on, 1941. 2. World War, 1939–1945—Influence.
3. Popular culture—United States. I. Title. II. Series.
D767.92.R67 2003
940.54'26—dc21   2003007553